i before e
(except after c)

Every man's memory is his private literature.

—ALDOUS HUXLEY

i before e
(except after c)

old-school ways
to remember stuff

JUDY PARKINSON

Reader's Digest

The Reader's Digest Association, Inc.
Pleasantville, New York/Montreal

A READER'S DIGEST BOOK

Copyright © 2008 Michael O'Mara Books Limited

Illustrations © Louise Morgan 2007
For www.artmarketillustration.com

All rights reserved. Unauthorized reproduction, in any manner, is prohibited.

Reader's Digest is a registered trademark of The Reader's Digest Association, Inc.

First published in Great Britain in 2007 by Michael O'Mara Books Limited
9 Lion Yard, Tremadoc Road
London SW4 7NQ

FOR MICHAEL O'MARA BOOKS
Illustrations by Louise Morgan
Cover design by Angie Allison
Front cover title lettering by Toby Buchan
Interior design by Martin Bristow

FOR READER'S DIGEST
U.S. Project Editor: Sandra Kear
Copy Editor: Marilyn Knowlton
Canadian Project Editor: Pamela Johnson
Associate Art Director: George McKeon
Project Production Coordinator: Wayne Morrison
Executive Editor, Trade Publishing: Dolores York
Production Manager: Elizabeth Dinda
Vice President, U.S. Operations: Michael Braunschweiger
Associate Publisher: Rosanne McManus
President and Publisher, Trade Publishing: Harold Clarke

Parkinson, Judy.
  I before E : old-school ways to remember stuff / Judy Parkinson.
    p. cm.
  ISBN 978-0-7621-0917-3
  1. Mnemonics--Handbooks, manuals, etc. I. Title.
  BF385.P37 2008 153.1'4--dc22

2007052006

The selected verses from "The History of the U.S." (1919) by Winifred Sackville Stoner Jr. were originally published in *Yankee Doodles: A Book of American Verse*, edited by Ted Malone (Whittlesey House, London/McGraw-Hill Book Company, New York, 1943)

Every effort has been made to trace and contact copyright holders of the materials in this book. The author and publisher will be glad to rectify any omissions.

We are committed to both the quality of our products and the service we provide to our customers. We value your comments, so please feel free to contact us.

The Reader's Digest Association, Inc.
Adult Trade Publishing
Reader's Digest Road
Pleasantville, NY 10570-7000

For more Reader's Digest products and information, visit our website:
www.rd.com (in the United States)
www.readersdigest.ca (in Canada)

Printed in the United States of America

7 9 10 8

Contents

Introduction		vi
1.	The English Language	1
2.	To Spell or Not to Spell	12
3.	Think of a Number	31
4.	Geographically Speaking	52
5.	Animal, Vegetable, Mineral	62
6.	Time and the Calendar	72
7.	The Sky at Night and by Day	82
8.	The World of Science	90
9.	World History	98
10.	Musical Interlude	114
11.	Foreign Tongues	121
12.	Religious Matters	127
13.	The Human Body	135
14.	Lifesaving Tips	145
15.	The World of Work	153
16.	Other Favorites	160

Introduction

"Thirty days hath September, April, June, and November…"

How many times, perhaps anxiously awaiting payday, have you repeated this saying to yourself? Or racked your brains for the name of the eleventh president of the United States in order to stump some impertinent know-it-all at a dinner party?

No doubt about it, memory's a funny business. But in a pre-Google, less hectic age, many useful, if not invaluable, facts were taught by mnemonics—simple memory aids, which once learned, fixed information in the brain forever. In fact, the concept of memory devices began in ancient Greece, before the written word. Rather than memorize information by rote, the Greeks developed a technique called the Method of Loci (pronounced LOW-sigh), or method of locations or places.

With this method a person creates an image that associates the necessary information with a location or place along a familiar and well-traveled route. To retrieve the items from memory, the person then mentally travels through that visualization, picking up the previously associated items.

As Cicero tells it in his work *De Oratore*, this method was invented by a Greek poet named Simonides of Ceos (c. 556-468 B.C.). After a recitation at a dinner party, Simonides was apparently called outside. While he was outside, the roof of the building he was in collapsed, killing all inside, many beyond recognition. Simonides was able to identify the victims by associating their names with their respective positions at the dinner table, and it is believed that through this tragedy, an ancient system of mnemonics was born.

Since then, hundreds of new mnemonic devices have been created that clearly give knowledge seekers an advantage. Studies have shown time and time again that people who use mnemonics remember at least twice as well as those who don't.

This book assembles many of those quirky and amusing ways that people have devised to remember tidbits of information in school—all of them still handy devices for solving today's problems. Packed with clever verses, entertaining acronyms, curious—and sometimes hilarious—sayings, *i before e (except after c)* includes all the mnemonics you could ever need (and some you probably don't).

This book is your one-stop shop for finding basic mnemonics. Soon you'll be recalling them to pass a test or include in a speech. They can help remind you when to turn your clocks back and forward, as well as important anniversaries and that special someone's birthday. Mnemonics could even save you from contacting poison ivy and may help you save a life. By the end of it, you'll definitely remember *i before e* as an amusing and handy collection of ingenious mind tricks devised to help us learn and understand the idiosyncrasies of this world and beyond.

1
The English Language

The Alphabet

Children, of course, must first learn the alphabet before they successfully embark upon reading the complete works of Shakespeare. So it is that for many of us, learning our ABCs to the tune of "Twinkle, Twinkle, Little Star" (made famous by *Sesame Street's* Big Bird) becomes our first introduction to the world of mnemonics.

It was Charles Bradlee, a Boston music publisher, who first copyrighted that combination in 1835, calling it "the ABC, a German air with variations for flute with an easy accompaniment for the pianoforte."

> *a–b–c–d–e–f–g,*
> *h–i–j–k–l–m–n–o–p,*
> *q–r–s–t–u–v,*
> *w–x–y and z.*
> *Now I know my ABCs,*
> *next time won't you sing with me?*

For the rhyme to work with the Z, you have to use the U.S. pronunciation of zee rather than zed. If you didn't sing your ABCs to the tune of "Twinkle, Twinkle, Little Star," then you might have used the tune of "Baa, Baa, Black Sheep" instead, which has a similar rhythm and the same melody.

Because the letters l—m—n—o—p have to be sung twice as fast as the rest of the letters in the rhyme, some children have mistakenly assumed that "elemenopee" is

a word. *Sesame Street's* DVD, "The Alphabet Jungle Game" pokes fun at this type of error. In the video Telly thinks he's been stumped when Zoe introduces the next letter after K, called "Elemeno." After some worrisome bantering, Elmo enlightens his friends to the error, and an animated short on each letter follows, in classic *Sesame Street* style.

In the nineteenth century, a popular way to teach

children the ABCs was through a rhyme entitled, "The Tragical Death of A, Apple Pie, Who Was Cut in Pieces, and Eaten by Twenty-Six Gentlemen, With Whom All Little People Ought To Be Very Well Acquainted." The text dates back as far as the reign of Charles II (1660–1685).

> **A** was an apple pie
> **B** bit it,
> **C** cut it,
> **D** dealt it,
> **E** eats it,
> **F** fought for it,
> **G** got it,
> **H** had it,
> **I** inspected it,
> **J** jumped for it,
> **K** kept it,
> **L** longed for it,
> **M** mourned for it,
> **N** nodded at it,
> **O** opened it,
> **P** peeped in it,
> **Q** quartered it,
> **R** ran for it,
> **S** stole it,
> **T** took it,
> **U** upset it,
> **V** viewed it,
> **W** wanted it,
> **X**, **Y** and **Z** all wished for
> and had a piece in hand.

The Five Vowels

The English alphabet has five soft vowels: **A E I O U**. This sequence of letters generally tends to roll off the tongue quite naturally, but for anyone who has trouble remembering the order of vowels, here are a couple of useful phrases:

Ann's **E**gg **I**s **O**n **U**s.

Anthony's **E**go **I**s **O**ver **U**sed.

The Parts of Speech

After learning the alphabet, the next step is to devise coherent sentences. The rhyme below categorizes each of the parts of speech, giving a clear example of each grammatical term. The rhyme dates back to 1855 and was written by educators David B. Tower and Benjamin F. Tweed:

A NOUN's the name of any thing;
As, *school or garden, hoop, or swing.*

ADJECTIVES tell the kind of noun;
As, *great, small pretty, white, or brown.*

Three of these words we often see
Called ARTICLES — *a, an,* and *the.*

Instead of nouns the PRONOUNS stand;

John's head, his face, my arm, your hand.

VERBS tell of something being done;
As, *read, write, spell, sing, jump,* or *run.*

How things are done the ADVERBS tell;
As, *slowly, quickly, ill,* or *well.*

They also tell us *where* and *when;*
As, *here,* and *there,* and *now,* and *then.*

A PREPOSITION stands *before*
A NOUN; *as, in,* or *through,* a door.

CONJUNCTIONS sentences unite;
As, kittens scratch *and* puppies bite.

The INTERJECTION shows surprise

A different rhyme called "The Parts of Speech" is similarly concise as a reminder of the different components of the English language. The origin of these verses is unknown.

Every name is called a **noun**,
As *field* and *fountain, street* and *town.*

In place of noun the **pronoun** stands,
As *he* and *she* can clap their hands.

The **adjective** describes a thing,
As *magic* wand and *bridal* ring.

The **verb** means action, something done—
To *read,* to *write,* to *jump,* to *run.*

How things are done, the **adverbs** tell,
As *quickly, slowly, badly, well.*

The **preposition** shows relation,
As *in* the street, or *at* the station.

Conjunctions join, in many ways,
Sentences, words, *or* phrase *and* phrase.

The **interjection** cries out, "Hark!
I need an exclamation mark!"

Through poetry, we learn how each
Of these make up the **Parts of Speech.**

What's a Preposition?

To further remember the function of a preposition, insert any word into the following sentence:

The squirrel ran____the tree.

For example, over, under, after, around, through, up, on, to, from, by, and so forth. Other prepositions include in, at, for, between, among, and of.

What's a Conjunction?

Conjunctions are words used to join two independent clauses. Most people are careless with punctuation, especially these days when shortcuts in e-mails and text messages have become commonplace. But this FAN

BOYS mnemonic helps if you want to remember the coordinating conjunctions, of which the most important are *and*, *or*, and *but*.

FAN BOYS

For, And, Nor, But, Or, Yet, So

The Rules of Punctuation

Cecil Hartley's poem from *Principles of Punctuation* or *The Art of Pointing* (1818) reveals the old-fashioned way that people were advised on how to interpret punctuation when reading sentences out loud.

> The stops point out, with truth, the time of pause
> A sentence doth require at ev'ry clause.
> At ev'ry comma, stop while *one* you count;
> At semicolon, *two* is the amount;
> A colon doth require the time of *three*;
> The period *four*, as learned men agree.

Though it's not a verse that most grammarians would encourage these days, it does give you an idea of the difference between each type of punctuation mark.

On Commas

A cat has claws at the ends of its paws.
A comma's a pause at the end of a clause.

On Colons

The English teacher and prominent lexicographer H. W. Fowler creates a useful visual image of the job done by the colon, which he says, "delivers the goods that have been invoiced in the preceding words."

On the Exclamation Point

The following anonymously authored seventeenth-century rhyme appeared in *Treatise of Stops, Points, or Pauses, and of Notes Which Are Used in Writing and Print* (1680):

> This stop denotes our Suddain Admiration,
> Of what we Read, or Write, or giv Relation,
> And is always cal'd an Exclamation.

Writing Stories

And when you put all these elements together to write your first novel, don't forget the main elements of storytelling:

Viewpoint
Mood
Plot
Characters
Theme
Setting

If the VMPCTS acronym doesn't roll easily off the tongue, this phrase should help to keep it firmly in mind:

Very **M**any **P**upils **C**ome **T**o **S**chool

Learning Lines

How do actors memorize scripts? Learning lines by repetition is the most obvious way, but many actors also refer to the beat of the script that is, the rhythm of the words, which actors literally tune into. Some plays are easier to learn than others. Shakespeare's texts are highly memorable because they are rich and full of puns (often extremely bawdy ones), rhymes, and alliterations.

> Whereat, with blade, with bloody blameful blade,
> He bravely breach'd his boiling bloody breast.

Another mnemonic secret of the English poetic tradition is the rhythm of the iambic pentameter. An iamb is a beat with one soft syllable and one strong syllable, and a series of five iambs forms the heartbeat of classic poetry: its familiarity makes it easy to remember, especially in the works of Shakespeare.

From *Hamlet*
To be / or not / to be / that is / the question.

From the Sonnets

Shall I / compare / thee to / a sum/mer's day?
Thou art / more love/ly and / more tem/perate:
Rough winds / do shake / the dar/ling buds / of May,
And sum/mer's lease / hath all / too short / a date.

Setting a text to a well-known tune and rhythm is a useful method of memorizing the words. Why not try singing Homer's *Odyssey*, Coleridge's "The Rime of the Ancient Mariner," or one of Shakespeare's sonnets to the tune of your favorite nursery rhyme or song? You can remember the words using a combination of rhymes, rhythms, and repetition.

English usage is sometimes more than mere taste, judgment, and education—sometimes it's sheer luck, like getting across the street.

— E. B. White

2
To Spell or Not to Spell

Although there are some people who can spell *supercalifragilisticexpialidocious* without blinking an eye, others draw blanks at the simplest word. Everyone has a different level of ability when it comes to spelling. For those who fall into the latter category, perhaps they weren't taught the right sort of spelling mnemonics...

I before E (except after C)

Teachers often drum this phrase into children's heads in grammar school, and it does apply in the sentence: "Receive a Piece of Pie." But all rules invariably have exceptions, just to make life difficult:

> *i* before *e*, except after *c*
> or when sounded like *a*
> as in *neighbor* and *weigh*.

A similar version ends with the line: "as in *weigh, neigh, or sleigh.*" Numerous exceptions to the rule include the words *neither, height, leisure,* and *weird.*

A rhyme with an extended rule used more commonly in British schools clarifies things a little further:

> When the sound is *ee*
> It's *i* before *e* except after *c*.

However, even the extended rule has a number of exceptions: words such as *caffeine, protein,* and *seize* are *e* before *i* despite having a long *ee* sound. Also, the plurals of *–cy* words end with *–cies*, which is another exception to this *i* before *e* rule, as are many *–cie* words, such as *science* and *conscience*.

Therefore, another addendum has been applied to the original saying:

> *i* before *e*, except after *c*
> Or when sounding like *a*
> As in *neighbor* and *weigh*.
> Drop this rule when *-c* sounds as *-sh*.

Words such as *ancient, efficient,* and *species* become covered by this additional rule.

The Complexities of English Spelling

The English language is full of convolutions and contradictions, which can make the spelling and pronunciations of certain words difficult to predict. The following poem, which appeared in the *NEA Journal*, a publication of the National Education Association, in 1966/67, by educator Vivian Buchan, expresses the idiosyncrasies and frustrations with so-called spelling rules.

Phony Phonetics

One reason why I cannot spell,
Although I learned the rules quite well
Is that some words like *coup* and *through*
Sound just like *threw* and *flue* and *Who;*
When *oo* is never spelled the same,
The *duice* becomes a guessing game;
And then I ponder over *though,*
Is it spelled *so,* or *throw,* or *beau,*
And *bough* is never *bow,* it's *bow,*
I mean the *bow* that sounds like *plow,*
And not the *bow* that sounds like *row*—
The *row* that is pronounced like *roe.*
I wonder, too, why *rough* and tough,
That sound the same as *gruff* and *muff,*
Are spelled like *bough* and *though,* for they
Are both pronounced a different way.
And why can't I spell *trough* and *cough*
The same as I do *scoff* and *golf?*

Why isn't *drought* spelled just like *route*,
or *doubt* or *pout* or *sauerkraut*?
When words all sound so much the same
To change the spelling seems a shame.
There is no sense—see sound like cents—
in making such a difference
Between the sight and sound of words;
Each spelling rule that undergirds
The way a word should look will fail
And often prove to no avail
Because exceptions will negate
The truth of what the rule may state;
So though I try, I still despair
And moan and mutter "It's not fair
That I'm held up to ridicule
And made to look like such a fool
When it's the spelling that's at fault.
Let's call this nonsense to a halt."

Commonly Misspelled Words

It has almost become cliché among educators and orthographers (who study spelling) to misspell the word *misspell* in order to prove a point. It does, however, demonstrate how easily words can run astray. You need only do an Internet search of the misspelled word *equiptment* to see how poor spelling has become commonplace.

Their/They're/There

Instructors and editors often find errors with this group of words, because the words all sound the same. They're all pronounced the same but spelled differently. The possessive is *their*, and the contraction of "they are" is *they're*. Everywhere else, it is *there*. Think directions for *there*: it's either *here* or *there*. The word *here* can be found in *there*. Think of ownership for *their:* children are *heirs* before they inherit *their* fortune. If there is an "*I*" in it, then it is the one that refers to people.

Principal/Principle

Remember the following spelling principle: the school *principal* is a *prince* and a *pal* (despite what you may think of him or her). The *principal's principle* dictates: a *principle* is a rule!

Lay and Lie

As a rule, irregular verbs pose problems for people who like neat, cut-and-dried methods to live and learn by. One forms the past and past participle of regular verbs by adding *-d* or *-ed* to the stem of the infinitive *(touch, touched)*, but this process does not apply to irregular verbs such as *lie*. So just remember the phrase:

You'll lay an egg if you don't lie down.

Affect or Effect?

The RAVEN mnemonic is useful when working out whether to use *affect* or *effect* in a sentence:

Remember: **A**ffect, **V**erb, **E**ffect, **N**oun

The woman was *affected* by the *effect* of the film.

A Useful Selection of Spelling Aids

Many of the words in the following list appear to have no logical spelling rule whatsoever, but reciting the clever mnemonic phrase that accompanies the word may help keep you out of the dunce's chair.

Accelerator
A Cruel **C**reature—imagine words and pictures to remind you to write two Cs.

Acceptable
Remember to accept any table offered, and you will spell this word correctly.

Accessible
—able or –ible?
Say out loud, "**I** am always accessible."

Accidentally
Two Cs and an ally. Make up a story:
Two cats accidentally scratched your friend and ally.

Accommodation
Again two Cs and two Ms,
And don't forget that second O after the second M.
Comfortable **C**hairs, **O**r **M**odern **M**ats, **O**r…

Address
Directly **D**elivered letters are **S**afe and **S**ound.

Aeroplane
All **E**ngines **R**unning **O**kay.

Almond
ALmonds are ov**AL**s.

Amateur
Amateurs need not be mature.

Argument
A Rude **G**irl **U**ndresses—**M**y **E**yes **N**eed **T**aping.

(Another way to check your spelling is to find short words within. Think of chewing GUM when you chew over an arGUMent.)

Arithmetic
A Rat **I**n **T**he **H**ouse **M**ay **E**at **T**he **I**ce **C**ream.

A Red **I**ndian **T**hought **H**e **M**ight **E**at **T**urkey **I**n **C**hurch.

Assassination
This word is comprised of four short words:

Ass Ass I Nation.

Asthma
The cause of Asthm**A**:

Sensitivity **T**o **H**ousehold **M**ites.

Autumn
There's an N at the end of autumn.

Think of N standing for November, because it's the end of autumn and the beginning of winter.

Bare or Bear
Imagine scenarios relating to the two words.

It's bath time with a bar of soap on your bare skin.

A bear is scary and fills you with fear.

Beautiful
Big **E**lephants **A**re **U**sually **BEAU**tiful.

Because
Big **E**lephants **C**an **A**lways **U**nderstand **S**mall **E**lephants.

Big **E**lephants **C**an't **A**lways **U**se **S**mall **E**xits.

Believe
This word obeys the *i* before *e* rule, and there's also a perfect word association within.

Do you beLIEve a LIE?

Biscuit
Some believe this word is derived from two French words—*bis cuit* meaning twice cooked. The easy way to remember how to spell it is with this phrase:

BIScuits are **C**rumbled **U**p **I**nto **T**iny pieces.

Broccoli
We know it's healthy, but it's tricky to spell.

Remember that broccoli would never **C**ause **COLI**c.

Calendar
Just remember that this word has an *e* between two *a*s. The last vowel is *a*.

Capital or Capitol
The capit**A**l city of Greece is **A**thens.

P**A**ris is the capital of Fr**A**nce.

Most capit**O**l buildings have d**O**mes.

There's a capit**O**l in Washingt**O**n.

Chaos
Cyclones, **H**urricanes **A**nd **O**ther **S**torms create chaos.

Character
CHARlie's **ACT** is **ER**otic.

Committee
Remember: **M**any **M**eetings **T**ake **T**ime—**E**veryone's **E**xhausted!

Conscience
It's not pronounced how it's spelled.

It's **S**cience with **C**on at the beginning.

Consensus
The census does not require a consensus, since they are not related.

Correspondence
CORRect your **CORR**espon**DEN**ce in the **DEN**.

Definitely
Find the word **FINITE** within.

Deliberate
It was a de**LIBERATE** plan to **LIBERATE** the hostages.

Desert (as in the Sahara) or Dessert (as in apple pie)
Remember that the sweet one has two **SugarS**.

Or that the double "s" in dessert stands for "sweet stuff."

Diarrhea
If you need to know how to spell this—here you go!

Dash **I**n **A** **R**eal **R**ush—**H**urriedly **E**vading **A**ccident.

Doubt
Sometimes it's only natural to **B**e in doubt.

Dumbbell
Even smart people forget one of the *b*s in this one. (So be careful whom you call one when you write.)

Eccentric
The word literally means "off center," so imagine an eccentric **C**razy **C**at, running around in circles.

Eczema
It's pronounced with an X, but there's no X factor with this problem:

Even **C**lean **ZE**alots **MA**y get eczema.

Embarrass
Do you turn **R**eally **R**ed **A**nd **S**mile **S**hyly when embarrassed?

Exaggerate
If he's br**AGG**ing, then he's surely exaggerating.

Fascinate
Are you fa**SCI**inated by **SCI**ence?

Fiery
The silent *e* on fire is so cowardly: it retreats inside the word rather than face the suffix -y.

Forty
FORget the *u* in four when you spell **FOR**ty.

Friend
FRIEs are for sharing with your **FRIE**nd.

Geography
General **E**isenhower's **O**ldest **G**irl **R**ode **A** **P**ony **H**ome **Y**esterday.

Grammar
There's no *e* in grammar.

Think about Grand**MA**, who teaches perfect grammar.

Grateful
You should be grateful to know that keeping "great" out of "grateful" is great.

Handkerchief
It's shortened to "hanky," but the long form has a **D**.

Think of holding a handkerchief in your **HAND**.

Heard or Herd
If you heard something, you used your **EAR**.

There are lots of animals in a herd, so there can't be a single one on its own in this word.

Indispensable
Only the most **ABLE** are indispens**ABLE**.

Interrupt
It's a fact that it's **R**eally **R**ude to interrupt.

Liaison
Dangerous and often misspelled.

To spot a liaison, use your two eyes (2 **I**s).

Lightning
Lighten the load of the word lightning by learning how to eliminate the e.

Memento
Commonly misspelled as "momento."

A souvenir from your holiday is a memento, and it represents happy **MEM**ories.

Millennium
A thousand years—**MILLE**—that's more than **N**inety-**N**ine years.

Miniature
It means tiny, and there are tiny words in the middle—**I** and **A**.

Misspell
The subject of this section of the book.

Don't mi**SS** that extra s in **M**i**SS**pell.

Necessary
Not **E**very **C**at **E**ats **S**ardines—**S**ome **A**re **R**eally **Y**ummy.

Or think of a shirt—it is necessary for a shirt to have one **C**ollar and two **S**leeve**S**.

Or think of your necessary coffee each morning with one **C**ream and two **S**ugar**S**.

Occasion
If it's a special one, you'd travel over two seas (**C**s).

Ocean
Only **C**at's **E**yes **A**re **N**arrow.

Parallel
There are three **L**s in parallel, but think of the middle ones acting as parallel lines next to each other.

Parliament
Think: **I AM** parliament.

People
People **E**at **O**ther **P**eople's **L**eftovers **E**agerly.

Pneumonia
People **N**ever **E**xpect **U**s to come down with **PNEU**monia.

Possession
Very sweet—four **S**ugar**S**.

Potassium
One **T**ea and two **S**ugar**S**.

Recommend
No need for confusion with this word.
It's simply commend with *re-* at the beginning.

Rhythm
Rhythm **H**elps **Y**ou **T**o **H**ear **M**usic.

Rhythm **H**elps **Y**our **T**wo **H**ips **M**ove.

Separate
The *e*s surround the *a*s.

Or think of your old Father or **PA** in his den as a se**PA**rate kind of person.

Stationery or Stationary
A or E? Every office intern gets the spelling of this word wrong at least once in his or her life. You only have to remember one, and by process of elimination, the other one must be right. Think of the initial *e* in envelope for stationery, or keep in mind the following sentences:

PEns are items of stationery.

CArs when parked are stationary.

Subtle
To **B**e subtle—**B**e silent.

Succeed
Succeed, **P**roceed, **E**xceed are the only three English words that end in **CEED**.

Take the initial letters of these words and think **SPEED**.

Together
Split it up into three separate words:

To get her.

Weather or Whether
WE look **AT HER** (the TV weather girl) to check the forecast and discover whether it will be sunny or rainy.

Wednesday
WE Do **N**ot **E**at **S**oup **D**ay.

Weird
Weird doesn't follow the *i* before *e* rule, because weird is just weird.

You're or Your
YOU'RE never going to get it right if you don't use **YOUR** head.

If something belongs to us, it is **OUR**s, just as something that belongs to you is **YOUR**s.

Eye halve a spelling checker
It came with my pea sea
It plainly marques for my revue
Miss steaks eye kin knot sea.

Eye strike a key and type a word
And weight four it to say
Weather eye am wrong oar write
It shows me strait a weigh.

As soon as a mist ache is maid
It nose bee fore two long
And eye can put the error rite
It's rare lea ever wrong.

Eye have run this poem threw it
Eye am shore your pleased two no
It's letter perfect awl the weigh
My checker tolled me sew.

—Margo Roark

www.spellingsociety.org/news/media/poems.php

3
Think of a Number

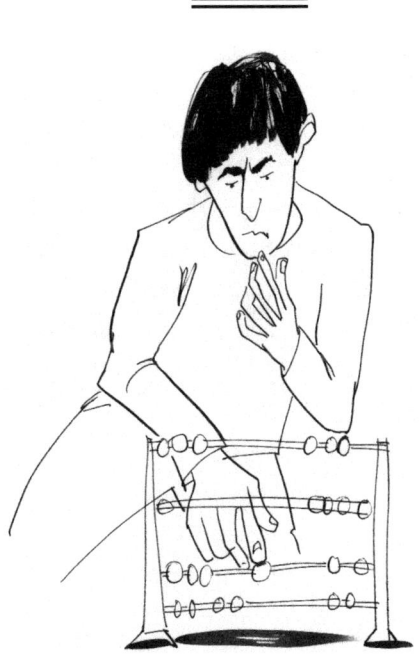

First Steps: Counting Rhymes

Learning to count is the first step to understanding arithmetic. Most children learn counting by reciting nursery rhymes, which contain the essential ingredients of mnemonics: imagery, rhyme, and fun. "One, Two, Buckle My Shoe" was devised many years ago as a fun way to teach children how to count to 20 using visual language and repetitive rhythm. Here are two slightly different versions of the famous verse:

> One, Two, buckle my shoe,
> Three, Four, knock at the door,
> Five, Six, pick up sticks,
> Seven, Eight, lay them straight,
> Nine, Ten, a big fat hen,
> Eleven, Twelve, dig and delve,
> Thirteen, Fourteen, maids a-courting,
> Fifteen, Sixteen, maids in the kitchen,
> Seventeen, Eighteen, maids in waiting,
> Nineteen, Twenty, my plate's empty.

> One, Two, buckle my shoe,
> Three, Four, knock at the door,
> Five, Six, pick up sticks,
> Seven, Eight, don't be late,
> Nine, Ten, a good fat hen,
> Eleven, Twelve, dig and delve
> Thirteen, Fourteen, maids a-courting,
> Fifteen, Sixteen, maids a-kissing,
> Seventeen, Eighteen, maids a-waiting,
> Nineteen, Twenty, I've had plenty.

"One, Two, Three, Four, Five," also known as "Once I Caught a Fish Alive," is another famous counting rhyme. Though its origins are unknown, its earliest date of publication has been traced back to 1888:

> One, two, three, four, five.
> Once I caught a fish alive.
> Six, seven, eight, nine, ten.
> Then I let it go again.
> Why did you let it go?
> Because it bit my finger so.
> Which finger did it bite?
> This little finger on my right.

This shorter counting rhyme was also popular with children:

> One, Two, Three, Four,
> Mary's at the cottage door.
> Five, Six, Seven, Eight,
> Eating cherries off a plate.

Writing Numbers

Mastering numbers out loud is one thing, but writing them down is something else entirely. However, the number-writing poem on the next page doubtless helped countless youngsters.

Around to the left to find my hero,
Back to the top, I've made a zero.

Downward stroke, my that's fun,
Now I've made the number 1.

Half a heart says, "I love you."
A line—now I made the number 2.

Around the tree, around the tree,
Now I've made the number 3.

Down and across and down once more
Now I've made the number 4.

The hat, the back, the belly—a 5.
Watch out! It might come alive.

Bend down low to pick up sticks,
Now I've made the number 6.

Across the sky, and down from heaven,
Now I've made the number 7.

Make an "S" and close the gate,
Now I've made the number 8.

An oval and a line,
Now I've made the number 9.

One (1) egg (0) laid my hen.
Now I've made the number 10.

Roman Numerals

Imagine doing sums using Roman numerals. They are still used today for indicating successive same-name successors to kings and queens, as well as for movie sequels, dates, Olympic Games, and the Super Bowl, but their usage is quite rare. I, V, and X are more commonly used, particularly on clock and watch faces, making it more familiar that they represent 1, 5, and 10 respectively. It's a good idea to remember that C stands for "century," i.e., 100 years:

I	**V**	**X**	**L**	**C**	**D**	**M**
1	5	10	50	100	500	1,000

The Romans did not have a notation for zero, which meant that early in the second millennium the system was gradually replaced by the Arabic numerals used today. Modern society rarely uses Roman numerals anymore; there's a danger that this system may become obsolete. This simple mnemonic helps keep the numbers in order:

I Value **X**ylophones **L**ike **C**ows **D**ig **M**ilk.

Remember the first three letters IVX, then recite the following to recall LCD and M:

Lucy **C**an't **D**rink **M**ilk.

The poem on the next page provides a rhythmic visual image for learning Roman numerals.

> X shall stand for playmates Ten,
> V for Five stout stalwart men,
> I for One as I'm alive,
> C for Hundred and D for Five,
> M for a Thousand soldiers true,
> And L for Fifty, I'll tell you.

As is this brief yet concise verse:

> M's mille—or 1,000 said,
> D's half—500 quickly read.
> C's just a 100—century
> And L is half again—50.
> So all that's left is X and V
> Or 10 and 5 and I is easy.

The Metric System

Metrication, or the decimal system, began in France in the 1790s. Although the United States has been slow to adopt metrics, it is gradually finding its way into the U.S. marketplace. Two-liter soft drinks are not uncommon; dental floss is often measured in meters; and prior to digitization, 35-mm film became a popular standard. Don't be terrified, get metrified. Here are some clever mnemonics to help you remember. Don't despair. If all else fails, use one of the many metric conversion calculators available on the Internet.

Kilometer	1,000 meters
Hectometer	100 meters
Decameter	10 meters
Meter (base)	1 meter
Decimeter	⅒ of a meter
Centimeter	1/100 of a meter
Millimeter	1/1000 of a meter

The first letters stand for the metric prefixes and base unit: Kilo, Hecto, Deca, Meter (base), Deci, Centi, Milli. The following phrases help to remember the correct order:

King **H**enry **D**ied **M**ightily **D**rinking **C**hocolate **M**ilk

Keep **H**er **D**iamond **M**ine **D**own **C**reek, **M**ister

King **H**enry **D**ied—**M**other **D**idn't **C**are **M**uch

King **H**ector **D**ied **M**iserable **D**eath—**C**aught **M**easles

If the base unit is a gram rather than a meter we would have:

King **H**enry **D**ied—**G**ranny **D**idn't **C**are **M**uch

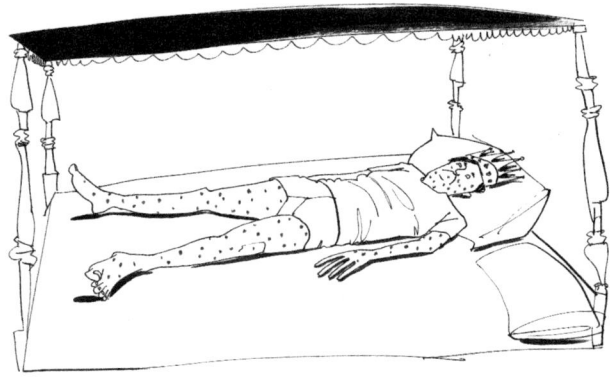

Times-Table Tricks

Ten Times-table

When multiplying a number by 10, add a zero to it. This is a simple mnemonic device— $3 \times 10 = 30$, just as $26{,}350 \times 10 = 263{,}500$. As the numbers get larger, add a zero and move the comma to the right by one place.

Nine Times-table

The study of arithmetic presents an infinite number of patterns to discover. One involves the nine times-table.

$$9 \times 1 = 9 \qquad 9 \times 6 = 54$$
$$9 \times 2 = 18 \qquad 9 \times 7 = 63$$
$$9 \times 3 = 27 \qquad 9 \times 8 = 72$$
$$9 \times 4 = 36 \qquad 9 \times 9 = 81$$
$$9 \times 5 = 45 \qquad 9 \times 10 = 90$$

Notice that the product of 9×5 inverts at 9×6 to 54:

$$9 \times 5 = 45;\ 9 \times 6 = 54$$

Also, up to 9×10, the digits in the products of numbers multiplied by 9 always add up to 9:

$$9 \times 2 = 18\ (1 + 8 = 9),\ 9 \times 3 = 27\ (2 + 7 = 9).$$

Nine Times-table: By Hand

Many people learned this clever way to remember our nine times-table.

First, hold your two hands up with the palms facing you, and number each digit from 1 to 10, starting with the thumb on your left hand (1) through to the thumb on your right hand (10).

For 9 × 2, you need to bend digit number 2 (your left index finger) to signify *times 2*. This leaves your thumb (1) outstretched to the left of your bent index finger, and 8 digits outstretched to the right of it. Put 1 and 8 together to form the product of 9 × 2.

For 9 × 6, you need to bend digit number 6 (your right pinky) to represent *times 6*. This leaves all the digits on your left hand outstretched (5) and the remaining digits on your right hand outstretched (4). Put 5 and 4 together to make the product of 9 × 6.

The key involves looking at the number of fingers to the left side of the folded-down finger to find the number for the tens column of the answer, and looking to the right of the folded-down finger to find the number for the ones column.

More Times-table Tricks

Eight Times-table
8 × 8 fell on the floor, when I picked it up, it was 64!
8 and 9 are nice, but I like seven, too (72).

Seven Times-table
Three 7s had drinks and fun, and so they must be 21.
7 × 7 were in a mine, it must be 1849.

Six Times-table
6 and 7 went on a date and secured a table four two (42).

Five Times-table
Learn to count by fives, and remember that the products always end with a 5 or an 0.

Four Times-table
To 4 × 4 it would seem, long ago was sweet 16.

Three Times-table
Three cats have nine lives before heaven, until they turn 27.

Two Times-table
To multiply by two is great; it must end in 0, 2, 4, 6 or 8.

Long Division

When it comes to the technique for remembering which steps to follow when doing long division—**D**ivide, **M**ultiply, **S**ubtract, **B**ring down—use one of these memorable phrases:

> **D**ad, **M**om, **S**ister, **B**rother.
> **D**ead **M**onkeys **S**mell **B**ad.

The Order of Calculation

The order to work out a sum is: **M**ultiply and **D**ivide before you **A**dd and **S**ubtract. Any mathematical statement with an "equals" sign is an equation; that is, one side of the equation equals the other side. For example, $1 + 1 = 2$ is an equation, just as $2 \times 10 = 4 \times 5$ is an equation.

Some people find that the following phrase helps them remember the MDAS correct order:

My **D**ear **A**unt **S**ally

When things get more complicated and several functions become necessary to solve for the sum, the PEMDAS order tackles the problem:

Parentheses **E**xponents **M**ultiplication
Division **A**ddition **S**ubtraction

Certain phrases are useful for keeping the correct order in mind:

Please **E**xcuse **M**y **D**ear **A**unt **S**ally.

Please **E**xecute **M**y **D**og **A**nd **S**oon.

Put **E**very **M**an **D**own **A**nd **S**hout.

The **BIDMAS** acronym offers another alternative, but works in exactly the same way:

Brackets **I**ndices **D**ivision **M**ultiplication
Addition **S**ubtraction

BIDMAS allows you to calculate the sum written as:

$$(8 - 3) \times 4 + \frac{15}{5} - 3 = 20$$

The B for Brackets in BIDMAS means the same as the P for Parentheses in PEMDAS, as does the I for Indices and the E for Exponents. The order of Division and Multiplication is flexible, so the order can either be DM or MD.

Finding Averages

Here is an excellent way to remember the names of the four methods of finding averages, using the **Medium-Range Mean Model** method:

Median—the number exactly in the middle when a set of numbers is listed in order.

Range—the difference between the highest and lowest numbers in a set.

Mean—the sum of a set of numbers, divided by the number of numbers in the set.

Mode—the number (or numbers) that appears most frequently in a set.

Isosceles Triangles

To help distinguish between an isosceles triangle and all other types of triangles, this song sung to the tune of "Oh, Christmas Tree" proved invaluable:

> Oh, isosceles, oh, isosceles,
> Two angles have
> Equal degrees.
> Oh, isosceles, oh, isosceles,
> You look just like
> A Christmas tree.

Dividing by Fractions

A fraction is a numerical quantity that is not a whole number, for example ½ or ¹⁹⁄₂₀, which are quantities that form part of a whole.

The definition of a fraction is a numerator divided by a denominator, but which is which?

Think of "Notre Dame":

NUmerator **U**p, **D**enominator **D**own.

Therefore, in ½, 1 is the numerator, 2 is the denominator.

In ¹⁹⁄₂₀, 19 is the numerator, 20 is the denominator.

This rhyme will help every student who gets into a muddle when dividing by fractions:

> The number you're dividing by,
> Turn upside down and multiply.

> e.g., 10 divided by ½ = 10 × ²⁄₁ = 20
> or 15 divided by ⅕ = 15 × ⁵⁄₁ = 75

The Value of Pi

Pi is the Greek letter π. It is a mathematical constant and calculated as the ratio of the circumference of a circle to its diameter. Pi is the number 3.14159, although in reality, it has an infinite number of decimal places.

The traditional way to remind yourself of the decimals is to use phrases containing word-length mnemonics, where the number of letters in each word corresponds to a digit.

Pi to six decimal places is:

> How I wish I could calculate pi = 3.141592

And to 14 places:

> How I like a drink,
> alcoholic of course,
> after the heavy lectures involving
> quantum mechanics = 3.14159265358979

And here's a rhyme to 20 decimal places of pi:

> Now, I wish I could recollect pi.
> "Eureka," cried the great inventor.
> Christmas Pudding, Christmas Pie,
> Is the problem's very center.
> = 3.14159265358979323846

And to 31 decimal places:

> Sir, I bear a rhyme excelling
> In mystic force, and magic spelling
> Celestial sprites elucidate
> All my own striving can't relate
> Or locate they who can cogitate
> And so finally terminate. Finis.
> = 3.1415926535897932384626433832795

Unfortunately, this useful method of remembering pi only works up to 31 decimal places, because the thirty-second number after the decimal point is 0.

Omni, the celebrated science magazine of the late 1970s and early 1980s, devised this fun verse to help students calculate the circumference of a circle using pi:

> If you cross a circle with a line,
> Which hits the center and runs from spine to spine,
> And the line's length is d
> The circumference will be d times 3.14159.

The area of a circle is calculated as π × r squared (where r is the radius) = πr².

To help remember the formula, think:

> Apple Pie Are Square.

The circumference of a circle is calculated as π × d (where d is the diameter) = πd.

One memorable way to recall the formula is to think:

> Cherry Pie Delicious.

The following rhyme helps teach the difference between circumference and area:

> Fiddlededum, fiddlededee,
> A ring round the moon is π times d.
> If a hole in your sock you want repaired,
> You use the formula πr squared.

Square Roots

Just as subtraction is the opposite of addition and division is the opposite of multiplication, so square roots are the opposite of squaring; that is, multiplying a number by itself, so the square root of 4 is 2 (i.e., 2 × 2 = 4).

This example shows a perfect square root and is therefore quite simple. Things get more interesting when math instructors explore more complicated concepts, such as the square root of 2. Which number multiplied by itself makes 2? It's not a round number, and so, as with pi, the length of each word in the following rhyme represents each digit:

> For the square root of 2,
> I wish I knew
> 1.414—the root of two.
>
> For the square root of 3,
> O, charmed was he
> 1.732—to know the root of three.
>
> For the square root of 5,
> So we now strive
> 2.236—to know the root of five.
>
> For the square root of 6,
> We need more logistics
> 2.449—to know the root of six.

Pythagoras's Theorem

Pythagoras (c. 580–500 B.C.) was a Greek mathematician and philosopher from Samos, sometimes known as the "Father of Numbers." His famous theorem is a math standard that reveals how to calculate the lengths of the three sides of a right-angled triangle.

In essence, Pythagoras's theorem states that the

square of the hypotenuse is equal to the sum of the squares of the other two sides, or HYPOTENUSE squared = BASE squared + HEIGHT squared.

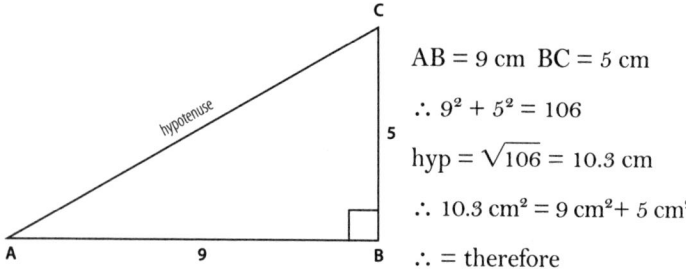

AB = 9 cm BC = 5 cm

∴ $9^2 + 5^2 = 106$

hyp = $\sqrt{106}$ = 10.3 cm

∴ 10.3 cm² = 9 cm² + 5 cm²

∴ = therefore

To help math students remember the formula, a visual aid in the form of the "teepee story" was devised, which featured a memorable mnemonic punch line:

> A Red Indian chief had three squaws in three teepees. When he came home late from hunting, he never knew which squaw was in which teepee, because it was always dark. One day he killed a hippopotamus, a bear and a buffalo. He put one hide from each animal into each teepee so that when he came home late he could feel inside the teepee and he would know which squaw was which. After a year, all three squaws had had children. The squaw on the bear hide had a baby boy, the squaw on the buffalo hide had a baby girl. But the squaw on the hippopotamus hide had a girl and a boy. And the moral of the story?
>
> *The squaw on the hippopotamus is equal to the sum of the squaws on the other two hides.*

Trigonometry: Sine Cosine Tangent

By definition, triangles are all about threes—sides and angles. If you know two elements of a right-angled triangle—whether it be sides, angles, or one of each—you can then calculate the third.

In a right-angled triangle, if the value of a second angle is given:

the **S**ine of the angle = the ratio of the **O**pposite side to the **H**ypotenuse

the **C**osine of the angle = the ratio of the **A**djacent side to the **H**ypotenuse

the **T**angent of the angle = the ratio of the **O**pposite and the **A**djacent sides

For example, in this diagram:

$\sin(A) = \dfrac{a}{c}$

$\cos(A) = \dfrac{b}{c}$

$\tan(A) = \dfrac{a}{b}$

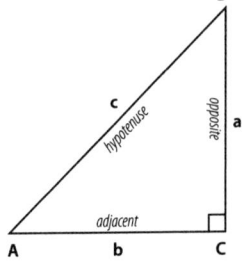

The initials spell **SOH–CAH–TOA**, which is easy to recall because it rhymes with Krakatoa, the volcanic island in Indonesia. If, however, the volcano comparison is less than effective, one of the examples on the next page might prove more memorable.

Smiles **O**f **H**appiness **C**ome
After **H**aving **T**ankards **O**f **A**le.

Some **O**ld **H**ag **C**aught
A **H**ippy **T**ripping **O**n **A**cid.

Some **O**ld **H**orse **C**aught **A**nother **H**orse
Taking **O**ats **A**way.

Graph Coordinates

From simple bar charts showing hours of sunshine against months of the year to advanced calculus graphs indicating rates of change, this is the rule for all graphs:

> X along the corridor,
> Y up and down the stairs.

The convention for labeling a pair of coordinates (x and y) is that x is the horizontal axis and y the vertical axis.

Converting Miles to Kilometers

Fibonacci numbers are named after the thirteenth-century mathematician Leonardo of Pisa, who was also called Leonardo Fibonacci. They are whole numbers in sequence: 0, 1, 2, 3, 5, 8, 13, 21, 34, 55, 89 ... and so on to infinity. Each number in the series is the sum of the previous two numbers.

There are approximately 8 (8.05 km) kilometers in 5 miles, and since both 8 and 5 are Fibonacci numbers, you can convert kilometers to miles and miles to kilometers by looking at the consecutive numbers. Just remember, there will always be more kilometers (longer word) than miles (shorter word).

$$8 \text{ km} = 5 \text{ miles}$$
$$13 \text{ km} = 8 \text{ miles}$$
$$21 \text{ km} = 13 \text{ miles}$$
$$34 \text{ km} = 21 \text{ miles}$$
$$55 \text{ km} = 34 \text{ miles}$$
$$89 \text{ km} = 55 \text{ miles}$$

> *The hardest arithmetic to master is that which enables us to count our blessings.*
>
> —Eric Hoffer
> *Reflections on the Human Condition*

4
Geographically Speaking

Learning Directions

The four main compass directions: north, south, east, and west form the introduction to many geography lessons. Remembering exactly where these points fall on a compass should be quite straightforward, but to avoid memory loss, a number of useful phrases have been devised.

Consider, for example, the acronym NEWS:

> **N**orth at the top
> **E**ast on the right
> **W**est on the left
> **S**outh at the bottom

Alternatively, the first letter of each word in these sentences indicates the points of the compass in clockwise order:

> **N**ever **E**at **S**hredded **W**heat.

Never Eat **S**limy **W**orms.
Never Enter **S**anta's **W**orkshop.
Never Eat **S**oggy **W**affles.
Naughty **E**lephants **S**quirt **W**ater.

Latitude and Longitude

If you've ever had problems remembering the direction of latitude and longitude lines, here are a few mnemonic pointers to ensure you won't get lost.

The Latin word *latus* means "side"; hence, latitude lines go from side to side.

The phrase "Lat is fat" should help remind us that the central lines of latitude go around the "belt" of the equator.

*Long*itude lines seem *long*er, going from top to bottom or north to south.

The Tropics of Cancer and Capricorn

These are two imaginary lines running parallel to the equator (the longest line of latitude that spans the center of the globe), which are based on the sun's position in relation to the earth at two points of the year. The sun is directly overhead at noon on the Tropic of Cancer on June 21 (the beginning of summer in the Northern Hemisphere and of winter in the Southern Hemisphere) and is again overhead at midday on the Tropic of Capricorn on December 21 (the beginning of winter in the Northern Hemisphere and of summer in the Southern Hemisphere).

The Tropic of Cancer lies 23.5° north of the equator and the Tropic of Capricorn lies at 23.5° south, and the following verse has helped many to remember this fact.

Ca**N**cer lies **N**orth of the equator.
Capric**O**rn lies on the **O**ther side of the equator.

Map Reading

Imagine you're a Girl Scout or Boy Scout on an expedition carrying no more than a Hershey bar and a topographical map, or a soldier in the field armed with just a map and a compass. Your map grid reference is 123456. To find your position on the map just think: "Onward and Upward."

Split your map reference into two sets of three figures: 123 and 456.

The 1 is the number of the grid line on the map going across—ONWARD—from west to east. The 2 and 3 give more precise coordinates within that grid.

The 4 is the grid line going up—UPWARD—from south to north. And the 5 and 6 give a more precise location.

The Seven Continents of the World

A continent is defined as a large continuous landmass, and geographers state that the world has seven of them:

Europe **A**sia **A**frica **A**ustralia
Antarctica **N**orth America **S**outh America

Although Europe is joined to Asia, the two areas are recognized as separate continents, with the Ural Mountains in Russia dividing the areas that we regard as East and West. Australia is the smallest continent and is also known as Oceania. Australia itself is an island of just under 3 million square miles. Asia is the largest continent at approximately 17 million square miles.

The following phrases are the most popular to remember the continents:

> **E**at **A**n **A**spirin **A**fter **A** **N**asty **S**andwich.
> **E**at **A**n **A**pple **A**s **A** **N**ice **S**nack.

The Five Oceans

For a long time, geography teachers categorized four oceans when teaching about the 70 to 75 percent of the earth that is blanketed with water. But in the spring of 2000, the International Hydrographic Organization officially established the Southern Ocean as number five, defining its often frozen perimeters. Now students need to memorize five oceans: Pacific, Atlantic, Indian, Southern, and Arctic (from largest to smallest). Form your own mnemonic to remember the PAISA acronym, such as:

> **P**acifiers **A**re **I**cky, **S**omeone **A**ttested.
> **P**ick **A**n **I**ndian **S**ummer **A**pple.

The Great Lakes

The five Great Lakes from west to east are: **S**uperior, **M**ichigan, **H**uron, **E**rie, and **O**ntario. As SMHEO is a less than memorable acronym, these short pithy sentences are far more effective:

> **S**ally **M**ade **H**enry **E**at **O**nions.
> **S**he **M**akes **H**im **E**at **O**reos.
> **S**uper **M**ario **H**eaved **E**arth **O**ut.

From east to west, try:

> **O**ld **E**lephants **H**ave **M**uch **S**kin.

An easier and more commonly used mnemonic acronym is HOMES, but this scrambles the correct geographical order.

Niagara Falls

Use the letters LENOR as a reminder of which two Great Lakes surround Niagara Falls. Picture the scene as if looking at a map where north is at the top of the page:

> **L**eft—**E**rie—**N**iagara—**O**ntario—**R**ight

Central America

There are seven Central American countries, namely: **G**uatemala, **B**elize, **H**onduras, **E**l Salvador, **N**icaragua, **C**osta Rica and **P**anama. If these names or the letters GBHENCP don't roll easily off your tongue, try using this mnemonic phrase to jog your memory:

Great **B**ig **H**ungry **E**lephant
Nearly **C**onsumed **P**anama.

The World's Longest Rivers

An unusual acronym used to remember the names of the world's longest rivers is NAYY CLAIM. The exact length of the two greatest rivers on Earth—the Nile and the Amazon—varies over time, and geographers disagree on their actual length. Therefore, this acronym is more of an aid to remembering the names of the rivers, rather than their exact pecking order, about which no one seems able to agree. In fact, this list changes significantly when all tributaries are included.

River	Continent	Length
Nile	Africa	4,160 miles (6,695 km)
Amazon	South America	4,150 miles (6,683 km)
Yangtze (Chang Jiang)	Asia	3,964 miles (6,380 km)
Yellow (Huang He)	Asia	3,000 miles (4,830 km)
Congo (Zaire)	Africa	2,880 miles (4,630 km)
Lena	Asia	2,734 miles (4,400 km)
Amur (Heilong Jiang)	Asia	2,703 miles (4,350 km)
Irtysh	Asia	2,640 miles (4,248 km)
Mekong	Asia	2,600 miles (4,180 km)

The three longest rivers in North America, including tributaries, can be recalled using the acronym MMR (think Measles, Mumps, and Rubella):

River	Country of Origin	Length
Mississippi-Missouri	United States	3,709 miles (5,970 km)
Mackenzie	Canada	2,635 miles (4,240 km)
Rio Grande	United States and Mexico	1,885 miles (3,034 km)

The Seven Hills of Rome

Rome was built on the seven hills east of the Tiber River. Clockwise from the westernmost hill, they are **C**apitoline, **Q**uirinal, **V**iminal, **E**squiline, **C**aelian, **A**ventine and **P**alatine, and they can be easily remembered with the following phrase:

Can **Q**ueen **V**ictoria **E**at **C**old **A**pple **P**ie?

Alternatively, if you start with the Quirinal, going in a clockwise direction, you could try remembering a slightly more amusing alternative:

Queen **V**ictoria **E**yes **C**aesar's **A**wfully **P**ainful **C**orns.

An even more memorable acronym is **PACE QVC**. *Pace*, the Italian word for "peace," is paired with QVC, the shopping channel.

Italian Geography

If you ever need a reminder of the location of Sicily, here's a verse guaranteed to help:

Long-legged Italy kicked little Sicily
Right into the middle of the Mediterranean Sea.

The Streets of Los Angeles

Mnemonics can be used to help tourists find their way in unfamiliar cities and towns. The following mnemonic mentions 10 primary east to west (actually SE to NW) streets in central LA:

> In LOS ANGELES, you MAINly SPRING onto BROADWAY, go up the HILL to OLIVE with the GRAND HOPE of picking FLOWERs on FIGUEROA.

Grand is actually an avenue not a street, but the idea allows the reader to navigate that part of the city with relative ease by memorizing one simple sentence.

When asked how the Beatles found America on their first U.S. visit:

Just turn left at Greenland....

—John Lennon

5
Animal, Vegetable, Mineral

Geological Periods

The list below details the geological classification of rock deposits, starting with the Cambrian, the first period in the Palaeozoic era.

Approximate number of years ago

Cambrian	570–510 million
Ordovician	510–439 million
Silurian	439–409 million
Devonian	409–363 million
Carboniferous	363–290 million
Permian	290–245 million
Triassic	245–208 million
Jurassic	208–146 million
Cretaceous	146–65 million
Palaeocene	65–56.5 million
Eocene	56.5–35.4 million
Oligocene	35.4–23.3 million
Miocene	23.3–5.2 million
Pliocene	5.2–1.64 million

| Pleistocene | 1,640,000–10,000 |
| Recent (Holocene) | 10,000–present day |

Large mammals flourished and became extinct as recently as the Pleistocene period, during which time anatomically modern humans most likely began to evolve. The Recent period marked the end of the last Ice Age and the start of the development of modern civilization.

Here's a memorable phrase to help you tell your Eocene from the Pliocene period, starting with the Cambrian era from more than 500 million years ago:

Camels **O**ften **S**it **D**own **C**arefully.
Perhaps **T**heir **J**oints **C**reak? **P**ossibly **E**arly **O**iling **Mi**ght **P**revent **P**ermanent **R**heumatism.

Components of Soil

When testing the soil for its age, geologists also need to know the main constituents of soil—namely, **A**ir, **H**umus, **M**ineral salts, **W**ater, **B**acteria and **R**ock particles—which can be remembered with this essential saying:

All **H**airy **M**en **W**ill **B**uy **R**azors.

The Hardness of Minerals

The Mohs Scale, devised in 1822 by German mineralogist Friedrich Mohs (1773–1839), lists 10 familiar, easily available minerals and arranges them in order of their "scratch hardness." Scratch hardness involves a mineral's resistance to fracture or its permanent deformation due to friction from a sharp object.

Minerals in order from softest to hardest:

1. **T**alc
2. **G**ypsum
3. **C**alcite
4. **F**luorite (fluorspar)
5. **A**patite
6. **O**rthoclase (feldspar)
7. **Q**uartz
8. **T**opaz
9. **C**orundum
10. **D**iamond

Groups 1–2 can be scratched by a fingernail.
Groups 3–6 can be scratched with a blade.
Groups 7–10 are hard enough to scratch glass.

A couple of useful mnemonics to memorize the Mohs Scale are:

Tall **G**irls **C**an **F**lirt **A**nd **O**ther **Q**ueer **T**hings **C**an **D**evelop.

TAll **GY**roscopes **CA**n **FL**y **AP**art **OR**biting **QU**ickly **TO** **CO**mplete **DI**sintegration.

Types of Fossils

One way of learning the different types of fossils is to remember the acronym IMAP, which stands for:

Imprint
Molds (or casts)
Actual remains
Petrified

Or keep in mind the following apt phrase:

I Marvel **A**t **P**etrification.

Stalactites and Stalagmites

Stalactites form when water containing calcium carbonate dissolves after seeping down through limestone or chalk, then evaporates leaving deposits of carbonates of lime to accumulate over time to form mineral columns in caves. Stalagmites develop in the same way when rain falls onto the floor of caves and minerals build up to form pillars.

The similarity between the spelling and pronunciation of the two words sometimes causes confusion, so several memory aids have been developed to help simplify matters.

The following example relies on the difference in spelling, using the C and the G to relate to the origin of the formation:

> StalaCtites are formed on the Ceiling.
>
> StalaGmites are formed on the Ground.

A slightly sillier way is to think of the reaction to having ants (mites) in your pants:

> When mites go up, the tights come down!

A couple of other suggestions have been:

> Stalactites hang *tight* from the roof;
> Stalagmites *might* reach the roof.

> Stalactites hang down like *tight*s on a clothesline;
> Stalagmites *might* bite if you sit on them.

Camels: One Lump or Two

There are two main types of camel—one has one hump and the other has two. But what's the best way to remember which is which?

> A **B**actrian camel's back is shaped like the letter B
> —it has two humps.
>
> A **D**romedary's back is shaped like the letter D
> —it has only one hump.

Both species of camel come from the dry deserts of Asia and North Africa. The Bactrian, or two-humped, camel inhabits central Asia. The Dromedary, or one-humped camel, is a light and fast breed, otherwise known as the Arabian camel. The name comes from the Greek word *dromas*—to run. The Dromedary is domesticated and no longer lives in the wild.

Elephants Never Forget

How do you tell the difference between an Indian (Asian) elephant and an African elephant? It's all in the size, as this rhyme proves:

> India's big, and its elephant there features,
> But Africa's bigger with much bigger creatures.

Generally the ears of an African elephant are bigger than those of its Indian counterpart. Imagine that those ears resemble the shape of the larger African continent, while those of the Indian elephant are the shape of India.

Insect Stings

From one of the world's largest creatures to two of the smallest. What home remedies will effectively treat a bee or a wasp sting?

> Use **A**mmonia for a **B**ee sting
>
> And **V**inegar for a **W**asp sting.
>
> **B** follows **A** and **W** follows **V**
> (Think of the VW car as well).

This is also a useful mnemonic with which to remember the Latin family classification of bees and wasps:

> **A**pidae are Bees.
>
> **V**espidae are **W**asps.

More correctly, the Apidae classification refers to the "superfamily" of bees, while Vespidae is the "family" classification for wasps.

Taxonomic Classifications

Not to be confused with the art of preparing, stuffing and mounting animal skins (taxidermy), alpha taxonomy is the principle of arranging groups of living organisms—that is, plants and animals—into groups based on similarities of structure and origin. To give an example of the classifications, here are the definitions of man or *homo sapiens:*

Kingdom	*Animalia*
Phylum	*Vertibrata*
Class	*Mammalia*
Order	*Primate*
Family	*Hominidae*
Genus	*Homo*
Species	*Sapiens*
Variety	—

To remember the different classifications including "variety," these two phrases supply strong visual memory aids:

> **K**rakatoa **P**ositively **C**asts **O**ff **F**umes **G**enerating **S**ulphurous **V**apors.

Kindly **P**lace **C**over **O**n **F**resh **G**reen **S**pring **V**egetables

Versions excluding reference to "variety" can be remembered by using the following phrases:

> **K**ids **P**refer **C**heese **O**ver **F**ried **G**reen **S**pinach.
> **K**im **P**ut **C**heese **O**n **F**rank's **G**reen **S**hoes.
> **K**ings **P**lay **C**hess **O**n **F**ine **G**reen **S**ilk.

Cedar Trees

Evergreen cedar trees in many parks and gardens come in three types:

>Atlas has Ascending branches.
>
>Lebanon has Level branches.
>
>Deodar has Drooping branches.

The Cedar tree has a long history, dating back to biblical times. The Cherokee Indians believed that cedar trees held the spirits of ancient ancestors. The Atlas cedar, was first introduced into the United States in 1845, makes a popular specimen tree, and is used today in some aromatherapies. Lebanon cedar trees were coveted in ancient times for their appearance, fragrance, and commercial value, particularly in the building industry and today they are a threatened conifer. The massive Deodar cedar tree can reach approximately 250 feet in its original Himalayan habitat. Deodar, from the Sanskrit *devadaru*, translates into "timber of the gods."

Firewood

If you are building a fire at home or making a campfire, consider this traditional poem on the opposite page to avoid suffocating smoke and flying sparks.

Beech wood fires are bright and clear,
If the logs are kept a year.
Chestnut's only good, they say,
If for long it's laid away.
Birch and fir logs burn too fast,
Blaze up bright and do not last.
It is, by the Irish said,
Hawthorn makes the sweetest bread
Elm wood burns like a churchyard mold,
Even the very flames are cold.
Poplar gives a bitter smoke,
Fills your eyes and makes you choke.
Apple wood will scent your room
With an incense like perfume.
Oak and maple, if dry and old,
Keep away the winter cold.
But ash wood wet and ash wood dry,
A king shall warm his slippers by.

6
Time and the Calendar

Spring Forward, Fall Back

The seasons change, the clocks go back and forth, time waits for no man, and woe betide the person who forgets to reset his or her clock at the beginning of autumn and spring.

Most of the United States now begins daylight saving time at 2:00 A.M. on the second Sunday in March and reverts to standard time on the first Sunday in November. The Energy Policy Act, passed by the U.S. Congress in July 2005, marked the start of this change. This act altered the time-change dates for daylight saving in the United States. The legislation was enacted in the hope that this change would result in energy savings.

Another advantage to daylight saving time is that many fire

[72]

departments urge people to change the batteries in their smoke detectors on the same day that they change their clocks. This provides a convenient reminder.

So in the **spring** the clocks move **forward** one hour to herald summer, and in autumn (or **fall**) they are set **back** one hour to welcome winter.

A similar saying to "Spring Forward, Fall Back" adapted to the new system reminds people of the change in time: "Forward March, back November." That is all you need to remember.

Thirty Days Hath September...

The words to this rhyme are possibly the most often-repeated of all memory aids. This verse, first learned in childhood, helps to recall how many days there are in each month.

The origin of the "Thirty Days Hath September" poem is obscure, but the use of "old" English in the verse suggests that it dates back to at least the sixteenth century. Several different endings to the last two lines of the verse have been recorded, two are listed below:

> Thirty days hath September,
> April, June, and November;
> All the rest have thirty-one
> Excepting February alone,
> And that has twenty-eight days clear,
> With twenty-nine in each leap year.

Which hath but twenty-eight, in fine,
Till leap year gives it twenty-nine.

The verse informs the reader that four particular months contain 30 days, and February has either 28 or 29. Therefore, by process of elimination we can work out that the remaining seven months all comprise 31 days. February was the last month in the Julian calendar year; that's the reason it was left to pick up the leftovers.

Days of the Months by Hand

A physical mnemonic trick that can help determine the days of each month is right on the back of your hands. Place your clenched fists together, side by side, and begin with your left hand, naming the knuckle of your little finger as January. The valley or dip between the first two knuckles is February, the knuckle of the ring finger is March, and the next valley is April. July marks the last knuckle on the left hand, and August marks the first knuckle on the right hand, since both months have 31 days. Carry on until you reach the penultimate knuckle on your right hand, representing December. The two thumb knuckles are both excluded from this technique.

All the knuckles represent months with 31 days, and the valleys the shorter months. As in the rhyme, remember that February is the exception. So if you can't remember the famous verse, you can rely on your own hands to jog your memory. A similar memory devise uses the piano keyboard, moving from January, represented by the "F" key, and moving up the keyboard in semitones—the black notes indicate the short months and the white the long months.

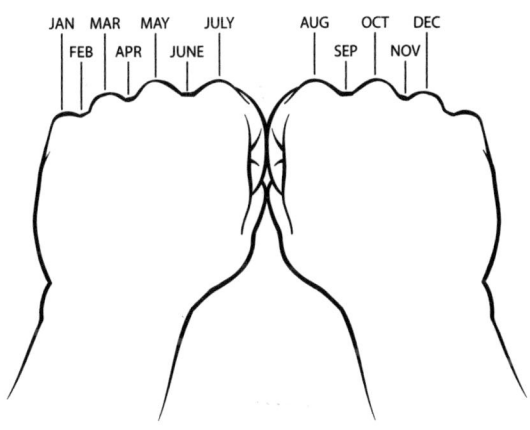

Teaching the Days of the Week

Teaching young children the days of the week poses a challenge for many parents and preschool teachers. The melody to "Clementine" *(Oh, my darlin', oh, my darlin', oh, my darlin', Clementine...)* provides a rhythmic background to the following verse:

> Sunday, Monday,
> Tuesday, Wednesday,
> Thursday, Friday, Saturday,
>
> There are seven days,
> There are seven days,
> There are seven days in a week.

Another musical variation uses the tune to the old TV show *The Addams Family:*

> Days of the week (clap, clap)
> Days of the week (clap, clap)
> There's Sunday and there's Monday
> There's Tuesday and there's Wednesday
> There's Thursday and there's Friday
> And then there's Sat-ur-day.
> Days of the week (clap, clap)
> Days of the week (clap, clap)
> Days of the week, days of the week, days of the week (clap, clap).

Teachers and parents can point to the days on a calendar as the children sing the song, to further help with placement and word identification.

How to Remember Dates

Writer and educator Grace Fleming writes a column on homework and study tips. She claims that an effective way to remember an important date is to think of a silly, visual term that rhymes with the date to imbed the thought into one's consciousness. She offers the following useful examples:

> You can leave off the century, so that 1861, the starting date for the Civil War, becomes 61.

Example:
  61 = Sticky gun

Imagine a Civil War soldier struggling with a gun that's been covered with honey. It may sound silly, but the technique works!

1773 was the date of the Boston Tea Party. To remember this, you could think:

  73 = Heavenly tea

Think of protesters, sipping lovely cups of tea right before tossing them into the water.

This strategy also works for the husband who can't seem to remember his wedding anniversary or wife's birthday:

> June 10, I married the hen.
> September 15, treat her like a queen.

Time Travel

When traveling long distances throughout the world, it helps to remember EWG and WEL to calculate if you'll be losing or gaining time during a journey:

East to **West** **G**ains and **West** to **East** **L**oses.

The Caribbean Hurricane Season

The people of the Caribbean and the southern United States are only too aware of the risks of hurricanes, as this mnemonic indicates:

June—Too Soon (first month)

July—Stand By (for any news of a storm)

August—You Must (prepare in case a storm comes)

September—Remember (to stand by)

October—It's All Over (last month)

The Signs of the Zodiac

Aries	The Ram	March 21 – April 20
Taurus	The Bull	April 21 – May 20
Gemini	The Twins	May 21 – June 20
Cancer	The Crab	June 21 – July 22
Leo	The Lion	July 23 – August 22
Virgo	The Virgin	August 23 – September 22
Libra	The Scales	September 23 – October 22
Scorpio	The Scorpion	October 23 – November 21
Sagittarius	The Archer	November 22 – December 21
Capricorn	The Goat	December 22 – January 19
Aquarius	The Water Bearer	January 20 – February 18
Pisces	The Fish	February 19 – March 20

The first letters of the words in this mnemonic sentence provide the signs of the astrological zodiac in order, which can be remembered with these phrases:

> **A**ll **T**he **G**reat **C**hancellors **L**ive **V**ery **L**ong
> **S**ince **S**hops **C**an't **A**lter **P**olitics.

A Tense **G**ray **C**at **L**ay **V**ery **L**ow
Sneaking **S**lowly, **C**ontemplating **A P**ounce.

Alternatively, if starting from January, the order changes:
Capricorn, **A**quarius, **P**isces, **A**ries, **T**aurus, **G**emini,
Cancer, Leo, **V**irgo, Libra, **S**corpio, **S**agittarius:

Can **A**ll **P**eople **A**lways **T**ake **G**ood **C**are
Lighting **V**aluable **L**amps **S**urrounding **S**aratoga?

To recall the list with a sense of rhythm instead, use the verse written by preacher, poet and hymn writer Isaac Watts (1674–1748), which starts with Aries:

> The *Ram*, the *Bull*, the Heavenly *Twins*,
> And next the *Crab*, the *Lion* shines,
> The *Virgin* and the *Scales*;
> The *Scorpion*, *Archer* and *Sea Goat*.
> The *Man* who held the watering out
> And *Fish* with glittering tails.

Or perhaps try this alternative from E. Cobham Brewer's *Dictionary of Phrase & Fable* (1899):

> Our vernal signs the *Ram* begins
> Then comes the *Bull*, in May the *Twins*;
> The *Crab* in June, next *Leo* shines,
> And *Virgo* ends the northern signs.
> The *Balance* brings autumnal fruits,
> The *Scorpion* stings, the *Archer* shoots;
> December's *Goat* brings wintry blast,
> *Aquarius* rain, the *Fish* come last.

The events in our lives happen in a sequence in time, but in their significance to ourselves they find their own order: the continuous thread of revelation.
—Eudora Welty

7
The Sky at Night and by Day

The Order of the Planets

Before August 2006, the planets of the solar system were **M**ercury, **V**enus, **E**arth, **M**ars, **J**upiter, **S**aturn, **U**ranus, **N**eptune, and **P**luto. Their initial letters lent themselves to all sorts of phrases:

My **V**ery **E**asy **M**ethod: **J**ust **S**et **U**p **N**ine **P**lanets.

My **V**ery **E**ducated **M**other **J**ust **S**erved **U**s **N**ine **P**izzas.

Mom's **V**ery **E**arly **M**orning **J**elly **S**andwiches **U**sually **N**auseate **P**eople.

In August 2006, the International Astronomical Union decided to downgrade the status of Pluto, and so some new mnemonic phrases that don't mention poor old Pluto have been devised for the new generation of stargazers:

My **V**ery **E**ducated **M**other **J**ust **S**erved **U**s **N**achos.

My **V**ery **E**nergetic **M**other **J**ust **S**ent **U**s **N**owhere.

My **V**ery **E**ducated **M**other **J**ust **S**ent **U**s **N**uts.

My **V**ery **E**xotic **M**istress **J**ust **S**erved **U**s **N**oodles.

The four planets closest to the sun are **M**ercury, **V**enus, **E**arth, and **M**ars. These are called the "rocky," or "terrestrial," planets. They are small in relation to other planets, and consist of similar materials to Earth:

> **M**y **V**isitor **E**ats **M**ice.
>
> **M**y **V**irgin **E**ats **M**en.
>
> **M**y **V**oice **E**xpects **M**ore.

The "gas" planets are **J**upiter, **S**aturn, **U**ranus, and **N**eptune, which all have rings and moons, and consist mainly of hydrogen, helium, frozen water, ammonia, methane, and carbon monoxide:

> **J**elly **S**andwiches **U**sually **N**eeded
>
> **J**oyful **S**usan's **U**nder-**N**ourished
>
> **J**ohn **S**mith **U**psets **N**eighbors

Saturn's Moons

Saturn has a number of moons. The count is currently 59 with three of them unconfirmed. The fifty-seventh (S/2007 S 1) was discovered on April 13, 2007, and the fifty-eighth and fifty-ninth (S/2007 S 2 and S/2007 S 3) on May 1, 2007.

Saturn moon spottings have increased significantly since the advent of the Voyager missions and the Hubble

Space Telescope; therefore, many books and websites are not accurate or up-to-date. A mnemonic, put into practice prior to the discovery of most of these moons, helped students to memorize the following nine moons of Saturn: Mimas, Enceladus, Tethys, Dione, Rhea, Titan, Hyperion, Iapetus, and Phoebe.

MET DR THIP

The Brightest Stars in the Sky

Positioned at the center of the solar system, the closest star to Earth is the sun. The brightest stars visible from Earth are listed below, along with the constellation where each is located:

Sir Can Rig A VCR, PA

Sir	Sirius in Canis Major
Can	Canopus in Carina
Rig	Rigil Kent in Centaurus
A	Arcturus in Boötes
V	Vega in Lyra
C	Capella in Auriga
R	Rigel in Orion
P	Procyon in Canis Minor
A	Achernar in Eridanus

The Sky at Night and by Day

The Earth's Atmospheres

Troposphere: extends from the Earth's surface to approximately 3.72–6.21 miles (6–10 km).

Stratosphere: extends to approximately 6.21–31.06 miles (10–50 km) above the Earth.

Mesosphere: located 31.06–49.7 miles (50–80 km) above the Earth's surface.

Thermosphere: located more than 49.7 miles (80 km) above the Earth.

Exosphere: the outermost layer of the atmosphere at 310.6–621.37 miles (500–1,000 km) above the Earth.

To help recall the order of the Earth's atmospheres, the following phrases may act as helpful reminders:

The **S**trong **M**an's **T**riceps **E**xplode.

The **S**traight **M**an's **T**hrottle **E**xcites.

Men on the Moon

Named after the Greek god of the sun, the Apollo program was a series of manned space flights that aimed to land a man on the moon by the end of the 1960s. On

July 20, 1969, Neil Armstrong accomplished this mission when he became the first man to walk on the moon. Armstrong was a member of the crew of Apollo 11, which we can remember by the double *ll* in "Apollo." The names of Armstrong and his fellow astronauts can be recalled with the simple use of ABC:

Armstrong

Buzz Aldrin

Michael **C**ollins

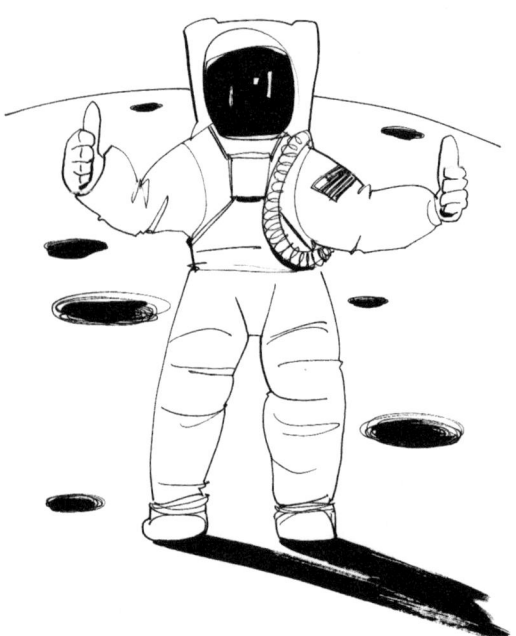

The Apollo program lasted until only 1975, when it was cut short due to rising costs. Only 12 men have ever walked on the moon: Neil Armstrong, Buzz Aldrin, Pete Conrad, Alan Bean, Alan Shepard, Edgar Mitchell, David Scott, James Irwin, John W. Young, Charles Duke, Eugene Cernan, and Harrison Schmitt.

Colors of the Rainbow

When a rainbow appears in the sky as a result of the refraction and dispersion of the sun's rays by light or other water droplets, the seven colors that are said to be visible are: **R**ed, **O**range, **Y**ellow, **G**reen, **B**lue, **I**ndigo, and **V**iolet.

"**R**ichard **O**f **Y**ork **G**ave **B**attle **I**n **V**ain" is the popular mnemonic phrase. It refers to the Battle of Bosworth in 1485, when King Richard III was defeated by Henry Tudor, who became, as Henry VII, the first king of the Tudor dynasty. However, it can also be fun to make up other phrases, such as:

Run **O**ff **Y**ou **G**irls, **B**oys **I**n **V**iew!

Ran **O**ut **Y**esterday, **G**ot **B**lotto **I**n **V**ineyard

Still, other people prefer to recall the colors by making up a man's name: **ROY G BIV**.

Nowadays, however, it is widely believed that indigo does not strictly appear in the spectrum but was merely included by Sir Isaac Newton, the seventeenth-century English physicist and mathematician, because seven colors were considered to be better than six.

Weather Forecasting

A red sky at night; shepherd's delight,
A red sky in the morning; shepherd's warning.

The origins of this rhyme can be traced back to St. Matthew's Gospel in the Bible:

When evening comes, you say, "It will be fair weather, for the sky is red," and in the morning, "It will be foul weather today, for the sky is red and overcast."

Although the words refer to a shepherd who would say that a red sky in the morning would indicate inclement weather to follow, the words could pertain to a sailor's predictions:

Red sky at night, sailor's delight;
Red sky at morning, sailors take warning.

Hundreds of years ago, before any accurate means of weather forecasting became available, people had to rely on those with knowledge and experience, such as sailors and shepherds, whose lives depended on the weather and its changing moods.

Fahrenheit and Celsius

With many countries converting to the metric system, deciding whether to pack a sweater or a coat can get awfully confusing. Here are two basic formulas to help navigate between the two:

> Celsius to Fahrenheit:
> Multiply C by 9
> Divide the answer then by 5
> Next, all you need to do, is to add 32.
>
> Fahrenheit to Celsius:
> From F, subtract 32
> Divide that by 9, but before you're through
> Multiply that whole by 5
> To Celsius, you will arrive.

8
The World of Science

Chemistry instructors expect their students to have a sound, working knowledge of the names and properties of the 100+ chemical elements of the Periodic Table. It's crucial that students learn not only a chemical's unique properties but also how it reacts with other elements, because getting it wrong can have disastrously flat, fizzy, or fiery consequences.

The Periodic Table of Elements

The Periodic Table was devised in 1869 by Russian chemist Dmitri Mendeleyev. The elements are arranged in increasing order of atomic number from left to right across the table so that elements with similar atomic structures and chemical properties appear in vertical columns. The horizontal rows are called periods, and the vertical rows are known as groups.

Setting a long list of strange names to music is a tried and tested way to remember them. Music has a structure and flow, so if the words fit, they fly off the tongue with ease. Singer-songwriter and mathematician Tom Lehrer concocted his own version of Gilbert and Sullivan's "I Am the Very Model of a Modern Major-General," a song from the comic opera *The Pirates of Penzance*. To hear the ditty sung live, simply type "The element song" into youtube.com.

> There's antimony, arsenic, aluminum, selenium,
> And hydrogen and oxygen and nitrogen and rhenium,
> And nickel, neodymium, neptunium, germanium,
> And iron, americium, ruthenium, uranium,
> Europium, zirconium, lutetium, vanadium,
> And lanthanum and osmium and astatine and radium,
> And gold and protactinium and indium and gallium,
>
> *[Gasp]*
>
> And iodine and thorium and thulium and thallium.
> There's yttrium, ytterbium, actinium, rubidium,
> And boron, gadolinium, niobium, iridium,
> And strontium and silicon and silver and samarium,
> And bismuth, bromine, lithium, beryllium and barium.
> There's holmium and helium and hafnium and erbium,
> And phosphorus and francium and fluorine and terbium,

And manganese and mercury, molybdenum, magnesium,
Dysprosium and scandium and cerium and caesium.
And lead, praseodymium, and platinum, plutonium,
Palladium, promethium, potassium, polonium,
And tantalum, technetium, titanium, tellurium,

[Pause for deep breath]

And cadmium and calcium and chromium and curium.
There's sulfur, californium, and fermium, berkelium,
And also mendelevium, einsteinium, nobelium,
And argon, krypton, neon, radon, xenon, zinc and rhodium,

And chlorine, carbon, cobalt, copper, tungsten, tin and sodium.

These are the only ones of which the news has come to Harvard,

And there may be many others, but they haven't been discavard!

In addition to the 102 elements listed above, there are a few more that complete the list; namely, lawrencium, rutherfordium, dubnium, seaborgium, bohrium, hassium, meitnerium, darmstadtium, iroentgenium, and seven others, which have yet to be named.

Here are some ways of remembering the first 18 elements in the periodic table, which occupy the first three periods:

Periods 1–2 (Elements 1–10)

H	Hydrogen
He	Helium
Li	Lithium
Be	Beryllium
B	Boron
C	Carbon
N	Nitrogen
O	Oxygen
F	Fluorine
Ne	Neon

Happy **H**enry **L**ikes **B**aking **B**ig **C**akes,
Not **O**mitting **F**loury **N**uggets.

Happy **H**enry **L**ikes **B**eer
But **C**ould **N**ot **O**btain **F**our **N**uts.

Period 3 (Elements 11–18)

Na	Sodium
Mg	Magnesium
Al	Aluminum
Si	Silicon
P	Phosphorus

S	Sulfur
Cl	Chlorine
Ar	Argon

Naughty **M**agpies **A**lways **S**ing **P**erfect **S**ongs **C**lawing **A**nts.

The Most Common Magnetic Material

The four most common magnetic materials are **N**ickel, **I**ron, **C**obalt, and **S**teel, which can be remembered by the clever saying:

> **N**ick **I**rons **C**reased **S**hirts.

Oxidation and Reduction

Oxidation is the loss of an electron by a molecule, an atom, or an ion. Reduction is the opposite; that is, the gain of an electron by molecule, atom, or ion. A simple example of an oxidation—reduction reaction (you can't have one without the other) is the reaction of hydrogen gas with oxygen gas to form water: $2H_2 + O_2 = 2H_2O$.

Many students have found the OILRIG acronym an invaluable method of understanding the process:

> **O**xidation **I**s **L**oss (of electrons)
>
> **R**eduction **I**s **G**ain (of electrons)

Parts of an Atom

PEN is possibly the simplest acronym in the history of mnemonics:

Proton, **E**lectron, **N**eutron

CFCs

CFCs have invaded the language and the atmosphere. Thomas Midgley, an organic chemist at General Motors Corporation, discovered chlorofluorocarbons (CFCs) in the 1920s. They are a group of gases believed to contribute to global warming by eroding the ozone layer. The gases that come from leaking air conditioners, refrigerators, and aerosols take 10 to 20 years to reach the stratosphere and remain there for 65 years.

Because the word chlorofluorocarbons doesn't exactly roll off the tongue, some thoughtful soul shortened the word to **CFC**, to keep this vital word in the forefront of our minds.

The Speed of Light

In the same way that it is possible to remember pi to different numbers of decimal places, a simple phrase also enables us to recall the speed of light in meters per second:

We guarantee certainty, clearly referring to this light mnemonic = 299,792,458 m/sec.

Chemistry Experiments: A Warning

And here's a warning to all would-be chemists about the dangers of confusing water with sulfuric acid:

> Johnny was a chemist,
> But Johnny is no more,
> For what he thought was H_2O,
> Was H_2SO_4!

The capacity to blunder slightly is the real marvel of DNA. Without this special attribute, we would still be anaerobic bacteria, and there would be no music.

—Lewis Thomas

9
World History

The Greek Philosophers

The names of the three most important Greek philosophers, in order of their dates of birth and also their influence, are:

Socrates (469–399 BC)
Plato (c. 429–c. 347 BC)
Aristotle (384–322 BC)

Socrates taught Plato, and Plato taught Aristotle. Together they created the foundations of Western philosophy. Use your visual memory and imagine them meditating in a health **SPA**. Or think of the phrase: **S**mart **P**eople of **A**thens.

Roman Emperors

After Julius Caesar, the Roman general and statesman who became dictator of the Roman Empire before his assassination in 44 BC, the first five emperors of Rome were all Caesars. The first emperor was Julius Caesar's adopted son (and great-nephew), Augustus, who handed down the title to his son-in-law Tiberius. From Augustus to Nero, Caesar's descendants, by adoption, marriage, or birth, all inherited the family name:

Augustus	(31 BC–AD 14)
Tiberius	(AD 14–37)
Caligula	(AD 37–41)
Claudius	(AD 41–54)
Nero	(AD 54–68)

Here's a phrase to help remember the names by which they were most commonly known:

Another **T**om **C**at **C**aught **N**apping.

The next six Roman emperors after Nero are **G**alba, **O**tho, **V**itellius, **V**espasian, **T**itus, **D**omitian:

> At The Cat Club Never Give Out
> Violent Vermin To Dogs

The Seven Wonders of the Ancient World

The seven wonders of the ancient world were chronicled in the second century B.C., but a list has been discovered in *The Histories of Herodotus* in the fifth century B.C. The final list of amazing monuments to religion, mythology, and art was compiled in the Middle Ages.

1. **S**tatue of Zeus at Olympia
2. **L**ighthouse (Pharos) of Alexandria
3. **M**ausoleum of Halicarnassus
4. **P**yramids of Egypt
5. **H**anging Gardens of Babylon
6. **T**emple of Artemis at Ephesus
7. **C**olossus of Rhodes

This mnemonic phrase has proved useful in remembering the seven wonders:

Seems **L**ike **M**ata Hari **P**icked **H**er **T**argets **C**arefully.

Mythological Matters

Mnemosyne is the Greek goddess of memory, daughter of Gaia and Uranus. She lay with Zeus for nine nights and gave birth to the nine Muses: **C**alliope, **E**uterpe, **C**lio, **E**rato, **M**elpomene, **P**olyhymnia, **T**erpsichore, **T**halia, and **U**rania.

Carol **E**ats **C**runchy **E**ggs,
Mashed **P**otatoes, **T**hen **T**hrows **U**p.

Clarrissa **E**ats **C**andy **E**very **M**orning,
Politely **T**aking **T**urns.

In classical art, the Muses are represented by emblems, or mnemonic symbols, of which the masks of comedy and tragedy are probably the most familiar.

Name	Association	Mnemonic symbol
Calliope	Chief of the muses and muse of epic poetry	writing tablet
Euterpe	Muse of music	flute
Clio	Muse of history	scroll and books
Erato	Muse of love poetry	lyre and crown of roses
Melpomene	Muse of tragedy	tragic mask
Polyhymnia	Muse of sacred poetry	pensive expression

Terpsichore	Muse of dance	dancing with a lyre
Thalia	Muse of comedy	comic mask
Urania	Muse of astronomy	staff and celestial globe

Joan of Arc

Also known as the Maid of Orléans, Joan of Arc (c. 1412–1431) a French national heroine, claimed that it was God's mission for her to reclaim her homeland from English domination toward the end of the Hundred Years War. She triumphed at the Siege of Orléans in 1429, which led to Charles VII's coronation at Reims, but was later captured at a skirmish near Compiègne. The English regent John of Lancaster, first Duke of Bedford, had her burned at the stake at Rouen when she was only 19. She was canonized in 1920.

This mnemonic phrase describes the short life of Joan of Arc:

ORLEANS CAMPAIGN RUIN

Orleans – victory – 1429

Compiègne – capture – 1430

Rouen – trial and death – 1431

The Six Wives of Henry VIII

Henry VIII (1491–1547) married six times in a quest to have a son and heir. His decision to divorce his first wife and remarry was the root of the split of the Roman Catholic Church, the dissolution of the monasteries, and the formation of the Church of England. The following is a list of Henry's wives in order of marriage dates from first to last:

1510—Catherine of Aragon (mother of Mary I)
1533—Anne Boleyn (mother of Elizabeth I)
1536—Jane Seymour (mother of Edward VI)
1540—Anne of Cleves
1540—Catherine Howard
1543—Catherine Parr

Use this rhythmic couplet to remember their first names:

Kate & Anne & Jane & Anne & Kate again & again!

Using the initial letters of their surnames gives the phrase:

All **B**oys **S**hould **C**ome **H**ome, **P**lease.

The following memorable rhyme reveals the ultimate fate of these six women:

> Divorced, beheaded, died,
> Divorced, beheaded, survived.

Brief History of the United States

The following verse was devised by American poet and former child prodigy Winifred Sackville Stoner, Jr. (1902–1983). She was best known for writing mnemonic rhymes and poems to help people recall important information, particularly for educational purposes. One of her most famous poems is "The History of the U.S." The poem contains 19 stanzas, but people often remember only the first one or two. It paints an often-unrealistic picture of U.S. history but serves as a clever mnemonic to remember those important historical dates. Below you will find the first five stanzas, which start in 1492, along with the final stanza, which brings the reader all the way to 1918 and the end of WWI.

> In fourteen hundred ninety-two,
> Columbus sailed the ocean blue

And found this land, land of the Free,
beloved by you, beloved by me.

And in the year sixteen and seven,
good Captain Smith thought he'd reach Heav'n,
And then he founded Jamestown City,
alas, 'tis gone, oh, what a pity.

'Twas in September sixteen nine,
with ship, Half Moon, a read Dutch sign,
That Henry Hudson found the stream,
the Hudson River of our dream.

In sixteen twenty, pilgrims saw
our land that had no unjust law.
Their children live here to this day
proud citizens of U.S.A.

In sixteen hundred eighty-three,
good William Penn stood 'neath a tree
And swore that unto his life's end
he would be the Indian's friend.

…Thank God in nineteen eighteen,
Peace on earth again was seen,
And we are praying that she'll stay
forever in our U.S.A.

The Pilgrim Fathers

In 1620 a group of English puritans who had fled to Holland to avoid religious persecution returned to England and sailed on the *Mayflower* from Plymouth to America. After a long, treacherous journey, they landed at Cape Cod, Massachusetts.

Nothing abbreviates this voyage more cleverly than the *Schoolhouse Rock* cartoon from the 1970s, "No More Kings."

> The pilgrims sailed the sea
> To find a place to call their own.
> In their ship, *Mayflower*,
> They hoped to find a better home.
> They finally knocked
> On Plymouth Rock
> And someone said, "We're there."
> It may not look like home
> But at this point I don't care.

The *Schoolhouse Rock* (SHR) revolution began in 1971, when David McCall, chairman of the ad agency McCaffrey & McCall, noticed that his son could sing all the Beatles and Rolling Stones lyrics but couldn't handle simple math. His solution was to link math with contemporary music. Grammar and history were added to the SHR mix, and the fact that many adults can still sing its phrases today solidly establishes video, combined with song, as an effective mnemonic device.

Declaration of Independence

The date 1776 marks the signing of the Declaration of Independence. The number of letters in each word in the following sentence stands for a numeral in the date:

I sighted Thomas's rights.

American poet Winifred Sackville Stoner, Jr.'s take on how to remember the date of the Declaration of Independence goes like this:

> Year seventeen hundred seventy-six,
> July the fourth, this date please fix
> Within your minds, my children dear,
> for that was Independence Year.

The Civil War

And regarding the dark days of the American Civil War, Winifred Sackville Stoner, Jr. wrote:

> In eighteen hundred and sixty-one,
> an awful war was then begun
> Between the brothers of our land,
> who now together firmly stand.

Author and certified holistic counselor Laurel Ann Browne offers the following civil war mnemonic on her parenting website:

> Four Bulls Ate Everything Vicky Grew.

It translates into chronological order the major events of the Civil War.

> **Four**: Fort Sumter, the first shots in the Civil War
> **Bulls**: Battle of Bull Run (First Manassas), the first major battle of the Civil War
> **Ate**: Antietam, the bloodiest battle in Civil War history with over 20,000 casualties
> **Everything**: Emancipation Proclamation, in which Lincoln abolished slavery

Vicky: The battle of Vicksburg, which controlled the Mississippi River for the North
Grew: The Gettysburg Address, four score and seven years ago...

Presidents of the U.S.

To date, 43 U.S. presidents have assumed office, which would make an incredibly long and complicated mnemonic phrase. The names of the first 11 presidents are:

> George Washington (1789–1797)
> John Adams (1797–1801)
> Thomas Jefferson (1801–1809)
> James Madison (1809–1817)
> James Monroe (1817–1825)
> John Quincy Adams (1825–1829)
> Andrew Jackson (1829–1837)
> Martin van Buren (1837–1841)
> William Henry Harrison (1841)
> John Tyler (1841–1845)
> James Polk (1845–1849)

Here's a question to ponder to help recall the first 11:

> Will **A** **J**olly **M**an **M**ake **A** **J**ust
> **B**ut **H**arshly **T**reated **P**resident?

And if 11 is too many to remember, here's a phrase for the first seven:

Washington **A**nd **J**efferson **M**ade **M**any **A** **J**oke

The names of the middle American presidents are:

Zachary Taylor (1849–1850)
Millard Fillmore (1850–1853)
Franklin Pierce (1853–1857)
James Buchanan (1857–1861)
Abraham Lincoln (1861–1865)
Andrew Johnson (1865–1869)
Ulysses S. Grant (1869–1877)
Rutherford B. Hayes (1877–1881)
James Garfield (1881)
Chester Arthur (1881–1885)
Grover Cleveland (1885–1889)
Benjamin Harrison (1889–1893)
Grover Cleveland (1893–1897)
William McKinley (1897–1901)

To recall this eminent list of 14, keep in mind the following phrase:

> **T**aylor **F**elt **P**roud **B**ut **L**incoln **J**ust **G**rinned **H**appily, **G**argling, **A**nd **C**ould **H**ardly **C**ontain **M**cKinley

And finally, the presidents of the twentieth century:

> **T**heodore Roosevelt (1901–1909)
> William H. **T**aft (1909–1913)
> Woodrow **W**ilson (1913–1921)
> Warren **H**arding (1921–1923)
> Calvin **C**oolidge (1923–1929)
> Herbert **H**oover (1929–1933)
> **F**ranklin D. Roosevelt (1933–1945)
> Harry S **T**ruman (1945–1953)
> Dwight D. **E**isenhower (1953–1961)
> John F. **K**ennedy (1961–1963)
> Lyndon B. **J**ohnson (1963–1969)
> Richard M. **N**ixon (1969–1974)
> Gerald **F**ord (1974–1977)
> Jimmy **C**arter (1977–1981)
> Ronald **R**eagan (1981–1989)
> George H. W. **B**ush (1989–1993)
> William J. **C**linton (1992–2001)

Though it's quite a lengthy list, this saying might just make life easier:

Theodore Takes Wilson's Hand,
Cool Hoovering Franklin's True Experiences.
Ken, Justly Noted For Candor, Ruled But Coolly.

The Heads on Mount Rushmore

Mount Rushmore is a world-famous national memorial in South Dakota, which represents the first 150 years of U.S. history with 60-foot-high granite carvings of the heads of four great U.S. presidents: **W**ashington, **J**efferson, **L**incoln, and **R**oosevelt.

We **J**ust **L**ike **R**ushmore.

World War I (The Great War)

Once called the War to End All Wars, this massive military conflict took 20 million lives. Many factors contributed to the outbreak of this global war. The word

ANIMAL assists people in remembering some of the most prominent causes.

> **A**ssassination—Archduke Franz Ferdinand of Austria-Hungary and his wife were assassinated on June 28, 1914.
>
> **N**ationalism—This time period saw a rise in strong patriotic sentiments and loyalty toward home countries.
>
> **I**mperialism—Colonization was common at the turn of the century, and countries competed for territory and economic advantage.
>
> **M**ilitarism—Britain and Germany had well-established military might, and an arms race ensued.
>
> **AL**liance System—War with any allied nation meant war with the whole alliance. This system was meant to discourage aggressive nations but failed.

We learn from history that we learn nothing from history.

—George Bernard Shaw

10
Musical Interlude

Music can be a mnemonic device all by itself: advertisers often use musical jingles to remind us of their products. For example, in just seven fluctuating notes composed by Steve Karmen in 1969 we have: "Nationwide is on your side." Karmen is also notorious for the New York State song "I Love New York." And who could forget the Chock Full O' Nuts song:

> *Chock Full O' Nuts is that heavenly coffee*
> *A better coffee a billionaire's money can't buy.*

Musical Notes

The first seven letters of the alphabet (A, B, C, D, E, F, G) are used in musical notation, which at least helps to keep it simple. In the 1965 film *The Sound of Music*, Julie Andrews's character Maria makes the learning of music seem so easy.

Do–Re–Mi–Fa–So–La–Ti

Do = doe – a female deer

Re = ray – a drop of golden sun
Mi = me – a name I call myself
Fa = far – a long, long way to run
So = sew – a needle pulling thread
La = la – a note to follow "so"
Ti = tea – a drink with jam and bread
Which will bring us back to "Do"

Musical Staves

Learning to read music notation is almost impossible without the use of mnemonic tools. The musical staff is the set of five lines and four spaces on which notes indicate pitch and rhythm. The treble staff (or clef), indicating higher notes, is generally played with the right hand on the piano, and the bass staff (or clef), indicating lower notes, with the left hand.

Treble Clef: Lines

The notes on the lines of the treble clef are, from the lowest, E, G, B, D, F. They can be remembered with the following common:

Every **G**ood **B**oy **D**eserves **F**avor

Favor may be replaced by fruit, fudge, or fun, depending on your taste.

Other variations include:

> **E**very **G**ood **B**oy **D**oes **F**ine.
> **E**very **G**irl **B**uys **D**esigner **F**ashions.
> **E**very **G**ood **B**ird **D**oes **F**ly.

Treble Clef: Spaces

The notes on the spaces on the treble clef are, from the lowest, F, A, C, E. This short rhyme may help with learning the order of notes:

If the note's in a space, together they spell FACE.

Bass Clef: Lines

The order of notes on the lines of the bass clef are G, B, D, F, A. "Good boys" return again in the catchy phrase devised to help musicians remember these basics:

> **G**ood **B**oys **D**eserve **F**ruit **A**lways.

"Fruit" can, of course, be substituted for another more suitable f-word if necessary.

Other variations include:

> **G**ood **B**oys **D**on't **F**ool **A**round.
>
> **G**reat **B**ig **D**ogs **F**ight **A**lways.
>
> **G**ood **B**ikes **D**on't **F**all **A**part.
>
> **G**reat **B**ig **D**ucks **F**ly **A**way.
>
> **G**entle **B**rown **D**onkeys **F**avor **A**pples.

Bass Clef: Spaces

And thus it follows that the notes in the spaces of the bass clef are A, C, E, G. The following sayings act as a useful reminder of the four-note order:

> **A**ll **C**ows **E**at **G**rass.
>
> **A**ll **C**ars **E**at **G**as.
>
> **A**ll **C**ats **E**at **G**oldfish.

The Cycle of Fifths

Music theory is not rocket science. There are 12 notes in Western music in one octave, and all you need to do is add, subtract, multiply, and divide. The notes—B, C, C#, D, D#, E, F, F#, G, G#, A, A#—are all half a tone apart.

Major chords are comprised of the root note and the higher third and fifth notes, plus the options of the seventh or eighth. Minor chords are made up of the root note and the minor third and fifth notes of the scale, with the option of the other notes. The cycle of fifths is based on taking the fifth note as the root for the next chord. For example, in an F chord the fifth note is C; therefore, the next chord is C, then G and so on—F, C, G, D, A, E, B:

Father **C**harles **G**oes **D**own **A**nd **E**nds **B**attle.

Other variations include:

Father **C**hristmas **G**ets **D**runk **A**fter **E**very **B**eer.

Fat **C**ats **G**o **D**eaf **A**fter **E**ating **B**ats.

Five **C**ool **G**uys **D**anced **A**way **E**very **B**eat.

And in reverse for the flat keys, the mnemonic can be reversed—B♭, E♭, A♭, D♭, G♭, C♭, F♭:

Battle **E**nds **A**nd **D**own **G**oes **C**harles's **F**ather.
Bottles **E**mpty **A**nd **D**own **G**oes **C**harles's **F**ather.
Be **E**xciting **A**nd **D**aring, **G**o **C**limb **F**ences.

Choral Voices

There are four different voice ranges that one can hear in a quartet, whose initial letters helpfully spell out STAB:

Soprano
Tenor
Alto
Bass

Musical Modes or Scales

The modes as based on the white piano keys beginning at C are:

Ionian mode—the familiar major scale in which most popular music is written.

Dorian mode—most often heard in Celtic music, with a melancholy feel.

- **P**hrygian mode—used especially by guitar soloists in counterpoint to an Ionian mode.
- **L**ydian mode—popular in jazz music, with a mix of major and minor chord progressions.
- **M**ixolydian mode—major feel with minor intervals and popular with soloists as a counterpoint to an Ionian mode.
- **A**eolian mode—in a minor key and produces a sense of sadness.
- **L**ocrian mode—the intervals are considered unsatisfactory and most composers find it unworkable.

Named after Greek cities that are thought to reflect the moods of the seven modes, one way of remembering the order of the modes is to recall this phrase:

I Don't **P**lay **L**ike **M**y **A**unt **L**ucy.

11
Foreign Tongues

French Plurals with an X

Here's a verse to tell you which French nouns require the letter "x" rather than "s" when they are used in the plural:

> *Bijou, caillou, chou,*
> *Genou, hibou, joujou . . .*
> *Pou!*

The English translation of the verse is:

> Jewel, pebble, cabbage,
> Knee, owl, toy . . .
> Flea!

Or commit this rhyme to memory:

> *Mes choux, mes bijoux,*
> *Lassez-vous joujoux,*
> *Venez sur mes genoux!*
> *Regardez ces mauvais petits garçons,*
> *Qui jettent des cailloux a ces pauvres hiboux!*

> My cabbages, my jewels,
> Stop playing with your toys, and come sit on my knees!
> Look at these bad little boys,
> Who throw stones at these poor owls!

Counting to Six in French

The correct words for one to six in French are *un, deux, trois, quatre, cinq,* and *six*. Try to picture the horror of this dark story of how to control the cat population:

Un, deux, trois, cat sank—cease, please!

French Verbs Using *Être*

All French verbs that use *être* in the perfect tense rather than *avoir* indicate a particular kind of movement. The

13 main verbs (and four derivatives) can be recalled using the popular mnemonic phrase **Dr. & Mrs. P. Vandertramp**:

Devenir **R**evenir **&** **M**onter **R**ester **S**ortir
Passer **V**enir **A**ller **N**aître **D**escendre **E**ntrer
Rentrer **T**omber **R**etourner **A**rriver
Mourir **P**artir

Alternatively, the acronym ADVENT is another useful way to recall the main *être* verbs. Each letter stands for one of the verbs and its opposite, with the thirteenth verb— *retourner*—standing alone.

Arriver—Partir
Descendre—Monter
Venir—Aller
Entrer—Sortir
Naître—Mourir
Tomber—Rester
Retourner

Japanese Vowels

The pronunciation and lexical ordering of the Japanese vowels is AIUEO. Using this short phrase, you can understand the pronunciation of the vowels:

Ah, we soon get old.

Counting to 10 in Japanese

Numeral	Japanese word	Sounds like
1	Ichi	Itchy
2	Ni	Knee
3	San	Sun
4	Shi	She
5	Go	Go
6	Roko	Rocko
7	Shichi	Shi Shi
8	Hachi	Hatchy
9	Kyu	Queue
10	Ju	Jew

Days of the Week in French, Spanish, and Italian

The seven-day week has been the norm for almost 2,000 years. The Romans allocated one of the seven planets to each of the days of the week: the sun, moon and the five planets that shine brightly in the night sky—Mars, Mercury, Jupiter, Venus, and Saturn.

	Planet	French	Spanish	Italian
Sunday	Sun	Dimanche	Domingo	Domenica
Monday	Moon	Lundi	Lunes	Lunedì
Tuesday	Mars	Mardi	Martes	Martedì

	Planet	**French**	**Spanish**	**Italian**
Wednesday	Mercury	Mercredi	Miércoles	Mercoledì
Thursday	Jupiter	Jeudi	Jueves	Giovedì
Friday	Venus	Vendredi	Viernes	Venerdì
Saturday	Saturn	Samedi	Sábado	Sabato

By recalling the planets after which the days were named, it helps to jog the memory when remembering the days of the week in the Latin-based languages.

Since many of the planets were named after the gods, this traditional rhyme borrows some of the characteristics of the planets or gods and pairs them with the corresponding days of the week:

> Monday's child is fair of face,
> Tuesday's child is full of grace,
> Wednesday's child is full of woe,
> Thursday's child has far to go;
> Friday's child is loving and giving,
> Saturday's child works hard for a living,
> But the child that is born on the Sabbath day
> Is bonny and blithe, good and gay.

The Greek Alphabet

To learn the Greek alphabet, you can memorize the order of the 24 letters by singing along to the tune of "Twinkle, Twinkle, Little Star," but if you're no longer a child, it might be better not to practice out loud . . .

> Alpha, Beta, Gamma, Delta,
> Epsilon, Zeta, Eta, Theta,
> Iota, Kappa, Lambda, Mu,
> Nu, Xi, Omicron, Pi,
> Rho, Sigma, Tau, Upsilon,
> Phi, Chi, Psi kai Omega.

NB: *K* (kai) means "and" in Greek.

The Runic Alphabet

The Runic alphabet is also known as FUTHARK, after the first six letters in this alphabet—namely *f, u, th, a, r,* and *k*. Runes were used by Scandinavians, and Anglo-Saxons used runes around the third century. There are 24 letters comprising 18 consonants and six vowels.

The Runic characters comprise a series of glyphs that represent sounds and ideas, based on the hieroglyphs of Ancient Egypt. They were not only used to convey sacred meaning but also mysteries and secrets. It is not known why the letters were ordered in this way, but the word FUTHARK is considered an ancient mnemonic.

12
Religious Matters

For Christians most religious instruction comes from Sunday school or religious-education classes. While children listen to countless Bible stories, many rhymes and sayings help to simplify certain matters of religion, keeping the vast subjects of the Old Testament and New Testament more clearly in their minds.

The Twelve Apostles

The twelve chief followers of Jesus are recalled in a well-known Sunday school rhyme:

> This is the way the disciples run
> Peter, Andrew, James, and John
> Philip and Bartholomew
> Thomas next and Matthew, too.
> James the less and Judas the greater
> Simon the zealot and Judas the traitor.

An alternative shorter method uses the following line:

Bart And John Fill (Phil) Tom's Matt with 2 Jameses, 2 Simons,* and 2 Judases.

*Peter was originally Simon or Simon-Peter, therefore there are two Simons in the second verse.

The Four Gospels

With regard to the first four books of the New Testament (the Gospels), religious leaders and Sunday school teachers have various rhymes to help children remember the names (and their order) more easily.

> Matthew, Mark, Luke, and John
> Went to bed with their trousers on.

The verse is probably derived from the following traditional poem, of which there are two versions:

> Matthew, Mark, Luke, and John
> Bless the bed that I lie on;
> Before I lay me down to sleep,
> I give my soul to Christ to keep.

> Matthew, Mark, Luke, and John
> Bless the bed that I lie on;
> Four corners to my bed,
> Four angels round my head;
> One to watch, one to pray,
> And two to bear my soul away!

The Ten Commandments

The Ten Commandments are a list of rules for living an honest and moral life. According to the Old Testament, they are the word of God, inscribed on two stone tablets and given to Moses on Mount Sinai. James Muirden, author of *The Rhyming Bible*, has cleverly compiled them into an unforgettable verse comprising six rhyming couplets:

> The First Law set by God in stone
> reads *Worship me, and me alone!*
> The next says Idols are profane;
> the Third, don't take my Name in vain;

the Fourth says keep the Seventh Day free;
the Fifth, treat Parents properly;
the Sixth says Murdering is wrong
(you knew the Seventh all along*);
the Eighth is crystal clear on Thieving,
as is the Ninth, on Not Deceiving;
and now the last of all His laws—
don't Covet things that are not yours.

*The Seventh, of course, forbids adultery.

Another way of remembering the commandments is the following:

One idle damn Sunday, Dad killed cheating thief
and lied to cover it.

That is, one God; no idols; don't swear; keep the Sabbath; honor your father (and mother); don't kill; don't commit adultery; don't steal; don't bear false witness; and don't covet.

Books of the Old Testament

Although there are a total of 39 books in the Old Testament (King James Bible), this memorable verse has made it much easier to remember them all in order:

That great Jehovah speaks to us,
In Genesis and Exodus,

Leviticus and Numbers see,
Followed by Deuteronomy,
Joshua and Judges sway the land,
Ruth gleans a sheaf with trembling hand;
Samuel and numerous Kings appear,
Whose Chronicles we wondering hear.
Ezra and Nehemiah now,
Esther, the beauteous mourner show.
Job speaks in sighs, David in Psalms,
The Proverbs teach to scatter alms.
Ecclesiastes then come on,
And the sweet Song of Solomon.
Isaiah, Jeremiah then,
With Lamentations takes his pen,
Ezekiel, Daniel, Hosea's lyres,
Swell Joel, Amos, Obadiah's.
Next Jonah, Micah, Nahum come,
And lofty Habakkuk finds room.
While Zephaniah, Haggai calls,
Rapt Zechariah builds his walls,
And Malachi, with garments rent,
Concludes the Ancient Testament.

RELIGIOUS MATTERS

The 10 Biblical Plagues of Egypt

From Exodus 7:14–12:36, these are the 10 catastrophes that God inflicted upon Egypt:

>**R**iver to blood
>**F**rogs
>**L**ice
>**F**lies
>**M**urrain (disease)
>**B**oils
>**H**ail
>**L**ocusts
>**D**arkness
>**F**irstborn

If the list proves too tricky to remember, the following sentence is a memorable means of recalling the order and initial letter of each plague:

Robert **F**rost **L**ikes **F**udge **M**ilk
Brownies **H**aving **L**ot of **D**ouble **F**udge

or

Flow **L**ike **F**resh **M**ilk
Behind **H**arry **L**ong's **D**eer **F**ence

The Seven Deadly Sins

There are seven days of the week, seven colors in the rainbow, seven wonders of the world, and for those who have not taken their Bible studies to heart, there are seven deadly sins:

Anger, **P**ride, **C**ovetousness, **L**ust, **S**loth, **E**nvy, **G**reed

To help make the list of sins easier to memorize, some God-fearing person devised the following mnemonic phrase:

All **P**rivate **C**olleges **L**eave **S**erious **E**ducational **G**aps.

Or to put it another way:

Pride, **E**nvy, **W**rath, **S**loth, **A**varice, **G**luttony, **L**ust
PEWS 'Ave GLu

The 10 States of Mind

In the Buddhist construct there are 10 states of mind:

1. **H**ell, the state of suffering
2. **H**unger, the state of base needs
3. **A**nimalism, the state of beastly power
4. **A**nger, the state of loathing
5. **N**eutrality, the state of neither one thing or another
6. **R**apture, the state of joy
7. **L**earning, the state of being mentally open
8. **R**ealization, the state of receiving/living wisdom
9. **B**odhisattva, the state of compassion
10. **B**uddha, the state of perfection

All of that mental agony and ecstasy gives us:

> **Has Hannah Arranged All Novices Running Late, Required Before Buddha?**

13
The Human Body

Young medics often face masses of dull and lengthy lists of complicated words, which represent the workings of the human body. Without a wide range of useful and often-amusing memory aids, it would be impossible for them to remember everything.

The Vital Processes of Life

Collectively, these are known as **MRS. GREN**:

Movement, **R**espiration, **S**ensitivity,
Growth, **R**eproduction, **E**xcretion, **N**utrition

The Human Brain

The brain is the most complex structure at the nub of all human decisions, communications, and activities. The cerebral cortex is divided into four sections, or lobes:

Frontal, **P**arietal, **O**ccipital, **T**emporal

First **P**lace **O**ften **T**rounces.

Cranial Bones

Occipital, **P**arietal, **F**rontal, **T**emporal,
Ethmoid, **S**phenoid

Old **P**eople **F**rom **T**exas **E**at **S**piders

Cranial Nerves

How many medical students learned the 12 cranial nerves sung to the tune of "The Twelve Days of Christmas?"

The first and second verses start off:

I (Olfactory)
On the first nerve of the cranium,
my true love gave to me:
My sense olfactory.

II (Optic)
On the second nerve of the cranium,
my true love gave to me:
Two eyes a-looking,
And my sense olfactory.

The song gets quite lengthy, so the final verse is:

XII (Hypoglossal)
On the twelfth nerve of the cranium,
my true love gave to me:
Twelve lovely lickings, (Hypoglossal)
Eleven heads a-tilting, (Spinal accessory)

Ten heartbeats a minute, (Vagus)
Nine quick swallows, (Glossopharyngeal)
Eight sounds, and balance, (Auditory)
Seven funny faces, (Facial)
Six sideways glances, (Abducens)
Mas-ti-ca-tion! (Trigeminal)
Four superior oblique muscles, (Trochlear)
Three cross-eyed glances, (Oculomotor)
Two eyes a-looking, (Optic)
And my sense olfactory. (Olfactory)

In addition to the song, there is also a catchy phrase to recall when remembering the names of the cranial nerves:

On **O**ld **O**lympus's **T**owering **T**op,
A **F**at-**A**ssed **G**erman **V**iewed **S**ome **H**ops.

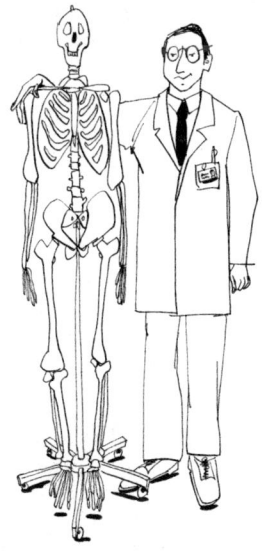

Bones of the Human Body

BONES OF THE UPPER LIMB OR ARM:
Scapula, **C**lavicle, **H**umerus, **U**lna, **R**adius, **C**arpals, **M**etacarpals, **P**halanges

Some **C**rooks **H**ave **U**nderestimated **R**oyal **C**anadian **M**ounted **P**olice.

BONES OF THE LOWER LIMB OR LEG:
Hip, **F**emur, **P**atella, **T**ibia, **F**ibula, **T**arsals, **M**etatarsals, **P**halanges

Help **F**ive **P**olice **T**o **F**ind **T**en **M**issing **P**risoners.

BONES OF THE WRIST (CARPAL):
Scaphoid, **L**unate, **T**riquetrum, **P**isiform, **T**rapezium, **T**rapezoid, **C**apitate, **H**amate

Some **L**overs **T**ry **P**ositions **T**hat **T**hey **C**an't **H**andle.

VERTEBRAE OR BONES OF THE SPINAL COLUMN (SUPERIOR TO INFERIOR):
Cervical, **D**orsal,* **L**umbar, **S**acrum, **C**occyx

Canned **T**una **L**ooks **S**o **C**ramped.

* Dorsal vertebrae are also known as Thoracic—therefore, the alternative phrase.

SHOULDER MUSCLES OR ROTATOR CUFF
Teres minor, **I**nfraspinatus, **S**upraspinatus, **S**ubscapular

Time **I**s **S**tanding **S**till.

Bone Fracture Types

Once medical students learn the specific bones, they can use the **GO C3PO** acronym to learn the ways in which the bones can get broken.

Greenstick, Open, Complete/Closed/Comminuted, Partial, Others

Skin Layers

Mnemonic sentences help medics to remember the order of skin layers or nerves so that when they become surgeons and start brandishing scalpels, they can identify which bit to cut through first. They use the aptly named **SCALP** acronym:

Skin, Connective tissue, Aponeurosis, Loose areolar tissue, Periosteum

Excretion

For the excretory organs of the body, think **SKILL**:

Skin, Kidneys, Intestines, Liver, Lungs

The Properties of Bile

Here's a catchy ditty to keep the properties of bile in mind:

> Bile from the liver emulsifies greases
> Tinges the urine and colors the feces
> Aids peristalsis, prevents putrefaction
> If you remember all this, you'll give satisfaction.

Doctors dealing with a patient who is a possible suicide risk will find the **SAD PERSONS** checklist quite handy:

Sex (male or female)

Age (old or young)

Depression

Previous suicide attempts

Ethanol and other drugs

Reality testing/**R**ational thought (loss of)

Social support lacking

Organized suicide plan

No spouse

Sickness/**S**tated future intent

Signs of Mania

Medics have to **DIG FAST** to identify key symptoms of manic behavior:

Distractibility
Indiscretion (excessive involvement
in pleasurable activities)
Grandiosity
Flight of ideas
Activity increase
Sleep deficit (decreased need for sleep)
Talkativeness (pressured speech)

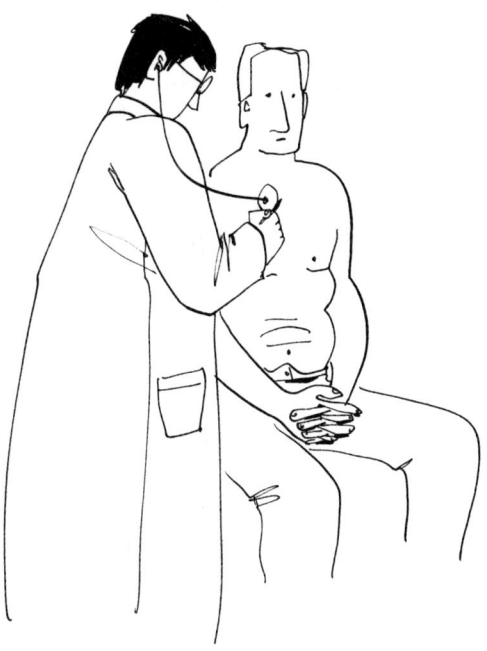

Signs of Schizophrenia

If doctors suspect a patient may have schizophrenia, they will check for **WHID**:

> **W**ithdrawn, **H**allucinations,
> **I**nappropriate emotional response, **D**elusions

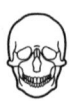

Signs of Anxiety Disorder

Your doctor will test for **MR FISC** if you're suffering from GAD—General Anxiety Disorder:

> **M**otor tension
> **R**estlessness
> **F**atigue
> **I**rritability
> **S**leep disturbances
> **C**oncentration difficulty

The Heart

The signs of heart failure are ABCDE:

> **A**cidosis, **B**lue skin, **C**old skin, **D**ilated heart,
> **E**dema

Doctors' Shorthand

Doctors-to-be develop their sense of humor as students and refine it throughout their careers. Consequently, doctors have been known to write F BUNDY on patients' notes if the prognosis is grim:

F***ed **B**ut **U**nfortunately **N**ot **D**ead **Y**et

Fever Facts

Your doctor will check the **FACTS** to diagnose influenza or just "man flu"; that is, a cold:

Fever
Aches
Chills
Tiredness
Sudden symptoms

Vitamins Are Healthy

Vitamins help maintain health. This rhyme reminds us of the important qualities of each and every vitamin:
>Vitamin **A** keeps the cold germs away
>And tends to make meek people nervy,
>**B**'s what you need
>When you're going to seed,
>And **C** is specific in scurvy.
>Vitamin **D** makes the bones in your knee
>Tough and hard for the service on Sunday,
>While **E** makes hens scratch
>And increases the hatch
>And brings in more profits on Monday.
>Vitamin **F** never bothers the chef
>For this vitamin never existed.
>**G** puts the fight in the old appetite
>And you eat all the foods that are listed.
>So now when you dine remember these lines;
>If long on this globe you will tarry.
>Just try to be good and pick out more food
>From the orchard, the garden, and dairy.

14
Lifesaving Tips

Learning and reviewing lifesaving techniques might be the best thing you ever do, so pay attention and refresh your memory regarding the many first-aid-related acronyms in existence.

The main aim of First Aid is the **3 Ps**:

Preserve life
Prevent deterioration in the patient's condition
Promote recovery

ABC is the traditional and essential way to remember what to check when administering cardiopulmonary resuscitation on a casualty:

Airways

Breathing

Circulation

Lifesaving Tips

Here are two groups of **3 Bs** to remember when dealing with an accident victim:

> Check **B**reath **B**efore **B**lood (flow)
> And then **B**lood **B**efore **B**ones

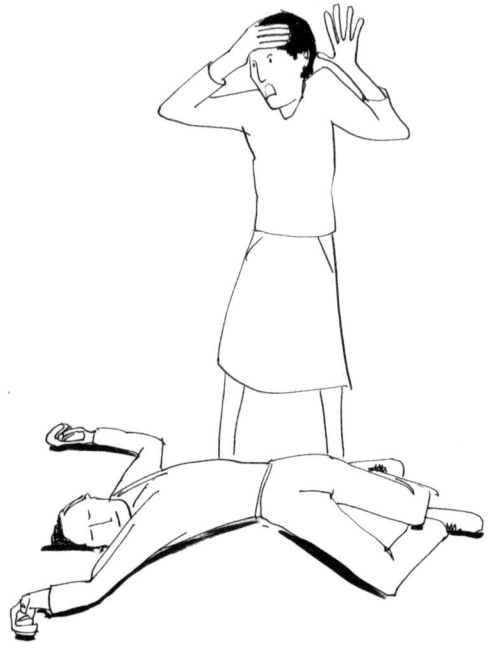

Keep calm in an emergency, and think **AMEGA**:

> **A**ssess the situation
> **M**ake the area safe
> **E**mergency aid
> **G**et help
> **A**ftermath

How alert is your casualty? Check for **AVPU**:

>**A**lert
>**V**oice
>**P**ain
>**U**nconscious

Is the victim in circulatory shock? Look for **PCFATS**:

>**P**ale
>**C**old and **C**lammy skin
>**F**ast pulse
>**A**nxious
>**T**hirsty
>**S**ick

Assess the injuries. Look at areas of soft tissue and bones, and think **RICE**:

>**R**est
>**I**ce/**I**mmobilize
>**C**ompression
>**E**levation

If your victim is lucid, ask these **AMPLE** questions:

Allergies—do they have any?
Medication—are they taking any?
Past history—do they have any prior medical problems?
Last meal—what/when did they last eat?
Environment—do they know where they are?

If the injured party is in a coma, it could be caused by any of the following **MIDAS** problems:

Meningitis
Intoxication
Diabetes
Air (respiratory failure)
Subdural/**S**ubarachnoid hemorrhage

Or by **COMA**:

CO$_2$ (carbon dioxide) and **CO** (carbon monoxide) excess
Overdose: drugs, such as insulin, paracetamol, etc.
Metabolic: BSL (blood sugar level), Na+ (sodium), K+ (potassium), Mg^2+ (magnesium), urea, ammonia, etc.
Apoplexy: stroke, meningitis, encephalitis, cerebral abscess, etc.

Keep the word **FAST** in mind when assessing the condition of a possible stroke victim:

Face: is one side of the face drooping downward?
Arm: can the person raise both arms?
Speech: is the person's speech slurred or confusing; is the person unable to speak?
Time: time is critical.
Call an ambulance immediately.

If you witness a person collapsing, what could have caused it? Think **I'VE FALLEN**:

Illness
Vestibular (balance problem)
Environmental
Feet or **F**ootwear
Alcohol and/or drugs
Low blood pressure
Low oxygen status
Ears or **E**yes
Neuropathy

Is the patient in shock? If so, he or she might be suffering from any one of the **R**egistered **N**urse **CHAMPS** range of shocks:

> **R**espiratory
> **N**eurogenic
> **C**ardiogenic
> **H**emorrhagic
> **A**naphylactic
> **M**etabolic
> **P**sychogenic
> **S**eptic

Survival Techniques

If it's a case of personal survival out in the wilds, use extreme survival expert Ray Mears's word **STOP**:

> **S**top
> **T**ake inventory
> **O**rientate
> **P**lan

In the event of discovering a fire, think **FIRE**.

Find the fire
Inform people by shouting out
Restrict the spread of fire (*if it is safe to do so*)
Evacuate the area/**Ex**tinguish the fire
(*if it is safe to do so*)
And don't forget to **S**top, **D**rop, and **R**oll to stay clear of the rising smoke.

Driving a Car

Mirror **S**ignal **M**aneuver is an essential phrase drummed into all student drivers, but it's one that drivers should never forget. Say it to yourself before you start, turn, change lane, reverse, and stop. It's a motorist's way of applying the "Look Before You Leap" principle.

Don't forget to buckle up, too:

Click it or Ticket

Road Safety

When learning to cross the road, children of all ages have been strongly advised to remember these lifesaving lines:

Lifesaving Tips

> Look Right, Look Left, Then Right Again
> Stop, Look and Listen

You may also remember the useful public-service announcement from the 1970s, which featured people from different walks of life, saying, "Cross at the green, not in between," in many different languages. In between their statements, the announcer firmly urges:

> No matter how you say it,
> it always means the same thing.
> Cross at the green, not in between.
> It means cross at the corner,
> never in the middle of the block;
> don't walk until the light turns green;
> always cross at corners
> where motorists expect you
> and where you can see them.
> Cross at the green, not in between
> In any language, it's a way of life.

15
The World of Work

The world of business and employment can be a cut-throat one, which is why it helps to be ahead of the game and gain an advantage over competitors whether individuals or entire companies.

Business Internet Domain Names

As with all aspects of selling yourself, choosing a name for your website is as vital as any other way of making sure people notice your business and, most important, remember it.

Here's the list that the UK Freeserve website defines as the key to success: **RAIL**

Recall	Will the name be easy to remember?
Aesthetics	How will the name look on the screen or on paper?
Impressions	First impressions always count.
Length	Keep it short and sweet. Less is definitely more.

Business Presentations

In any type of public meeting, seminar, or lecture, never forget your **ABC** and always be:

Accurate, **B**rief, and **C**lear

PPPPP

To give a good presentation, plan ahead and remember the **5 Ps**:

Proper **P**lanning **P**revents **P**oor **P**erformance.

PRIDE

Whatever line of work you're in—take **PRIDE** in what you're doing:

Personal **R**esponsibility **I**n **D**aily **E**fforts

To B or Not to B

Be **B**rave and **B**elieve; and don't be **B**oring or **B**ashful.

KISS

No matter how you earn a living, never forget to:

Keep **I**t **S**imple, **S**tupid.

The **KISS** acronym is applied to principles of business, advertising, computer operating systems to science and learning. Albert Einstein's maxim was: "Everything should be made as simple as possible, but no simpler."

SWOT Analysis

SWOT is a study of four crucial elements of a business's planning process:

Strengths, **W**eaknesses, **O**pportunities, **T**hreats

Never ASSUME Anything

Every business person knows that making assumptions is the mother of all screwups:

To assume makes an **ASS** out of **U** and **ME**.

Office Egos

In the world of employment and life in general, it's sometimes wise to keep your ego under control to avoid making enemies of at least half the population. Stick to the **FASTA** technique:

Focus on your goals, not just on yourself.
Ask for other people's opinions.
    You can learn from others.
Say thank you. Always a good idea in any situation.
Treat everyone as your equal.
    Other people know stuff that you don't.
Allow yourself to fail.
    You learn from your mistakes.

Sales Techniques

If you have something to sell, always **PLAN** in advance:

Prepare with research (don't forget your 5 Ps)
Lose time, lose all
Analyze the situation
Never just call (always have a viable reason)
    to make contact if you are making a "cold call."

During a sales pitch, meeting, or presentation, these should be your **AIMS**:

> **A**rrest the senses
> **I**nterest by questions and novelty
> **M**ove by proof and demonstration
> **S**ucceed in getting a "yes."

Think **ETC** after the pitch has been made:

> **E**valuate the outcome
> **T**each yourself and others
> **C**heck for results.

How to Interview

The first mnemonic a journalist learns is the five Ws and the H. The worst moment during an interview is when the subject gives only *yes* or *no* answers. Phrasing a question with these words gets people talking and should prevent single-word replies.

Who? **W**hen? **W**here? **W**hat? **W**hy? **H**ow?

SMART

Use this mnemonic for setting goals. It's a powerful tool for personal planning and kick-starting your career. Setting goals is all about knowing what you want to achieve and where to concentrate your efforts. You have to be **SMART**! Your daily "to do" list must be:

Specific, **M**easurable, **A**ttainable, **R**elevant, **T**ime bound

AIDA

Advertisers need to urge people to buy their products, so they design arresting images and messages for consumers. The key principles of advertising are:

Attract **A**ttention—"Look at that!"
Arouse **I**nterest—"Mmm, that looks interesting!"
Create **D**esire—"I want it!"
Urge **A**ction—"Now!"

Job Interview Techniques

Preparing for meetings is vital in business, and job interviews are possibly the most important meetings in your business life. Your aim at an interview is to sell yourself—you are the product. Hence the need for the **STAR** system:

Situation—Describe your previous experience regarding situations that you have managed successfully.
TAsk—Give details of exactly how you managed the situation. What was your contribution to the task? A tip from the professionals—don't make it up, and don't exaggerate, because you'll be found out!
Result—Congratulations. You're hired!

16
Other Favorites

Champagne Bottles

Name	Capacity	No. of Bottles
Quarter	18.75 cl	—
Half-bottle	37.5 cl	—
Bottle	75 cl	1
Magnum	1.5 l	2
Jeroboam	3 l	4
Rehoboam	4.5 l	6
Methuselah	6 l	8
Salmanazar	9 l	12
Balthazar	12 l	16
Nebuchadnezzar	15 l	20

One way to recall the names of different-sized bottles of champagne is to think of a detective in the company of some ancient men:

> **M**agnum—1980s TV private detective (or gun)

OTHER FAVORITES

Jeroboam—Founder and first king of Israel,
931–910 BC
Rehoboam—Son of Solomon, king of Judah,
922–908 BC
Methuselah—Biblical patriarch who lived
to the age of 969
Salmanazar—King of Assyria, 859–824 BC
Balthazar—Son of Nabonide, Regent of Babylon, 539 BC
Nebuchadnezzar—King of Babylon, 605–562 BC

Otherwise this rude mnemonic could jog your memory:

My Joanna Really Makes Splendid Burping Noises.

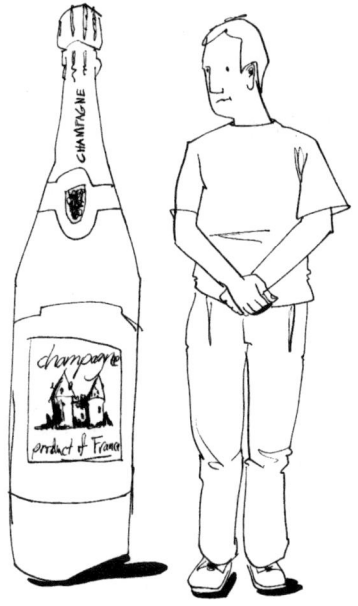

Alcohol Tips

Few people need tips on drinking alcohol, but some drinkers swear by the advice offered in this rhyme:

> Beer on whisky? Very risky!
> Whisky on beer, never fear . . .

Mixing drinks isn't a wise thing to do, but the warning quote below says it succinctly and honestly:

> Never mix grape with the grain.

Steering a Boat

If you find yourself behind the wheel of a boat, it helps to recall which side of the boat is port (the left side with red lights) and starboard (the right side with green lights). Fortunately, there are several ways to jog one's memory:

> PORT has four letters and so has LEFT.
>
> P (port) comes before S (starboard) in the alphabet, as L (left) comes before R (right).
>
> PORT wine should be LEFT alone when it is RED (therefore starboard is RIGHT).
>
> There's a little RED PORT LEFT in the bottle.

Five Sailing Essentials

This handy phrase reminds the crew of a boat of the "Five Essentials" of sailing:

Can The Boat Sail Correctly?

- **C**ourse to steer—the course might be a particular bearing (as, say, 250 degrees) or at a particular angle to the apparent wind.
- **T**rim—the fore and aft balance of the boat. The movable ballast on the boat is of course the crew, and the aim is to achieve an even keel.
- **B**alance—the port and starboard balance. This is also about adjusting the weight inboard or outboard.
- **S**ail—this is to ensure the sails are set correctly until they fill with wind. The front edge, or luff, of the sail should be in line with the wind.
- **C**enterboard—if the boat has a movable centerboard, it should be lowered when sailing close to the wind. It is raised on a downwind course to reduce drag.

Left and Right

An oft-heard criticism of some organizations is that the right hand doesn't know what the left hand is doing, which is a bit of a problem if you can't even tell the difference.

A quick physical mnemonic you can use to remember is to place your left-hand palm down, rotate your left thumb 90 degrees clockwise so that the forefinger and thumb make the shape of L for Left.

Interest Rates

Every city slicker knows this one:

> When rates are low
> Stocks will grow.
> When rates are high
> Stocks will die.

A Game of Bridge

The order of suits from highest to lowest are:

Spades, **H**earts, **D**iamonds, **C**lubs

If the order of suits just won't stick in your mind, try remembering the following fact:

Sally **H**as **D**irty **C**hildren.

Basic DIY Techniques

So you've found the screwdriver, climbed the ladder, but you don't know which way to turn the screw, because it was secured so tightly the last time round? This invaluable expression will guarantee that you don't waste precious minutes trying to unscrew a screw the wrong way:

> Righty-tighty,
> Lefty-loosey.

Or how about:

> Right on; left off.

And the mantra of every smart woodworker:

> Measure twice,
> Cut once.

OTHER FAVORITES

The Great Outdoors

If you're invited on a huntin', shootin' and fishin' weekend with the boss, remember the following acronym: **BRASS**.

Breathe, **R**elax, **A**im, **S**ight, **S**queeze

By keeping this sequence in mind, it might help you to shoot a rifle without missing your targets by a mile, or at least make you seem as if you know what you're doing ....

Setting a Table

When preparing for your next holiday or dinner party, remember that items to the left of the plate have EVEN letters, like the word LEFT (4) FORK (4) and NAPKIN (6). Items to the right of the plate have ODD letters, like the word RIGHT (5), KNIFE (5), SPOON (5), GLASS (5).

Enjoy These Other Reader's Digest Best-Sellers

Fun and interesting facts and quips about authors and books sure to delight the bibliophile and make anyone the life of the literary party. Covering both modern and classic literature—and those popular guilty pleasures—this book will interest both bookworms and trivia buffs.

$14.95 hardcover
ISBN 978-1-60652-034-5

Make learning fun again with these light-hearted pages that are packed with important theories, phrases, and those long-forgotten "rules" you once learned in school.

$14.95 hardcover
ISBN 978-0-7621-0995-1

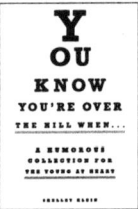

This laugh-out-loud collection of heartwarming jokes, quips, and truisms about the joys of aging will keep you entertained for hours.

$14.95 hardcover
ISBN 978-1-60652-025-3

Confused about when to use "its" or "it's" or the correct spelling of "principal" or "principle"? Avoid language pitfalls and let this entertaining and practical guide improve both your speaking and writing skills.

$14.95 hardcover
ISBN 978-1-60652-026-0

Do you know who really designed and sewed the first flag? It wasn't Betsy Ross! The answer to this and hundreds of other fascinating myth-debunking facts of U.S. history will delight history buffs and trivia lovers alike.

$14.95 hardcover
ISBN 978-1-60652-035-2

Reader's Digest books can be purchased through retail and online bookstores.
In the United States books are distributed by Penguin Group (USA), Inc.
For more information or to order books, call 1-800-788-6262.

I Used to Know That

stuff you forgot from school

Caroline Taggart

Reader's Digest

The Reader's Digest Association, Inc.
Pleasantville, New York / Montreal

For Jon and Nic, who are old enough to start forgetting this sort of stuff; and for Mishak and Camille, who are just beginning to learn it.

A READER'S DIGEST BOOK

Copyright © 2009 Michael O'Mara Books Limited

All rights reserved. Unauthorized reproduction, in any manner, is prohibited.

Reader's Digest is a registered trademark of The Reader's Digest Association, Inc.

First published in Great Britain in 2008 by Michael O'Mara Books Limited, 9 Lion Yard, Tremadoc Road, London SW4 7NQ

READER'S DIGEST TRADE PUBLISHING
U.S. Project Editor: Kimberly Casey
Consulting Editor: Sandra Kear
Copy Editor: Barbara Booth
Canadian Project Editor: Pamela Johnson
Canadian Consulting Editor: J. D. Gravenor
Project Production Coordinator: Wayne Morrison
Senior Art Director: George McKeon
Executive Editor: Dolores York
Manufacturing Manager: Elizabeth Dinda
Associate Publisher: Rosanne McManus
President and Publisher: Harold Clarke

Library of Congress Cataloging-in-Publication Data:

Taggart, Caroline.
  I used to know that : stuff you forgot from school / Caroline Taggart.
    p. cm.
  "A Reader's digest book"--T.p. verso.
  "First published in Great Britain in 2008 by Michael O'Mara Books"--T.p. verso.
  ISBN 978-0-7621-0995-1
  1. Handbooks, vade-mecums, etc. I. Title.
  AG105.T14 2009
  031.02--dc22
                                                            2008033112

The author would like to thank Ana, who wanted me to write this book; Silvia, for making it happen and for sharing my loathing of *Wuthering Heights*, and the other Ana, for neck-breaking design. Thanks, also, to everyone who has entered into the spirit of it and made enthusiastic suggestions, even if I haven't had room to include them all. Special thanks to Bob for vetting the math and science chapters and pointing out that pi isn't a recurring decimal. I used to know that.

Reader's Digest is committed to both the quality of our products and the service we provide to our customers. We value your comments, so please feel free to contact us:
The Reader's Digest Association, Inc., Adult Trade Publishing,
Reader's Digest Road, Pleasantville, NY 10570-7000

For more Reader's Digest products and information, visit our website:
www.rd.com (in the United States)
www.readersdigest.ca (in Canada)

Printed in the United States

9 10 8

CONTENTS

Introduction	6
☞ ENGLISH	8
☞ LITERATURE	19
☞ MATH	55
☞ SCIENCE	79
☞ HISTORY	105
☞ GEOGRAPHY	141
☞ GENERAL STUDIES	162

Introduction

When I started to write this book, I realized that I did remember lots of different things, but I didn't always remember those facts completely, or necessarily accurately. I knew, for example, that "The Assyrian came down like a wolf on the fold" was a perfect example of—what—a dactyl or an anapest? I had to look it up. I remembered a bit about sines and cosines but had no idea why they were important. I used to know most of the principal bones in the body. How did that song go? "The head bone's connected to the neck bone, the neck bone's connected to the…" Hmmm. And after years of study, I could not seem to name the dates of important wars or, for that matter, why they were fought (I'm still having some trouble with that).

Geography was especially challenging—just when I thought I knew the capital of Burma, they change everything. Myanmar is tragically all over the news, and I'm left scratching my head in bewilderment as to where it is exactly. There's also a wealth of general information that I thought I knew, like Roman numerals and the Roman equivalent to the Greek gods.

Sometimes I hear a symphony and all I can remember is that it was composed by a man whose last name starts with V…or was it B?

In the course of talking to other people about what I should include in this book, I discovered two things: one, that everybody I spoke to had been to school, and two, that that was pretty much all they had in common. They had all forgotten completely different things. So with every conversation the book seemed to grow longer. One chat with an editor friend sent me rushing to add the active and passive voices to the English chapter. Another friend could recite British poetry verbatim but could not remember if the poem she so eloquently performed was by Keats or Shelley. Yet another friend confessed that she had completely forgotten what a square root was (though I have no idea why she suddenly wanted to know). In the end I had to stop discussing it, or this book would have surpassed the size of *War and Peace*. I also found in the course of researching the things I used to know that I learned more than a few things that I didn't.

All of which is a roundabout way of saying that I hope you, too, will learn something new or find things here that strike a chord, however faintly. Things that make you say, "Oh, yes, I used to know that." Because by the time you read this, I will almost certainly have forgotten most of them again.

ENGLISH

Learning to read and write was just the beginning. After you had mastered that, you had to study how the language worked and, when you started to write your own stories, how to stay focused, develop content, organize material, maintain a consistent voice and style, *and* use proper grammar. If (perish the thought) you had to write poetry as well, there was a whole new set of conventions....

Parts of Speech

This is a way of categorizing words according to the function they perform in a sentence, and there are nine of them:

adjective: a describing word. Some examples include *tall, short, brown,* and *blue*. With one possible exception— *blond/blonde*—adjectives in English (unlike most European languages) are invariable; that is, they don't change according to the number and gender of the thing they are describing.

adverb: a word that describes a verb, an adjective, or another adverb. Adverbs answer such questions as how, when, or where: *She walked aimlessly; light brown hair* (where *light* is an adverb describing the adjective *brown*); *they lived fairly frugally* (where *fairly* is an adverb describing the adverb *frugally*). Most, but by no means all, adverbs in English are formed by adding *-ly* to the adjective.

article: *Merriam-Webster* defines an article as "any small words or affixes...used with nouns to limit or give definiteness to the application." That's not very helpful, is it? It may be easier just to remember that the definite article is *the* and the indefinite articles are *a* and *an*.

conjunction: a joining word. Examples include *and, but, though,* and so on. Conjunctions link two words, phrases, or clauses together: Pride **and** Prejudice *is Jane Austen's most popular book,* **but** *I also love* Sense **and** Sensibility, ***though*** *Marianne can be really annoying.*

interjection: a word to express emotion. For example, *Aha!* or *Alas!*

noun: a naming word. There are three categories:
- Collective nouns describe a group of things. However, they are funny things. There are some genuinely useful ones to describe animals that live in groups—you wouldn't talk about a gaggle of elephants, for example, or a flock of lions. But at some stage in history, someone thought it was useful to give collective names to almost a hundred birds where you might have thought that *group*, *colony*, or *a whole bunch* would serve the purpose. And there are many variations. If you are talking about a group of ducks, for example, you could say a *badelynge, brace, bunch, dopping, flock, paddling, plump, raft, safe, skein, sord, string,* or *team. A charm of goldfinches, an exaltation of larks,* and *a parliament of owls* are often quoted but rarely used in real life—but once you start Googling for this sort of thing, you also come across *a dopping of goosanders.* (Goosanders? Some people have too much time on their hands.)

- Proper nouns name a person, place, or thing that requires a capital letter, such as *Caroline, Paris,* or the *Smithsonian Institution.*
- Common nouns cover general terms, such as *street, book,* and *photograph.*

preposition: a word that links nouns, pronouns, and phrases and indicates their relationship to the object in a sentence. Prepositions include words such as *beside, through, over, during, at, in, to, on: The boy stood* on *the burning deck; it was Greek* to *me.*

pronoun: a word that stands in the place of a noun. For instance, *Caroline has forgotten a lot of stuff. That is why* she *is writing this book*—where the pronoun *she* in the second sentence takes the place of the proper noun *Caroline* in the first. Other examples include *it, he, her, his, me,* and *they.*

verb: a doing word. A verb indicates the occurrence or performance of an action, or the existence of a state or condition, such as *to be, to do, to run, to happen.* This form of a verb (normally containing the word *to*) is called the **infinitive.** Verbs change their form according to tense, person, and number: *I am, I was, you were, he is, they are.* Verbs can also be in the **active** or **passive voice**—*I bake the bread* is active; *the bread is baked* is passive. English also has three verb moods: the **indicative** makes a simple statement—*I bake the bread*; the **subjunctive** indicates something that is wished or possible—*If I were you, I would bake the bread*; and the **imperative** gives a command—*Bake that bread!*

Phrases and Clauses

Now it is time to take a look at the building blocks of sentences: phrases and clauses. Each depends on the other to express a complete thought, but knowing the difference between them can be quite confusing. Generally, you can rely on the following definitions:

- A **phrase** is a group of words (in a sentence) that does not contain a subject or predicate—or either one: *In the afternoon,* we went to the store.
- A **clause** does contain a subject and a verb and may stand alone as a sentence or as part of a sentence. However, in the sentence *He loves dogs but doesn't have one,* the clause *but doesn't have one* is the subordinate clause.

Sentences—and each clause of a sentence—can be divided into a **subject** and a **predicate**.

- The **subject** is the noun or noun phrase that the sentence is about, the thing that does the action expressed in the verb.
- The **predicate** is everything else. In sentences involving the verb *to be*, what follows the verb is known as the **complement**, as in *Silence is golden,* where *golden* is the subjective complement of the verb.
- A verb may be **transitive** or **intransitive,** which means it may or may not need a direct object in order to make sense. The **object** is the thing on which the subject performs the action of the verb. In the sentence *He hit the ball*, the object is *ball*.

To see some examples of all this, consider a line from *A Midsummer Night's Dream:*

I know a bank whereon the wild thyme blows.

The main statement or principal clause is *I know a bank*. Not very interesting, but it stands alone as a sentence. *I* is the subject, *know a bank* is the predicate and can be subdivided into the verb *know,* and the object (answering the question What do I know?), is *bank*. *Know* in this sentence is a transitive verb—it doesn't make much sense without the object.

The subordinate clause is *whereon the wild thyme blows*. The clause has a verb (*blows*) with a subject (*the wild thyme*, which is a noun phrase), but it isn't a sentence. Note, however, that *blows* makes sense on its own—it doesn't need an object, so it is intransitive.

Blow is one of many verbs that can be either transitive or intransitive, depending on context: The wind blows intransitively, but you can blow a horn or blow glass in a transitive way.

Taking a sentence apart to analyze its components is called **parsing**. You may remember drawing a parse tree or **sentence diagram** in elementary school.

Synonyms, Antonyms, and the Like

The suffix *-nym* derives from the Greek for *name*, but in fact, these words are currently used to refer to meaning. So a **synonym** is a word that has the same or similar meaning as another, while an **antonym** has the opposite meaning.

Here are some examples:
- *Spooky, scary, frightening,* and *eerie* are **synonyms,** as are *pale, wan,* and *ashen.*
- *Mean* is an **antonym** of *generous.*

Illogically, a **homonym** is a word that has the same spelling as another, but a different meaning. A **homophone** sounds like another word but doesn't have the same spelling. Confused?

English abounds in homonyms and homophones, which are often completely unrelated in the etymological sense.
- *Eerie* (spooky) is a homophone of *eyrie* (an eagle's nest).
- *Pale* (light in color) is a homonym of *pale* (a fence, as in *beyond the pale*) and a homophone of *pail* (a bucket).
- *Mean* (miserly) is a homonym of *mean* (intend) and a homophone of *mien* (appearance).

All those silly mistakes that spell-checkers fail to detect, such as *there* and *their*, are homophones.

Diphthongs

Diphthongs are complicated things. What most people think of as a diphthong is actually a digraph or ligature, and true diphthongs are often written as a single letter, which makes them less obvious to readers.

Huh?

OK. *Merriam-Webster* defines a diphthong as "a gliding monosyllabic speech sound that starts at or near the articulatory position of one vowel and moves to or toward the position of another."

Try it for yourself and feel the difference when you say *late* and *bat* or *loud* and *catch*. Listen for the glides (*y* or *w*) at the end of the vowel sound.

Diphthongs may be written as a single letter (the *i* in *white* and the *o* in *no*, for example) or as two (*ui* in *fruit*, *ea* in *heat*). Any combination of two letters, whether vowels or consonants that produces a single sound is known as a *digraph,* so that includes not only the *ui* in *fruit* and the *ea* in *heat* but also the *ph* in *photograph* and the *dg* in bridge.

Many North American words that are spelled with a single letter are represented by two letters in their British counterparts. The *ae* written together in the British spelling of *encyclopaedia* or *mediaeval* is, strictly speaking, a ligature, which means that the two letters are joined together as one. This has its origins with medieval scribes who were simply trying to save time and space by combining the two letters on the same block when it was transferred to hot metal type. Modern typesetting doesn't recognize ligatures, so the tendency since the 1950s has been to write the two letters separately or, increasingly, to drop one of them altogether—with the result that, in British English, *encyclopaedia* and *mediaeval* look rather old-fashioned, while in American English *encyclopedia* and *medieval* have become the standard.

Figures of Speech (and other devices for spicing up your writing)

A figure of speech is technically an expression used in a nonliteral (that is, a figurative) way, such as when you say *My lips are sealed.* Obviously, this is not possible unless you have put glue over them. When most people learn ways to expand their writing style, they are often directed to utilize such techniques as **alliteration** and **onomatopoeia**, which poets also use for effect. Here is a basic list that you may (or may not) remember:

alliteration: when a number of words in quick succession begin with the same letter or the same letter is repeated. For example, *Full fathom five thy father lies*, as Ariel sings in *The Tempest*.

assonance: similar to alliteration, but now with the repetition of vowel sounds. For example, *And so, all the night-tide, I lie down by the side/ Of my darling—my darling—my life and my bride,/ In the sepulchre there by the sea,/ In her tomb by the sounding sea.* (Edgar Allan Poe, *Annabel Lee*)

euphemism: replacing an unpleasant word or concept with something less offensive, as in substituting the term *Grim Reaper* for *death*. Some are also intended to be funny, as when morticians refer to *corpses* as *clients*.

hyperbole: Pronounced hy-PER-bo-lee. Not HY-per-bowl. Exaggeration for effect, as in *I've told you a hundred times*. This is the opposite of…

litotes: understatement for effect, as when *not bad* means *completely wonderful*. Litotes can be interpreted differently, depending on culture and verbal emphasis.

metaphor: an expression in which a word is used in a nonliteral sense, saying that *x is y* rather than *x is like y*, which would be a simile. For example, Macbeth's *Life's but a walking shadow, a poor player, That struts and frets his hour upon the stage.*

metonymy: *Merriam-Webster* defines this as "a figure of speech consisting of the name of one thing for that of another of which it is an attribute or with which it is associated." For example, the term *press*, which originally was used for printing press, now connotates the news media. Easily confused with synecdoche.

onomatopoeia: a word or phrase that sounds (a bit) like the sound it is meant to convey: *buzz, purr,* or Tennyson's *the murmuring of innumerable bees.*

oxymoron: an apparent contradiction for effect, the classic example being *jumbo shrimp.*

personification: giving human qualities, such as emotions, desires, and sensations to an inanimate object or an abstract idea. Emily Dickinson's *The Railway Train* is often cited as an example of personification:

> *I like to see it lap the miles,*
> *And lick the valleys up,*
> *And stop to feed itself at tanks;*
> *And then, prodigious step*
> *Around a pile of mountains...*

simile: a comparison that—unlike a metaphor—expresses itself as a comparison, usually with the words *as* or *like.* Examples include *dead as a dodo* or *like a bat out of hell.*

synecdoche: a form of metonymy, but in this instance specifically "a whole for the part or a part for the whole." For example, *a set of wheels* used to denote the term *automobile,* or the command *All hands on deck* to summon a crew of sailors.

Prosody

Confusingly, prosody has nothing to do with prose—it is defined by *Merriam-Webster* as "the study of versification; especially: the systematic study of metrical structure."

The basic unit of a line of poetry—normally comprising two or three syllables—is called a **foot**, and the most common feet are:

iamb (adj. **iambic**): a short syllable followed by a long one. The most widely used foot in English poetry. Much of Shakespeare's verse is written in *iambic pentameter,* which means that a line consists of five iambic feet, or ten syllables in all:

Shall I / compare/ thee to/ a sum/ mer's day?
(*Sonnet 43*)

If mu/ sic be/ the food/ of love,/ play on
(*Twelfth Night*)

trochee: a long syllable followed by a short one, although the final syllable is often missing:

*Tiger!/ Tiger!/ burning/ bright
In the/ forest / of the/ night*
(Blake, *The Tiger*)

dactyl: a long syllable followed by two short ones (again, the final syllable is often dropped). It produces a gentle, flowing rhythm:

This is the/ forest prim/ eval. The/ murmuring/ pines and the/ hemlocks

(Longfellow, *Evangeline*)

anapest: two short syllables followed by a long one. In contrast to a dactyl, this conveys pace and action. It is often used in comic verses such as the nonsense poem by Lewis Caroll, *The Hunting of the Snark:*

In the midst of the word he was trying to say/ In the midst of his laughter and glee/ He had softly and suddenly vanished away/ For the Snark <u>was</u> Boojum, you see.

spondee: two long syllables, giving a heavy, rhythmical effect. The following example combines spondee and trochee so that you can almost hear the soldiers marching along:

We're / foot—slog/ —slog—slog/ —sloggin'/ over/ Africa—

Foot—foot/—foot—foot/—sloggin'/ over/ Africa—

(Boots—boots/—boots—boots/—movin'/ up and/ down a/ gain!)

(Kipling, *Boots*)

LITERATURE

Oh, those dreadful textbooks and anthologies. Who could ever forget the detailed chapter on tying knots in *Moby Dick*? Perhaps *Julius Caesar* was your particular nemesis. On the other hand, *Macbeth*, *Frankenstein*, and just about any of Poe's dark stories could deliciously disturb your evenings for nights on end. After all, as a teenager, it was sometimes hard to immerse yourself in the literature of serious life-and-death situations. So here's your second chance.

British Authors and Playwrights

There are some authors who embody the definition of "classic" literature. We all recognize the names: Austen, the Brontë sisters, Dickens, and Shakespeare. However, could you pass a pop quiz on their greatest works? Here's a brief rundown to review—just in case.

☞ JANE AUSTEN (1775–1817)

Jane Austen completed only six novels, which makes it easy to do a rundown of her complete works. In no particular order:

Emma: Emma Woodhouse is the most important young lady in her village, living alone with her aging father (the one who thinks that the sooner any party breaks up the better). Clever and pleased with herself, she amuses herself with matchmaking.

Despite the disapproval of her friend and neighbor, Mr. Knightley, she persuades her protégée, Harriet Smith, not to marry a respectable farmer, Robert Martin, thinking that Harriet (despite being poor, ignorant, and illegitimate) should set her sights on the new vicar, Mr. Elton. Mr. Elton, however, has set his sights on Emma and is deeply offended when she rejects him. He promptly marries someone else entirely, and Harriet, recovering from her disappointment, falls in love with Mr. Knightley instead. Emma's eyes are suddenly opened to the fact that no one should marry Mr. Knightley but herself. Fortunately, this turns out to be what he has always wanted.

Mansfield Park: Jane Austen's least appealing heroine is the virtuous but dull Fanny Price, who is sent to live at Mansfield Park with her aunt, Lady Bertram, and promptly falls in love with her cousin Edmund, another deeply virtuous person. The arrival of the worldly Crawfords, brother and sister Henry and Mary, upsets the calm of the neighborhood, with Edmund becoming smitten with Mary despite his disapproval of her character, and Henry attracting the attention of both Bertram sisters, Maria and Julia, despite the fact that both have admirers of their own. Henry, however, falls in love with Fanny, who is almost persuaded that her good influence can redeem his character, but then he elopes with Maria, now Mrs. Rushworth. Amid all the scandal and disappointment, Edmund finally recognizes Fanny's worth.

Northanger Abbey: Catherine Morland's head is full of ghoulish Gothic novels, so when she is invited to Northanger Abbey by her friend Elinor Tilney (with whose brother, Henry, she is already in love), she thinks she has discovered a horrific mystery: Elinor's father, the general, has murdered his wife. It turns out to be nonsense, of course, and she is deeply embarrassed that Henry should know of her silly suspicions. General Tilney now discovers that Catherine is not, as he has been led to believe, an heiress, and turns her out of the house. She is back at home thinking gloomy thoughts about her future when Henry appears and...

Persuasion: Eight years before the novel starts, Anne Elliot was persuaded by her proud father, Sir Walter, and her well-meaning friend Lady Russell to break off her engagement to Captain Frederick Wentworth. Now twenty-six, she has never met anyone else she can care for (and indeed has turned down a proposal from a neighbor, Charles Musgrove, who subsequently marries her sister, Mary). Chance brings Captain Wentworth, now wealthy, back into the neighborhood, but throws him together with Charles Musgrove's sisters, Henrietta and Louisa. Anne is forced to watch in silence as he apparently becomes involved with Louisa, whose steadfastness of character seems to appeal to him more than the weakness he has not forgiven in Anne. An outing to Lyme Regis ends with Louisa insisting on jumping off the Cobb, falling and causing herself serious injury. Just as Captain Wentworth's feelings toward Anne are reawakening, he finds that all his friends believe he is committed to Louisa, and he cannot honorably renege on this perceived promise. But Louisa, in the course of her convalescence, conveniently falls in love with Captain Wentworth's friend Captain Benwick, and Wentworth is free again.

Pride and Prejudice: Spirited but poor Elizabeth Bennet (Lizzy) takes a stand against the proud but extremely wealthy Mr. Darcy, particularly when he destroys the chances of her sister Jane marrying his friend Mr. Bingley. Darcy falls in love with Lizzy much against his better judgment and is tactless enough to tell her so. Scandal hits the Bennet family when the youngest daughter, Lydia, elopes with the charming but feckless Wickham, but Darcy saves the day. An unlikely scenario for bringing lovers together, but it does, as many readers predict, and the two "deserving" daughters make the happy marriages at the end of the novel. After all, "a single man in possession of good fortune must be in want of a wife."

Other characters include two more Bennet sisters, plain and studious Mary and silly Kitty; their parents, the empty-headed Mrs. Bennet and introverted, sarcastic Mr. Bennet; Mr. Bennet's cousin and heir, the bumbling clergyman Mr. Collins; and his haughty patroness Lady Catherine de Bourgh, who also happens to be Darcy's aunt.

Sense and Sensibility: The Dashwood sisters, Elinor and Marianne, are completely different in temperament, and, when Marianne falls in love with the dashing Willoughby, the whole world knows it. Elinor, on the other hand, suffers her disappointment over Edward Ferrars in silence. Willoughby is summoned to London just as he appears to be on the brink of proposing to Marianne and instead becomes engaged to a wealthy woman. Marianne's heartbreak is eventually healed by the less dashing Colonel Brandon, and Elinor gets Edward in the end.

Jane Austen also wrote fragments of two other novels, *The Watsons* and *Sanditon*, which have been published in their incomplete forms and variously completed by other authors.

☞ THE BRONTËS

There were three sisters who wrote novels—Anne (1820–49), Charlotte (1816–55), and Emily (1818–48). All, especially

Emily, were also poets of some distinction. Charlotte wrote *Shirley, Villette,* and *The Professor,* but her most famous novel is *Jane Eyre:*

***Jane Eyre* by Charlotte Brontë:** A poor orphan girl secures a job as governess to the ward of Mr. Rochester at Thornfield Manor, a place where strange noises tend to emanate from the attic. Jane and Rochester fall in love, but their wedding is stopped by the intervention of Mr. Mason, who announces that Rochester is, in fact, married to his sister, Bertha. And indeed he is, but she is mad and confined to the attic and watched over by the fearsome Grace Poole. Jane runs away and seeks refuge with her cousins, the Rivers; on the point of accepting a proposal of marriage from St. John Rivers, she thinks she hears Rochester calling her and insists on returning to Thornfield. There she finds that Bertha has broken out of her attic, set fire to the house, perished in the flames, and left Rochester blind, disfigured, and dependent. "Reader," as she famously says, "I married him."

***The Tenant of Wildfell Hall* by Anne Brontë:** Although Anne wrote *Agnes Gray,* a story about the horrors of being a governess in Victorian England, *The Tenant of Wildfell Hall* is slightly better known, perhaps for its public-television BBC series. This work could exemplify one of the first feminist novels, since it illustrates the inequities sometimes evident between men and women in marriage. The story involves the arrival of a mysterious new tenant, Helen Huntingdon, who with her young son moves to a small village in Yorkshire. A farmer falls in love with her, only to learn that she is still married to a wealthy man back in London. The husband becomes ill, inevitably from his life of debauchery, and eventually dies, leaving Helen free. You can likely guess what happens next.

***Wuthering Heights* by Emily Brontë:** This *extremely* dark tale of unrequited, misguided love and revenge oftentimes reaks with an uncomfortable intensity. Heathcliff is a wild orphan brought home to Wuthering Heights by kindly Mr. Earnshaw, Cathy's father. The two fall passionately in love, but Cathy refuses to marry a nobody and instead marries their drippy neighbor, Edgar Linton. Heathcliff, in revenge, marries Edgar's sister, Isabella, and cruelly mistreats her. Cathy dies in childbirth. Heathcliff goes a bit bonkers and ends up pretty much killing himself so as to be reunited with Cathy in death.

☞ CHARLES DICKENS (1812–70)

Love him or hate him, Dickens inspired many great films, and everyone knows what *Dickensian* means.

A Christmas Carol: The miserly Ebenezer Scrooge tries to ignore Christmas and is haunted by the ghost of his former partner, Marley, and by the ghosts of Christmases Past, Present, and Yet to Come, who show him the error of his ways.

David Copperfield: Dickens's favorite—the life story of a boy who is sent to boarding school by his evil stepfather, runs away to his eccentric aunt, becomes a lawyer, and then a writer. Sounds pretty dull, but really it is about growing up, learning from experience, and coming to terms with life. It's full of colorful characters such as Mr. Micawber, always hoping that something will turn up; the ever so 'umble Uriah Heep; Aunt Betsy Trotwood; and her mad companion, Mr. Dick, who is obsessed with the execution of Charles I; not to mention the Peggotty family, the deeply drippy Dora, and the saintly Agnes.

Oliver Twist: About the boy from the workhouse who is kicked out after he "wants some more" food and finds his way into a gang of pickpockets led by Fagin. The novel contains considerably more misery and rather less singing and dancing than the musical version.

If you don't remember much about Dickens, chances are most of the characters you do recall are from the ones previously mentioned from *David Copperfield;* the Artful Dodger, Nancy, the evil Bill Sikes, and Mr. Bumble the beadle from *Oliver Twist;* and Bob Cratchit and Tiny Tim from *A Christmas Carol.* But here are a few more stories that may ring bells:

The plot of *Bleak House* centers around the ongoing case of Jarndyce vs. Jarndyce, which eventually eats up all the money that is being disputed; the Circumlocution Office, Dickens's savage attack on civil service bureaucracy, appears in *Little Dorrit;* and *Barnaby Rudge* is set against the background of the Gordon Riots (anti-Catholic riots in London in 1780).

☞ SHAKESPEARE (1564–1616)

William Shakespeare wrote 37 plays, 154 sonnets, and a number of much longer poems. There isn't room in this book to summarize all the plays, so here are—arguably—the 10 best known.

Hamlet, Prince of Denmark: Another one where everyone dies. Hamlet's father, also Hamlet, has died in suspicious circumstances, and his widow, Gertrude, has married—with indecent haste—Hamlet senior's brother, Claudius. The ghost of King Hamlet tells his son that he has been murdered by

Claudius. Prince Hamlet then spends much of the play worrying about what to do and talking to himself—hence all the famous soliloquies. He has previously been attached to Ophelia, daughter of Polonius, the lord chamberlain, but he now rejects her ("Get thee to a nunnery"). Talking to his mother in her room, Hamlet realizes that someone is eavesdropping behind a wall hanging, and Hamlet stabs the individual, believing it to be Claudius. It is, in fact, Polonius. Ophelia goes mad and drowns herself. Her brother, Laertes, is determined to avenge his family, so Claudius arranges a fencing match in which Laertes will have a poisoned sword. Laertes wounds Hamlet; then there is a scuffle in which the two exchange swords and Hamlet wounds Laertes. Knowing that he is dying, Laertes confesses, Hamlet stabs Claudius, and Gertrude drinks poisoned wine that Claudius had prepared as a fallback for outing Hamlet. "Good night, sweet prince," says his friend Horatio as he prepares to clear up the mess.

Hamlet contains more quotations than the other plays. For example, Polonius's paternal advice to his son Laertes:

> Neither a borrower nor a lender be:
> For loan oft loses both itself and friend;
> And borrowing dulls the edge of husbandry.
> This above all—to thine own self be true;
> And it must follow, as the night the day,
> Thou canst not then be false to any man.

And a bit of Hamlet's most famous soliloquy...

> To be, or not to be; that is the question:
> Whether 'tis nobler in the mind to suffer
> The slings and arrows of outrageous fortune,

> *Or to take arms against a sea of troubles,*
> *And by opposing end them? To die, to sleep;*
> *No more; and by a sleep to say we end*
> *The heart-ache and the thousand natural shocks*
> *That flesh is heir to,—'tis a consummation*
> *Devoutly to be wish'd. To die, to sleep;*
> *To sleep! Perchance to dream: ay, there's the rub;*
> *For in that sleep of death what dreams may come,*
> *When we have shuffled off this mortal coil,*
> *Must give us pause.*

Julius Caesar: A number of Roman citizens, notably Caesar's close friend Marcus Brutus and his brother, Cassius, are worried that Caesar is becoming too powerful, so they kill him ("*Et tu, Brute?* Then fall Caesar"). But that happens in Act III Scene I, only halfway through the play. The rest is about the fallout from the assassination: the vengeance wrought on the conspirators by Caesar's supporters, led by Mark Antony; the conflict between Brutus and Cassius (the one who has "a lean and hungry look—he thinks too much; such men are dangerous."); the effect on them and their feelings of guilt; and their eventual defeat and suicide. And speaking of rabble-rousing, Antony's funeral oration, which works the crowd up into a frenzy so that they will avenge the murder, runs fairly close to *Henry V*:

> *Friends, Romans, countrymen; lend me your ears;*
> *I come to bury Caesar, not to praise him...*
> *He was my friend, faithful and just to me:*
> *But Brutus says he was ambitious;*
> *And Brutus is an honorable man...*

and so on and so forth, until the mob is fairly baying for Brutus's blood.

King Lear: Lear is "the foolish, fond old man" who decides to retire and divide his kingdom among his three daughters, Goneril, Regan, and Cordelia. The two eldest make fancy speeches about loving their father above all else; Cordelia refuses to play this game and is promptly exiled. Lear plans to spend half his time with Goneril and half with Regan, but these two wicked sisters have other ideas and soon kick him out. He wanders around in the rain, goes mad, meets up with Cordelia again, and then everyone dies. There is a subplot concerning the Earl of Gloucester's bastard son Edmund, who plots against everyone and becomes betrothed to both Goneril and Regan (despite the fact that they are both married). They all die, too.

Macbeth: The Scottish play. Three witches prophesy that Macbeth will become Thane of Cawdor and subsequently king. When he is proclaimed Thane of Cawdor, he starts wondering about hurrying the second prophecy along. Egged on by his wife, he murders King Duncan and is proclaimed king in his place. And it's all downhill from there. One murder leads to another, he is haunted by guilt (personified by the ghost of his friend Banquo, who appears at a banquet), Lady Macbeth goes mad and dies (after the famous "Out damned spot" hand-washing/sleepwalking scene), and Macbeth is finally killed in battle. Ultimately, Duncan's son Malcolm is restored to the throne.

The Merchant of Venice: Shylock the Jewish moneylender hates Antonio the Christian merchant. When Antonio needs to borrow money from him to help out his friend Bassanio, Shylock makes him sign a bond promising that he will pay

Shylock one pound of his own flesh should he fail to repay the loan. Bassanio takes the money and successfully courts the wealthy Portia. Antonio's ships are lost at sea, and he is unable to pay Shylock, who claims his pound of flesh. Portia disguises herself as a lawyer and rescues Antonio by pointing out that, contractually, Shylock is entitled to take a pound of flesh but no blood—a logistical impossibility. Her speech beginning "The quality of mercy is not strained" comes from this scene. A happy ending—unless you are Shylock.

A Midsummer Night's Dream: The one about the fairies. Three plots interwoven: In a wood outside Athens, two pairs of young lovers brush up against the squabbling king and queen of the fairies, Oberon and Titania, and Oberon's servant Puck. In the same wood a group of workmen, including Bottom the Weaver, are rehearsing the play *Pyramus and Thisbe* to perform at the forthcoming wedding of the Duke of Athens. Oberon has a magic potion that, when squeezed on the eyelids of someone who is asleep, makes that person fall in love with the first object he or she sees upon awakening. As a result, Titania falls in love with Bottom, whom Puck has given an ass's head, and Puck confuses the young lovers so that they keep falling in and out of love with the wrong partners. But in the end "all is mended."

Othello, the Moor of Venice: Othello is a successful general, but the problem is that he is black and has secretly married a white girl, Desdemona. The other problem is that Iago hates him, partly because Othello has promoted a young lieutenant, Cassio, over Iago's head. Iago persuades Othello that Cassio is having an affair with Desdemona. Mad with jealousy ("the green-eyed monster"), Othello smothers Desdemona in her bed. Iago also tries to have Cassio murdered, but the plot fails, and letters proving Iago's guilt and Cassio's innocence are discovered. Othello realizes that he has murdered Desdemona for no reason and kills himself. Othello was the man who loved "not wisely but too well," and it was Iago who said, "Who steals my purse steals trash." (But he was lying, of course.)

This section ends with words from one famous sonnet—number 18—whose first four lines have provided titles for at least two novels:

> *Shall I compare thee to a summer's day?*
> *Thou art more lovely and more temperate;*
> *Rough winds do shake the darling buds of May,*
> *And summer's lease hath all too short a date.*

Romeo and Juliet: The original star-crossed lovers. Romeo is a Montague, Juliet a Capulet, and the two families hate each other. Romeo and Juliet secretly marry. However, Juliet has already been commissioned to marry her cousin, Paris. To get out of this, Juliet comes up with one of those clever schemes that you just know will go wrong: She takes a potion that puts her into a coma for a couple of days so that everyone thinks she is dead. The message telling Romeo about this goes astray (of course), and he arrives at her tomb believing that she is dead. He poisons himself just before she wakes up, so Juliet, discovering him dead, stabs herself with his dagger.

The balcony scene is full of famous lines. For example, when Romeo lurks in the garden, Juliet appears on the balcony above and, talking to herself, says:

> *O Romeo, Romeo! Wherefore art thou Romeo?...*
> *What's in a name? That which we call a rose,*
> *By any other name would smell as sweet.*

And at the end of the scene, she says:

> *Good-night, good-night! Parting is such sweet sorrow*
> *That I shall say good-night till it be morrow.*

The Taming of the Shrew: Katharina is too bad-tempered to secure a husband, but her father will not allow her younger (and better behaved) sister, Bianca, to accept any of her many suitors until Katharina is married. Petruchio comes along and accepts the challenge, more or less beating Kate into submission. Twenty-first-century feminists do not care for this play, although Cole Porter's musical version, *Kiss Me Kate,* is wonderful.

Twelfth Night: Twins Viola and Sebastian become separated in a storm, and each believes the other dead. Viola disguises herself as a boy, Cesario, and enters the service of Duke Orsino, with whom she falls in love. Orsino, however, is in love with Olivia and uses Cesario as a messenger to woo her. Olivia—you guessed it—falls in love with Cesario, and it takes the reappearance of Sebastian to make everyone live happily ever after. The subplot concerns Olivia's pompous steward, Malvolio, who is conned by Olivia's uncle and his friends into believing that Olivia is in love with him and that she wishes to see him wearing yellow stockings and cross garters. The well-known saying "Some are born great, some achieve greatness, and some have greatness thrust upon them" appears in the letter that Malvolio believes Olivia has written to him.

Other Notable British Authors

Name	Major Works	Notes
William Blake (1757–1827) poet and artist	*Songs of Innocence*	Painter, and a bit of a religious upstart.
The Brownings, Elizabeth Barrett (1806–1861) and **Robert** (1812–1889) poets	"How Do I Love Thee" from *Sonnets for the Portuguese*, and "Grow Old Along with Me" from *Rabbi Ben Ezra*	Secretly married in 1846. He loved her despite her frail health. In 1861 she died in her husband's arms.
Sir Arthur Conan Doyle (1859–1930)	Sherlock Holmes stories, *The Lost World*	Started writing when his medical practice slowed.
George Eliot (1819–1880) pen name	*Middlemarch, Silas Marner*	Real name was Mary Ann Evans, but she changed it so her work would be taken more seriously; also because of her relationship with a married man.
E. M. Forster (1879–1970)	*A Room with a View, Howards End, Where Angels Fear to Tread, A Passage to India, The Longest Journey, Maurice*	Recent PBS series, *A Room with a View*, contained an alternative ending. Most of his novels were adapted for film.
John Galsworthy (1867–1933)	*The Forsyte Saga* and its sequels	Pulitzer Prize for Literature, 1932. People skipped church to see the BBC adaptation of *The Forsyte Saga* in the 1960s!
William Golding (1911–1993)	*Lord of the Flies, Pincher Martin, Darkness Visible, To the Ends of the Earth*	Was in D-Day invasion in Normandy. Won Booker Prize and Nobel Prize. Knighted by Queen Elizabeth II.
Ted Hughes (1930–1998) poet	*Crow, Tales from Ovid, Birthday Letters*	Poet Laureate. Married to Sylvia Plath. Great poet but merciless philanderer.

Name	Major Works	Notes
D. H. Lawrence (1885–1930)	*Sons and Lovers, The Rainbow, Women in Love, Lady Chatterley's Lover*	His work, considered scandalous for its time, was burned and banned.
C. S. Lewis (1898–1963) Irish-born	*The Chronicles of Narnia, A Grief Observed, Mere Christianity, The Allegory of Love*	*The Lion, the Witch, and the Wardrobe* and *Prince Caspian* recently adapted for film.
Christopher Marlowe (1564–1593) playwright, poet	*Edward II, Doctor Faustus, The Passionate Shepherd to His Love* ("Come live with me and be my love and we will all the pleasures prove")	Killed in Deptford tavern; some speculate that he spied for Elizabeth I. Freethinker and contemporary to Shakespeare.
Somerset Maugham (1874–1965)	*Of Human Bondage, The Razor's Edge, The Moon and Sixpence*	WWI spy; *Ashenden* influenced Ian Fleming's Bond series.
George Orwell, (1903–1950) pen name	*Animal Farm, 1984*	Real name was Eric Arthur Blair; died of tuberculosis at 46.
Alexander Pope (1688-1744) poet	"A Little Learning is a dangerous thing." *Essay on Man, The Rape of the Lock*	Also from *Essay on Man;* "To err is human, to forgive, divine."
Robert Louis Stevenson (1850–1894) Scottish	*Treasure Island, A Child's Garden of Verses*	Loved to travel despite poor health. Died at 44.
Jonathan Swift (1667–1745) Anglo-Irish	*Gulliver's Travels*	Wrote his own obituary.
J. R. R. Tolkien (1892–1973)	*The Hobbit, The Lord of the Rings*	"All that is gold does not glitter; not all those that wander are lost."
Virginia Woolf (1882–1941)	*A Room of One's Own, Mrs. Dalloway, To the Lighthouse, Orlando*	Filled her pockets with stones and drowned herself in the River Ouse.

North American Authors

There is a countless number of American writers who have earned their rightful place in literary history. While it is tricky to capture all of them in one relatively brief chapter, here are some that many students have come to know very well.

☞ PEARL BUCK (1892–1973)

Winner of both the Nobel Prize in Literature and the Pulitzer Prize, Buck wrote more than 100 titles, as well as short stories, plays, a book of verse, children's books, biographies, and a cookbook—much while sitting in her office at her Bucks County, Pennsylvania farmhouse watching her eight children play outside her window. Brought to China from Virginia as a young girl, Buck lived among the missionaries and based much of her work on her travels to Asia. In addition to the best-selling The *Good Earth*, a few other works by Buck include *Dragon Seed, East Wind: West Wind*, and the *House of Earth* trilogy. She also founded the charitable organization Pearl S. Buck International, which helps children around the world who have been marginalized due to mixed heredity, disease, hunger, poverty, or other tragic circumstances.

☞ STEPHEN CRANE (1871–1900)

Writer and journalist, Crane died at 28 years old and will forever be remembered for the required-reading novel, the *Red Badge of Courage*, which details the horrors of war experienced by a young soldier. This classic is based on memoirs and interviews with Civil War veterans.

☞ RALPH WALDO EMERSON (1803–82)

Essayist, philosopher, abolitionist, and poet, Emerson greatly influenced the transcendentalist movement of the mid-1800s. His associations include Henry David Thoreau (Walden Pond was on his property) and Nathaniel Hawthorne and his neighbor Louisa May Alcott. His collected essays included "Self-Reliance," which warned people to avoid conformity and to follow their own ideas and instincts. "Nature," "Circles," and "The Poet" are a few of his other most successful pieces.

☞ WILLIAM FAULKNER (1897–1962)

Known for his stream of consciousness, Faulkner's literary technique depicts what is going on in the speaker's head rather than simply relating the person's dialogue with others. In his novel *As I Lay Dying*, Faulkner presents 15 different points of view. Other well-known novels include *The Sound and the Fury; Light in August; Absalom, Absalom;* and *The Unvanquished*.

☞ F. SCOTT FITZGERALD (1896–1940)

Francis Scott Key Fitzgerald was the namesake and second cousin three times removed of the author of the United States' National Anthem. His six finished novels, including *Tender Is the Night* and *This Side of Paradise* and many short stories evoke the Jazz Age and his tumultuous relationship with his wife, Zelda Sayre. Like a fine wine, his masterpiece *The Great Gatsby* is about the futility and moral decay of the wealthy that gets even better with age. Fitzgerald died at 44, considering himself a failed writer. However, *Gatsby* continues as a best seller and is often required reading for many high school and college students.

☞ NATHANIEL HAWTHORNE (1804–1864)

Who could forget the *Scarlet Letter*'s all-too-human Hester Prynne, who—after being separated from her cool-hearted husband (Chillingworth)—has a passionate affair with her charismatic minister. The Puritans chide her and force her to wear a scarlet "A" upon her breast, advertising her sin. Hester dutifully (and wisely) protects Pastor Dimmesdale from public scorn, but his conscience catches up to him. The story warns of the scourge of sin and that people can be downright self-righteous. A few other examples from his published works include *The House of the Seven Gables;* a short-story collection, *Twice-Told Tales,* and the short stories "The Birthmark" and "Young Goodman Brown."

☞ JOSEPH HELLER (1923–1999)

Although he is often regarded as one of the best post-World War II satirists, Heller's career included stints as a blacksmith's apprentice, a B-25 bombardier, and an advertising copywriter. However, his novel *Catch-22* is one of the few whose title has created an idiom rather than employing an existing quotation. The plot centers on a group of American fighter pilots in Italy during World War II and their efforts to avoid flying suicidal missions. The problem is that the only way they can get out of flying missions is if they are crazy—but the moment they ask to be grounded because flying the missions is crazy, they are deemed to be entirely sane, and therefore fit to fly.

☞ ERNEST HEMINGWAY (1899–1961)

Remember the determined Santiago, the aging Cuban fisherman who struggles with a marlin in the Gulf Stream? *The Old Man and the Sea* won the Nobel Prize in Literature in 1954 and has been heavily analyzed in classrooms for its symbolism ever since. Hemingway, however, is posthumously quoted in a 1999 issue of *Time* ("An American Storyteller") as saying, "No good book has ever been written that has in it symbols arrived at beforehand and stuck in.... I tried to make a real old man, a real boy, a real sea and a real fish and real sharks. But if I made them good and true enough, they would mean many things." Hemingway was frank and wickedly tough, evident in some of his other great works: *The Sun Also Rises*, *A Farewell to Arms*, and *For Whom the Bell Tolls*.

☞ ZORA NEALE HURSTON (1891–1960)

Once criticized for her cultural depictions and political views, Hurston's work, *Their Eyes Were Watching God*, has grown into a seminal work for African-American and feminist writers, and it is a darn good read. The story relates the struggles of Janie Sparks, who in the end says, "Two things everybody got tuh do fuh theyselves. They got tuh go tuh God, and they got tuh find out about livin' fuh theyselves." Hurston's work grew from the Harlem Renaissance and was revived in the 1970s after an article in *Ms.* by *Color Purple* author Alice Walker.

☞ WASHINGTON IRVING (1783–1859)

Known for the *Legend of Sleepy Hollow*, which tells of the unfortunate disappearance of Ichabod Crane one autumn night after being pursued by the infamous headless horseman (the ghost of a Hessian soldier who had his head blown off during the American Revolution). Irving also wrote the Grimm-influenced (some say stolen) *Rip Van Winkle,* where a henpecked husband who hates his honey-do list heads for the hills. He then takes the drink of some bowling ghosts and falls asleep for a mere 20 years, waking up to a changed geographical and political landscape, a foot-long beard, and a deceased wife. Rip, however, resumes his old walks and habits.

☞ HENRY JAMES (1843–1916)

Although born in New York City, James eventually settled in England, becoming a British subject shortly before his death. James often wrote books that crossed the continents. *The Portrait of a Lady* was adapted for film in 1996, directed by Jane Campion. The story involves a newly wealthy, young American woman who travels to Europe and becomes scammed into marriage by two U.S. expatriates. James's other admired works include *Washington Square, The Bostonians,* and his shorter pieces, "The Aspern Papers," and "The Turn of the Screw."

☞ HARPER LEE (1926–)

Born in Monroeville, Alabama, Lee was a childhood friend and next-door neighbor of novelist Truman Capote. In 1956 some close friends gave her a year's salary for Christmas so she could take the time to write. Within that time she wrote one book, *To Kill a Mockingbird,* which was published in 1960 and won the Pulitzer Prize for fiction in 1961. The novel depicts the story of a white lawyer in a Deep South town who defends a black man who is wrongly accused of raping a white girl.

☞ HERMAN MELVILLE (1819–91)

You either love him or hate him, but one thing is for sure: After you read *Moby Dick,* you will know how to tie several different knots. Melville's immense detail and multileveled symbolism combine to make what is often called the epitome of American Romanticism (of epic proportions). The first chapter opens with the famous line "Call me Ishmael." Then soon the reader is afloat on this vessel as it ventures forth, fighting to surmount both fate and nature. Melville wrote other works, such as *Pierre* and the unfinished *Billy Budd.*

☞ LUCY MAUD MONTGOMERY (1874–1942)

Her works would become a favorite of young women around the world, and whose famous protagonist Anne Shirley once said, "Marilla, isn't it nice to think that tomorrow is a new day with no mistakes in it yet?" Some other "Anne" books include: *Anne of Green Gables, Anne of Avonlea, Anne of the Island, Anne of Windy Poplars,* and *Anne's House of Dreams.* In 1985 a miniseries based on her first novel was among one of the highest-rated programs of any genre to air on Canadian television and won several awards. The films starred Megan Follows as Anne and Colleen Dewhurst as Marilla Cuthbert.

☞ EDGAR ALLAN POE (1809–1849)

Poe's major success, *The Raven,* was published two years before the death of his first wife (his 13-year-old first cousin). After this unfortunate event and scandalous allegations of amorous indiscretions, Poe became dejected and began drinking. Two years later he was scraped off the streets of Baltimore, sick and delirious, and he died soon after. His wife's death influenced his writing, such as in *Annabel Lee*. Poe has a long list of bone-chilling stories, including *The Cask of Amontillado, The Fall of the House of Usher, The Masque of the Red Death,* and *The Pit and the Pendulum.* Many of his tales were adapted for film in the 1960s and starred horror legend Vincent Price.

☞ J. D. SALINGER (1919–2010)

The reclusive Salinger's biggest success is *The Catcher in the Rye,* the ultimate disaffected-teenager novel. It is told in the first person by sixteen-year-old Holden Caulfield, who loathes everything to do with his life and his parents' "phony" middle-class values. Although the novel was written in 1951, it remains popular and sells approximately 250,000 copies a year.

☞ JOHN STEINBECK (1920–68)

While growing up Steinbeck worked as a hired hand on nearby ranches, which fostered his impressions of the California countryside and its people. These thoughts contributed to the Pulitzer Prize-winning novel, *The Grapes of Wrath*. The book tells the story of the Joad family, who after the Oklahoma dust bowl disaster of the 1930s abandon their land and head for what they imagine is "Promised Land" in California, only to find that life is no easier there. His novels *Tortilla Flat* and *Cannery Row* also achieved critical acclaim.

☞ HARRIET BEECHER STOWE (1811–96)

Best known as the author of *Uncle Tom's Cabin,* a violent antislavery novel (published in 1852, when this was *the* political hot potato in America). According to legend, when Abraham Lincoln met Stowe in 1862 he said, "So you're the little woman who wrote the book that started this Great War!" Her writing career spanned 51 years, during which she published 30 books and countless shorter pieces as well as raising seven children. A year after she and her family moved into their Hartford, Connecticut house, Samuel Clemens, also known as Mark Twain, moved into a house just across the lawn.

☞ HENRY DAVID THOREAU (1817–62)

Sometimes called the father of environmentalism, he stated, "Thank God men cannot fly and lay waste the sky as well as the earth." He retreated to the woodland, isolating himself from society and wrote *Walden,* an account of simple living in natural surroundings. He also wrote an essay on Civil Disobedience after being arrested for not paying his taxes, which he did to protest slavery and the Mexican-American War.

☞ MARK TWAIN (1835–1910)
(Samuel Langhorne Clemens)

Drawing on his experience as a river pilot, this author's pen name comes from a riverboat term for two fathoms or 12 feet when the depth of water is sounded; "Mark twain" means that it is safe to navigate. Although Twain was also a popular humorist, satirist, and lecturer, he is best known as the author of *The Adventures of Tom Sawyer,* which drew on his childhood in the Mississippi River port of Hannibal, Missouri, and *The Adventures of Huckleberry Finn,* a much more serious book—sometimes called the Great American Novel—that had the issue of slavery at its heart.

☞ BOOKER T. WASHINGTON (1856–1915)

A former slave, freed after the Civil War, this author and educator worked tirelessly through school. He later became a noted educator and major proponent of education and rights for African Americans, working to establish vocational schools so they could learn trades, obtain jobs, and bolster their standing in society. The details of his life can be found in his compelling autobiography and best seller, *Up from Slavery*.

~~~

☞ EDITH WHARTON (1862–1937)

She became the first woman to win the Pulitzer Prize for Literature in 1921, for *The Age of Innocence*, which deals with upper-class society in New York City during the turn of the century, where marriage for connection was encouraged. Wharton could subtly poke fun at the upper classes, while displaying a warm, sympathetic tone. She had ample time and opportunity to observe her subjects, since her maiden name was Edith Newbold Jones, the wealthy family associated with the adage "Keeping up with the Joneses." Some of her other notable works include *The House of Mirth, Ethan Frome,* and her unfinished work (finished in 1993 by Marion Mainwaring) *The Buccaneers,* which was adapted for Masterpiece Theatre in 1995—a series that was soon forgotten.

British Poets

The myths, legends, and romance of the major British poets have sparked millions of imaginations. The following list mentions just a handful of the most familiar ones.

☞ W(YSTAN) H(UGH) AUDEN (1907–73, English)
Shot to renewed fame 20 years after his death, thanks to the film *Four Weddings and a Funeral*. *Stop all the clocks, cut off the telephone,* which is recited at the funeral, is taken from his "Twelve Songs."

☞ ROBERT BURNS (1759–96, determinedly Scottish)
His birthday was January 25, and for some reason many people still celebrate the event by eating haggis and reciting his poetry. In addition to the wonderfully bloodthirsty "Address to a Haggis," he also wrote "To a Mouse" (*Wee sleekit, cow'rin' tim'rous beastie* and *The best laid schemes o' mice an' men/ Gang aft a-gley*) and the words of *Auld Lang Syne*.

☞ GEORGE GORDON BYRON, LORD BYRON
   (1788–1824, English/Scottish)
The one who *awoke one morning and found myself famous* after the publication of *Childe Harold's Pilgrimage*. He led a wild life, left England after one scandal too many, lived in Italy, where he was friendly with Shelley, then fought for Greek insurgents against the Turks. He died at Missolonghi, in Greece, of rheumatic fever.

☞ GEOFFREY CHAUCER (c.1340–1400, English)

Chaucer is credited as being one of the first great poets to write in English rather than in French or Latin. Although his language is pretty unfamiliar to the uninitiated, he is best known for *The Canterbury Tales,* in which a party of outrageous pilgrims travel from the Tabard Inn in Southwark, London, to Canterbury Cathedral, where they tell stories to pass the time. The prologue presents a vivid portrait of 14th-century life; among the best-known tellers of tales are the Knight, the Miller, the Man of Law, and the Wife of Bath.

☞ SAMUEL TAYLOR COLERIDGE (1772–1834, English)

He wrote only two famous poems—one of them unfinished—but what successes they were: "The Rime of the Ancient Mariner" (that's the one about the wedding guest and the albatross) and "Kubla Khan" *(In Xanadu did Kubla Khan/ A stately pleasure-dome decree).* His friend Wordsworth could have learned a useful lesson about quality versus quantity.

☞ JOHN DONNE (1572–1631, English)

The greatest of the metaphysical poets (a loose term for a group of 17th-century poets whose work investigated the world using intellect rather than intuition). His most famous line, *"No man is an Island, entire of itself,"* oft misquoted, is from a book of devotions rather than a poem.

☞ T(HOMAS) S(TEARNS) ELIOT (1888–1965, American-born, worked in England)
Author of "The Wasteland" *(April is the cruellest month)* and "The Love Song of J. Arthur Prufrock."

~~~~~~

☞ THOMAS GRAY (1717–71, English)
Gets a mention here because we all have read his *Elegy Written in a Country Churchyard:*

> *The curfew tolls the knell of parting day,*
> *The lowing herd wind slowly o'er the lea,*
> *The plowman homeward plods his weary way,*
> *And leaves the world to darkness and to me.*

If you wrote only one poem in your life, you probably would have been quite happy to have written that one.*

~~~~~~

☞ JOHN KEATS (1795–1821, English)
Another great Romantic, he's the one who died at the intimidatingly young age of 26 of consumption in Rome—you can visit his house, located near the Spanish Steps. "La Belle Dame Sans Merci" *(O what can ail thee, knight-at-arms/ Alone and palely loitering?),* "Ode to a Nightingale" *(My heart aches, and a drowsy numbness pains/ My sense, as though of hemlock I had drunk),* "On First Looking into Chapman's Homer" *(Much have I travelled in the realms of gold)* and "To Autumn" *(Season of mists and mellow fruitfulness).*

---

* There are four poems by Gray in the *Oxford Book of English Verse*, one of them the endearingly named *"On a Favourite Cat, Drowned in a Tub of Gold Fishes."*

☞ RUDYARD KIPLING (1865–1936, English)

Prolific chronicler of the soldier's lot in South Africa and India, but best known for "If:"

> *If you can keep your head while all about you*
> *Are losing theirs and blaming it on you...*
> *If you can meet with Triumph and Disaster*
> *And treat those two impostors just the same...*
> *Yours is the Earth and everything that's in it,*
> *And—which is more—you'll be a Man, my son!*

☞ JOHN MILTON (1608–74, English)

Best known for his epic poems, *Paradise Lost* and *Paradise Regained*, which were composed in his later years while blind; *Areopagitica*, Milton's treatise on censorship, also earned him recognition.

☞ PERCY BYSSHE SHELLEY (1792–1822, English)

One of the great Romantic poets, married to Mary, the author of Frankenstein. Lived mostly in Europe, latterly Italy, where he drowned in a boating accident. Author of "Ode to a Skylark" *(Hail to thee, blithe Spirit!)*, "Ozymandias" *(Look on my works, ye Mighty, and despair!)* and *Adonais*, an elegy on the death of Keats.

☞ EDMUND SPENSER (c.1552–99, English)

Author of *The Faerie Queene*, an epic poem celebrating the Tudor dynasty and Elizabeth I, and known to his peers as "the prince of poets." His poem "Epithalamion" has 365 long lines, representing the sum of 52 weeks, 12 months, and 4 seasons of the annual cycle, and 24 stanzas, corresponding to the diurnal and sidereal hours.

☞ **ALFRED LORD TENNYSON** (1809–92, English)
Another prolific one. His great work is "In Memoriam," written on the early death of his friend Arthur Hallam; but most people are probably more familiar with "Come into the Garden," "Maud," and "The Lady of Shalott":

> *Out flew the web and floated wide;*
> *The mirror crack'd from side to side;*
> *'The curse is come upon me!' cried*
> *The Lady of Shalott*

☞ **DYLAN THOMAS** (1914–53, Welsh)
Famous drunkard, but you forgive him most things for having written "Under Milkwood" and enabling Richard Burton to record it for posterity.

☞ **WILLIAM WORDSWORTH** (1770–1850, English)
The most important of the Lake Poets (the others were Coleridge and Robert Southey). I have to say, I think "prolix" rather than "prolific" is the *mot juste* for Wordsworth. He churned it out, and goodness he was dull. The often-quoted "Daffodils" (*I wander'd lonely as a cloud*) is one of his, as is the "Sonnet Written on Westminster Bridge" *(Earth hath not anything to show more fair).*

☞ **W(ILLIAM) B(UTLER) YEATS** (1865–1939, Irish)
Theosophist and Rosicrucian as well as poet and playwright; dedicated his early poems to Maud Gonne. Best known are "The Song of Wandering Aengus" and "The Lake Isle of Innisfree" *(I will arise and go now, and go to Innisfree).*

North American Poets

Although this is an extremely short list of extraordinary poets, the writers listed here captured the voice and history of their generations. Hopefully they will inspire you to seek out the many remarkable poets that followed in their footsteps.

☞ **ANNE BRADSTREET** (1612–72)
A puritan, she immigrated with her family in 1630 to the New World. Anne, who was used to an Earl's manor, had to adjust to near-primitive living conditions. She struggled to take care of her home and raise eight children but still found time to write and became the first female writer to publish work in colonial America. Some notable poems include "The Prologue" and "To My Dear and Loving Husband."

☞ **EMILY DICKINSON** (1830–1886)
Dickinson spent a large part of her 55 years writing about death and immortality. After all, her home overlooked the Amherst, Massachusetts, burial ground, and since Emily was a bit of a recluse and spent a large part of her adult life caring for her ailing mother, she had plenty of time to contemplate life and death through her window. Fewer than a dozen of

her poems were actually published during her lifetime. Some of her well-known poems include "Because I could not stop for Death," "Success is counted sweetest," and "A wounded deer"—leaps highest, which contains the line *Mirth is the mail of Anguish.*

☞ ROBERT FROST (1874–1963, American)
Probably second only to Whitman as "the great American poet," Frost won the Pulitzer Prize three times. His works include "Stopping by Woods on a Snowy Evening" *(And miles to go before I sleep)* and "The Road Not Taken" *(Two roads diverged in a wood, and I—/I took the one less traveled by).*

☞ HENRY WADSWORTH LONGFELLOW (1807–1882)
He is known for his lyric poetry—"Paul Revere's Ride," "Evangeline," and "The Song of Hiawatha" *(By the shore of Gitche Gumee,* which, incidentally, is Lake Superior). Hiawatha may be the most mocked and parodied poem of all time, receiving reconstruction from agents such as Lewis Carroll ("Hiawatha's Photographing") and the producers of *Saturday Night Live.*

☞ WALT WHITMAN (1819–92, American)
The great American poet of the 19th century. His masterwork is *Leaves of Grass,* a massive collection of short poems, including "O Captain! My Captain!" and "When Lilacs Last in the Dooryard Bloom'd," both from the section "Memories of President Lincoln," inspired by the president's assassination.

International Authors

Most of us had teachers of English or general studies who encouraged us to broaden our horizons by reading some of the foreign "greats" in translation. Keeping this to a Top 10 has meant cheating a bit on the Greek tragedians and leaving out Horace, Ovid, Rabelais, Molière, Schiller, Balzac, Zola… and that's before I really hit the 20th century. But I think these are the ones you are most likely to have read without knowing the original language.

☞ **DANTE ALIGHIERI** (1265–1321, Italian)
Known for *The Divine Comedy,* Dante divided his epic into three parts: *Inferno* (Hell), *Purgatoria,* and *Paradiso.* It narrates Dante's journey through these three worlds, the first two guided by Virgil, the final by Beatrice, a woman with whom he had been madly in love since he was nine, although it seems they met only twice. Hell is depicted as having various circles, indicating degrees of suffering, depending on how bad you had been in life: the ninth and worst contained the poets.

☞ **MIGUEL DE CERVANTES** (1547–1616, Spanish)
One of the most influential works of Spanish literature is Cervantes's *Don Quixote.* The novel is about a man who becomes obsessed with books on chivalry and decides to go out into the world to do noble deeds. Toward this end, he imagines that a local village girl is the glamorous lady in whose name these deeds will be carried out, and he christens her Dulcinea del Toboso. His steed is actually a broken-down old horse called Rosinante, which means "previously a

broken-down old horse." Along with other foolish whims, he adopts Sancho Panza as his squire and goes around attacking windmills because he thinks they are giants.

☞ **FYODOR DOSTOEVSKY** (1821–81, Russian)
Often credited as a founder of 20th-century existentialism, Dostoevsky graduated as a military engineer. However, he soon resigned that career, began writing, and joined a group of utopian socialists. He was arrested and sentenced to death, but the punishment was commuted and he spent eight years in hard labor and as a soldier. His best-known works include *Crime and Punishment,* an account of an individual's fall and redemption, *The Brothers Karamazov,* a tale of four brothers involved in their father's brutal murder.

☞ **GUSTAV FLAUBERT** (1821–80, French)
One of the most important novels of the 19th century, *Madame Bovary* was attacked for its obscenity when it was published more than 150 years ago. The novel focuses on Madame Bovary—Emma—who is married to a worthy but dull provincial doctor, Charles. She longs for glamour and passion and has adulterous affairs, rebelling against the accepted ideas of the day. The novel served to inspire the beginnings of feminism.

☞ **JOHANN WOLFGANG VON GOETHE**
    (1749–1832, German)
Once called "Germany's greatest man of letters," Goethe is best known for his two-part drama *Faust,* the tragic play about a

man who sells his soul to the devil—here called Mephistopheles—in return for worldly success. Surprisingly, he is saved by angels. Christopher Marlowe's play *Doctor Faustus* was the inspiration for Goethe's work. Goethe's influence spread, extending across Europe, becoming a major source of inspiration in music, drama, poetry, and philosophy.

☞ **HOMER** (*c.* 9th century B.C., Greek)

The great epics the *Iliad* and the *Odyssey* are the basis of pretty much everything we know about the Trojan War and about Odysseus (Ulysses)'s 10-year journey to get home to Ithaca. A quick rundown on the Trojan War: Paris, prince of Troy, abducted Helen, the beautiful wife of Menelaus, who was the King of Sparta (in Greece). Various Greek heroes—Odysseus, Achilles, Agamemnon—were pledged to fight to bring her back. They laid siege to Troy for 10 years before finally hitting on the idea of a wooden horse: Soldiers hid inside it, the Trojans were fooled into taking it within the city walls, the soldiers leaped out, and the Trojans were defeated. The Trojan hero was Paris's older brother, Hector. Their parents were Priam and Hecuba, and their sister Cassandra was the one who made prophecies that no one believed. Then Odysseus set off for home, encountering Circe, Calypso, and the Cyclops Polyphemus on the way. Back home his wife, Penelope, had promised her suitors that she would marry one of them when she had finished the piece of weaving she was doing, but she secretly unraveled the day's work every night.

☞ **VICTOR HUGO** (1802–85, French)
One of the most notable French Romantic writers, Hugo created his own version of the historical novel by combining historical fact with vivid, imaginative details. His great achievements were *Notre-Dame de Paris,* known to us as *The Hunchback of Notre-Dame,* and *Les Miserables.* The hunchback Quasimodo is the bell ringer at Notre-Dame, and the plot concerns his love for the Gypsy girl Esmeralda. *Les Miserables,* known to many because of its successful stage adaptations, is set in Paris in 1815, at the time of the Battle of Waterloo. The central character, Jean Valjean, is a reformed thief who is persecuted by the police agent Javert.

☞ **SOPHOCLES** (*c.* 496–406 B.C., Greek); **EURIPIDES** (*c.* 480–406 B.C.); **ARISTOPHANES** (*c.* 448–380 B.C.)
Oedipus Rex, also known as *Oedipus the King,* is the play about the man who accidentally married his mother. It is the first in Sophicles's *Oedipus* Trilogy, followed by *Oedipus at Colonus* and then *Antigone. Medea*, the play about the woman who murdered her children to avenge herself on their father is by **Euripides**, who lived around the same time. And while we're at it, there was the comic playwright **Aristophanes**, who wrote *Lysistrata,* about the women who put a stop to the Peloponnesian War by refusing to have sex with their husbands.

☞ LEO TOLSTOY (1828–1910, Russian)

Born into Russian nobility and widely regarded by fellow writers as one of the world's greatest novelists, Tolstoy is best known for his epic, *War and Peace.* A rich tale of early 19th century czarist Russia under Alexander I, it discusses the absurdity and shallowness of war and aristocratic society. Tolstoy's *Anna Karenina* is the book he considered to be his first novel. Considered a true example of realist fiction, it centers on adultery and self-discovery while social changes storm through Russia.

☞ VIRGIL (70–19 B.C., Roman)

His most famous work is *The Aeneid,* the story of the Trojan prince Aeneas, the ancestor of the Roman people (also an ancestor of Romulus and Remus, who actually founded the city). Some of *The Aeneid* was inspired by Homer and relates to the story of the fall of Troy. Escaping from Troy, Aeneas eventually reached Italy but stopped off en route in Carthage, where he had an affair with the queen, Dido, who burned herself alive when he left her. The first words of the *Aeneid* are "*Arma virumque cano*"—"*I sing of arms and the man*"—which is where the title of George Bernard Shaw's play comes from.

MATH

Remember when you used to harangue your parents about why you needed to know "this stuff"? It was only later that you found out why as you wrestled with the challenges of chemistry, engineering, physics, architecture or more ordinary kinds of problems such as figuring your income tax and balancing your checkbook. That math you found so useless as a child is not so useless after all, is it? But perhaps over the years you have found yourself floundering for some of those rules and answers you might have known if you hadn't been doodling on your notebook during class. Well, flounder no more....

Arithmetic

Arithmetic is all about sums—adding, subtracting, multiplying, and dividing—each with its own vocabulary:

- If you add two or more numbers together, their total is a **sum**. So 7 is the sum of 4 + 3.
- With subtraction you find the **difference** between two numbers. The difference between 9 and 7 is the smaller number subtracted from the larger: 9 – 7, and the difference is 2.
- If you multiply two or more numbers together, the answer is a **product**. So 30 is the product of 6 x 5.
- With division you divide a **divisor** into a **dividend** and the answer is a **quotient**. If there is anything left over, it is called a **remainder**. So 15 divided by 2 gives a quotient of 7 with a remainder of 1.

☞ LONG MULTIPLICATION

If you are old enough to have taken math exams without the aid of a calculator, you will have learned the times tables. The easiest one is the 11 times table because it goes 11, 22, 33, 44, and so on—but it all goes a bit wrong after 99. Many people learn by rote up to 12 x 12 = 144; beyond that a person really needs to understand what they are doing. For example:

$$\begin{array}{r} 147 \\ \times\ 63. \\ \hline \end{array}$$

After the number 9, you have to use two digits. The right-hand digit in any whole number represents the units; to the left are the tens and then the hundreds and so on. So 63 is made up of 6 tens, or 60, plus 3 units. And in this problem, you need to multiply 147 by each of those elements separately.

Start from the right: 3 x 7 = 21, so you write down the 1 and "carry" the 2 to the next column;

3 x 4 = 12, plus the 2 you have carried = 14. Write down the 4 and carry the 1;

3 x 1 = 3, plus the 1 you carried = 4.

So 3 x 147 = 441.

To multiply 147 by 60, put a 0 in the right-hand column and multiply by 6 (because any number multiplied by 10 or a multiple of 10 ends in 0);

6 x 7 = 42, so write down the 2 and carry 4;

6 x 4 = 24, plus the 4 you have carried = 28. Write down the 8 and carry 2;

Arithmetic

6 x 1 = 6, plus the 2 you have carried = 8.

So 60 x 147 = 8,820;

63 x 147 is therefore the sum of 60 x 147 (8,820) and 3 x 147 (441), which equals 9,261.

Or

$$\begin{array}{r} 147 \\ \times\ 63 \\ \hline 441 \\ 8820 \\ \hline 9261. \end{array}$$

Songwriter and mathematician Tom Lehrer plays a tune about New Math, in which he does his problem in base 8. If you do a search on Youtube.com for Lehrer's New Math, you'll see why this section avoids that technique.

☞ LONG DIVISION

Division is multiplication in reverse, so start with 9,261 and divide it by 63.

If you have a divisor of 12 or less, the times tables does or did the work for you: You *know* or knew that 72 divided by 8 was 9, without having to work it out. But with a number larger than 12, you need to be more scientific:

$$63 \overline{)\ 9261.}$$

With division you work through the number from left to right.

You can't divide 63 into 9, for the simple reason that 63 is larger than 9. So look at the next column. You *can* divide 63 into 92—once—so you write a 1 at the top of the sum. But it doesn't go into 92 once exactly—there is a remainder, which is the difference between 92 and 63; in other words, 92 minus 63, which is 29.

Carry 29 forward into the next column and put it in front of the 6 to give you 296. Does 63 go into 296? Yes, it must, because 296 is bigger than 63, but how many times? Well, look at the left-hand figures of the two numbers and you'll see something that you can solve using the times table: 6 into 29. That's easy: Four 6s are 24, so 6 goes into 29 four times, with a bit left over. So it's likely that 63 will go into 296 four times with a bit left over. Indeed 4 x 63 = 252, and the bit left over is 296 minus 252, which equals 44.

Write 4 at the top of the sum, next to the 1, and carry 44 forward into the next column to make 441. How many times does 63 go into 441? Well, 6 goes into 44 seven times (6 x 7 = 42), so let's try that. And, conveniently, 63 x 7 = 441. Which means that 63 goes into 441 exactly seven times, with nothing left over, and that answers the problem: 147.

Fractions, Decimals, and Percentages

☞ PROPER FRACTIONS
A **fraction** is technically any form of number that is not a whole number; what most people think of as fractions—numbers such as ½, ⅔, ¾, and so on—are properly called vulgar, simple, or common fractions (as opposed to decimal fractions; see page 60).

The top number in these fractions is called the **numerator**, the bottom one the **denominator** (remember, **d**enominator **d**own).

In fact, the examples given above are all **proper** fractions, with the numerator smaller than the denominator (the fraction represents less than 1). In an **improper** fraction the reverse is true, as in ²²⁄₇ (an approximation for pi, see page 73), which can also be written as 3¹⁄₇, because 7 goes into 22 three times, with a remainder of 1.

If you want to solve problems that involve fractions, it is important to know that if you divide or multiply both the numerator and denominator by the same number, you produce a fraction that is the same value as the original fraction. Take ½. Multiply both numerator and denominator by 2 and you get ²⁄₄. Which is still a half, because 2 is half of 4. Or multiply ½ by 3 and you get ³⁄₆. Which again is still a half, because 3 is half of 6.

The same principle applies to division: If you start with ³⁄₆ and divide top and bottom by 3, you reduce your fraction down to ½ again. This process is called canceling. When you can't cancel anymore, the fraction is in its lowest terms.

With addition and subtraction, however, you can only add and subtract fractions that have the same denominator. You can add ½ + ½ and get ²⁄₂, which equals 1, because two halves make a whole. But what you have done is add the two numerators together. The denominator stays the same, because you are adding like to like. (It's no different from adding 1 apple to 1 apple to get 2 apples.)

Now say you want to add ½ + ⅓. It's easy to do, but first you must convert them so they have the same denominator. The lowest common denominator of 2 and 3 (the smallest number into which both will divide) is 6. To turn ½ into sixths, you need to multiply both parts of the fraction by 3:

$$\frac{1 \times 3}{2 \times 3} = \frac{3}{6}.$$

So ½ is the same thing as ³⁄₆.

To convert ⅓ into sixths, you need to multiply both parts by 2:

$$\frac{1 \times 2}{3 \times 2} = \frac{2}{6}.$$

So ⅓ is the same thing as ²⁄₆.

Now you have something that you can add, on the same principle of adding the numerators together:

$$\tfrac{3}{6} + \tfrac{2}{6} = \tfrac{5}{6}.$$

The same applies to subtraction:

$$\tfrac{7}{10} - \tfrac{3}{10} = \tfrac{4}{10}.$$

But both 4 and 10 can be divided by 2, to give the simpler fraction ⅖.

☞ DECIMAL FRACTIONS

The word decimal refers to anything *with the number 10,* and the English system is based on multiples of 10. As previously mentioned in the multiplication section, a single-digit number—say, 6—means that you have six units of whatever it is. When you have more than nine, you have to use two digits, with one digit representing the tens on the left and one digit representing the units on the right.

Decimal fractions work on the same principle, except that they go from right to left. The fraction is separated from the whole number by a dot called a **decimal point.** The figure immediately to the right of it represents tenths, to the right of that is hundredths, and so on. So 1.1 (pronounced one point one) = 1 plus one tenth of 1; 1.2 = 1 + ²⁄₁₀ (or ⅕); 1.25 (pronounced one point two five) = 1 + ²⁄₁₀ + ⁵⁄₁₀₀, or 1 + ²⁵⁄₁₀₀.

An interesting example is 1.25, because it is the same as 1¼. How do we know that? Well, return to the idea of dividing numerators and denominators by the same thing. For example, ²⁵⁄₁₀₀ can be divided by 5 to give ⁵⁄₂₀. But 5 and 20 are both also divisible by 5, giving ¼. (Once you've got your numerator down to 1, you know that you have simplified the fraction as far as it will go.) So 1.25 is exactly the same as 1¼.

Decimal fractions that are less than 1 can be written either 0.25 or just .25—it's the same thing.

☞ RECURRING DECIMALS

Not everything divides neatly into tens, so sometimes a decimal fraction can be no more than an approximation. For example, ⅓ is 0.333 recurring—no matter how many threes you add, you will never get a decimal that is exactly equal to one third.

If a decimal recurs, you can be certain that it's the same as some common fraction. For example, 0.222 recurring is ²⁄₉;

0.142857142857142857 recurring is ⅐. A recurring decimal is sometimes indicated with a dot above the last digit, which is sort of the equivalent of ellipses (…) or "etc., etc., etc."

Pi is different (see page 73). Its decimal expansion goes on forever but without recurring, because it isn't the same as any common fraction. Pi is called a **transcendental** number, and it's probably the only one you'll ever meet.

☞ PERCENTAGES

Percent means *by a hundred*, so anything expressed as a percentage is a fraction (or part, if you prefer) of 100. So 25 percent is twenty-five parts of 100, or ²⁵⁄₁₀₀ or 0.25. If you've been paying attention, you'll know that this is the same as ¼.

Similarly, 50 percent is ⁵⁰⁄₁₀₀, which can be canceled down to ²⁵⁄₅₀, which is ⁵⁄₁₀, which is ½.

Mean, Median, and Mode

In arithmetical terms, **mean** is simply a fancy word for **average**. You calculate a mean by adding a group of numbers together and dividing by the number of numbers. (Strictly speaking, this is the **arithmetic mean**—there are other sorts of mean, too, but of interest only to mathematicians.) So the mean of 4, 8, 12, and 16 is the total of the four numbers, divided by 4:

$$4 + 8 + 12 + 16 = 40 \text{ divided by } 4 = 10.$$

And it works for any number of numbers. For example, if a class of 11 children gets the following marks on an exam—55, 57, 57, 65, 66, 69, 70, 72, 75, 79, and 83—the total of the marks is 748. Divide that by 11, and you get a mean of 68.

The **median** of a set of values is literally the middle one. In the set of grades above, it is 69. There are five marks lower than 69 and five marks higher than 69—never mind their actual values. The median of an even number of values is the average of the middle two. For example, the median of 1, 4, 9, 16, 25, and 36 is 12.5—halfway between 9 and 16.

The **mode** of a set of values is the most common value. The mode of our set of marks is 57, because it is the only one that occurs more than once.

Measurements

Metric units and imperial (or what we will refer to as American) units are two different ways to measure the same things. Just as Fahrenheit and Celsius both measure temperature but in different ways (see page 94), so the metric system and system of American units quantify length, weight, and all sorts of other things, using different units. Metric units are also sometimes called SI units, which stands for Système Internationale.

The metric system calculates in tens or multiples of tens. The system of American units doesn't, and to the uninitiated it can seem pretty random. (American units used to mean something sensible, such as the foot was the length of a man's foot and the yard was the distance from his nose to the tip of his outstretched arm.)

☞ LENGTH
In American units length is measured in inches, feet, yards, and miles, and occasionally also in chains and furlongs. There are 12 inches in a foot, 3 feet (36 inches) in a yard, 22 yards

in a chain, 10 chains in a furlong, and 8 furlongs (1,760 yards, 5,280 feet) in a mile. Other units are still in use for some special purposes, such as the fathom (6 feet) for measuring the depth of the sea, and the hand (4 inches) for measuring the height of a horse.

The basic unit of length in the metric system is the meter, with subdivisions and multiples for measuring little things and big things. Most commonly used are the millimeter (a thousandth of a meter), the centimeter (a hundredth of a meter, or ten millimeters), and the kilometer (a thousand meters).

To convert between the two:
- 1 inch = 2.54 centimeters, so to convert inches to centimeters, multiply by 2.54. To convert centimeters to inches, divide by 2.54. Remember that a centimeter is shorter than an inch, so you should have a larger number of centimeters.
- 1 yard = 0.91 meters; 1 meter = 1.09 yards, or 3.3 feet. Yards and feet are shorter than meters, so you will have a larger number of them.
- 1 mile = 1.6 kilometers; 1 kilometer = 0.625 (⅝) of a mile. This time the metric unit is smaller, so you have more kilometers than miles.
- A nautical mile is about 1.15 miles, or *exactly* 1,852 meters.

☞ WEIGHT

In American units weight is measured in ounces, pounds, a hundredweight (short), and tons: 16 ounces (oz.) = 1 pound (lb., from *libra,* Latin for pound); 100 pounds = 1 hundredweight (short); 200 hundredweight (2,000 lb.) = 1 ton. This is sometimes called a short ton, because the imperial system in the U.K. uses a long ton of 2,240 lb. And they also use a measurement of stones (14 pounds = 1 stone).

In the metric system weight is measured in grams or kilograms. (You can have milligrams and centigrams, but a gram is already pretty small, so unless you're a pharmacist or something of that sort, you don't often need them.) A kilogram is 1,000 grams.

- 1 gram (or g) = about 0.0353 ounce, so to convert grams to ounces, multiply the number of grams by .0353. To convert ounces to grams, divide by .0353.
- 1 kilogram (or kilo or kg) is about 2.2 pounds, so multiply kilograms by 2.2, divide pounds by 2.2.
- A metric ton is 1,000 kilograms, or 2,205 pounds, just a bit more than an American ton.

☞ VOLUME

In the American system volume is measured in fluid ounces, pints, quarts, and gallons; in the metric system it is measured in liters. This becomes even more complicated because the value of the units in the United States differs from the imperial system in the U.K.

In the United States 16 fluid ounces make a pint. But the U.S. pint and gallon are smaller than the U.K. ones. To convert U.S. pints to liters, divide by 2.1.

In the U.K. 20 imperial fluid ounces make 1 imperial pint, 2 imperial pints make 1 imperial quart, and there are 4 quarts (8 pints) in an imperial gallon. A liter is about 1.75 pints, so to convert imperial pints to liters, divide by 1.75; to convert liters to imperial pints, multiply by 1.75 (pints are smaller, so you will have more of them).

Algebra and Equations

Algebra is the branch of math that uses symbols (normally letters of the alphabet) to represent unknown numbers, along the lines of $a + b = 5$. If you assign a value to a, you can calculate b: If $a = 2$, then $b = 3$. This is known as an **algebraic equation**.

The main thing to remember when solving equations is that one side of the = sign is equal to the other side, so anything that you do to one side, you need to do to the other.*

For example, to solve the equation

$$3a + 1 = 16 - 2a,$$

you first add $2a$ to each side, giving:

$$5a + 1 = 16.$$

Then subtract 1 from each side, giving

$$5a = 15.$$

Now you can divide both sides by 5 and announce proudly that $a = 3$.

☞ SIMULTANEOUS EQUATIONS

A simultaneous equation is a more complicated form of

---

*You're allowed to do almost anything to an equation, as long as you do the same thing to both sides. You are not allowed, however, to a) take square roots; or b) divide by 0. You wouldn't normally divide anything by 0 anyway, but if you were to divide something by, say, a–3 and it turned out that a equaled 3, you would get some very odd answers. More on square roots later in this section.

algebraic equation, in which you have two or more unknowns. The general rule is that you must have exactly the same number of equations as you have unknowns in order to find the value of each. If you have fewer equations, there will be lots of solutions and no way to choose between them. If you have too many equations, there will be no solution at all.

This assumes that the equations are all different and don't contradict each other. For example:

$$a + b = 6,$$
$$2a + 2b = 12$$

are no good as a pair of simultaneous equations, because they both say exactly the same thing, while:

$$a + b = 6,$$
$$a + b = 7$$

will not work either, because there's no way both of them can be true at the same time.

Here's a look at a better-behaved set of simultaneous equations:

$$a+b = 6,$$
$$a-b = 2.$$

A way of solving these is to add the two equations together, so

$$a + a + b - b = 6+2$$

or, more simply, $2a = 8$ (because the $+b$ and $-b$ cancel each other out).

From there you can calculate that $a = 4$ and, because $a + b = 6$, b must equal 2. Which is verified by the second equation, $4 - 2 = 2$.

The principle remains the same regardless of how many unknowns you have:

$$a + b + c = 24,$$
$$a + b - c = 16,$$
$$2a + b = 32.$$

Add the first two equations together and you get $2a + 2b = 40$ (because this time the c's cancel each other out).

Now look at the third equation. It's very similar to the sum of the first two. Subtract one from the other:

$$(2a + 2b) - (2a - b) = 40 - 32.$$

The a's cancel each other out, so $2b - b$ (in other words, b) = 8.

Go back to the third equation, which contains only a's and b's, and substitute 8 for b:

$$2a + 8 = 32.$$

Deduct 8 from each side of the equation to give

$$2a = 32 - 8 = 24,$$

which means that $a = 12$.

Now go back to the first equation and substitute both a and b:

$$12 + 8 + c = 24,$$
$$20 + c = 24,$$
$$c = 24 - 20 = 4.$$

Verify this by going to the second equation:

$$12[a] + 8[b] - 4[c] = 16,$$

which is true.

☞ QUADRATIC EQUATIONS

These are more complex again, because they involve a square—that is, a number multiplied by itself and written with a raised ^{2} after it—so 16 is 4^2, and 36 is 6^2. Thus, 4 is the square root of 16, and 6 is the square root of 36. The symbol for a **square root** is $\sqrt{}$. Actually, $(-4)^2$ is also 16, so 16 has two square roots: +4 and −4. Any positive number has two square roots. A negative number doesn't have any square roots at all, because if you multiply a negative by a negative, you get a positive.

An algebraic expression can also be a square: the square of $a + 4$ is $(a + 4) \times (a + 4)$. You do this by multiplying each of the elements in the first bracket by each of the elements in the second:

$$(a \times a) + (a \times 4) + (4 \times a) + (4 \times 4)$$
$$= a^2 + 8a + 16.$$

To solve a quadratic equation, you need to turn both sides of it into a perfect square, which is easier to explain if we look at an example:

$$a^2 + 8a = 48.$$

The rule for "completing the square" in order to solve a quadratic equation is, "Take the number before the a, square it, and divide by 4." For example, 8 squared (64) divided by 4 is 16, so we add that to both sides; reassuringly, we already know that adding 16 to this equation will create a perfect square, because we just did it in the previous equation:

$$a^2 + 8a + 16 = 48 + 16 = 64.$$

Taking the square root of each side gives:

$$a + 4 = 8 \text{ (because 8 is the square root of 64)}.$$

Again, we know that $a + 4$ is the square root of $a^2 + 8a + 16$, because it was part of the sum we did on the previous page. Anyway, we now have a simple sum to establish that $a = 4$.

Wait a minute, though. Taking the square root of both sides of an equation is not allowed. Why is this? Because a positive number like 64 has *two* square roots, +8 and –8. So the truth of the matter is that actually

$$a + 4 = +8 \text{ or } -8,$$

so *a* equals either +4 or –12.

Although this example is an easy one, the beauty of algebra is that the same principle applies whatever the numbers involved. So, to repeat: The rule for "completing the square" in order to solve a quadratic equation is, Take the number before the *a*, square it, and divide by 4.)

So if your equation is

$$a^2 + 12a + 14 = 33,$$

A **cone** is effectively a pyramid with a circular base, so the pyramid formula applies: A cone with a base 6 inches in diameter and a height of 10 inches has a base area of π x (6 x 6) = approximately 113 square inches, and a volume of:

$$\frac{10 \times 113}{3}$$

or

$$\frac{1130}{3},$$

which equals approximately 377 cubic inches.

☞ TRIANGLES

The area of a triangle is calculated by:

$$\frac{base \times height}{2}.$$

There are three types of triangles, depending on the length of their sides:
- An **equilateral** triangle has three sides of equal length.
- An **isosceles** triangle has two sides of equal length.
- A **scalene** triangle has three sides that are all of different lengths.

The sum total of the angles of a triangle, whatever its shape, is 180°. A **right angle** is 90°; any angle smaller than 90° is called an **acute angle,** while anything above 90° but lower than 180° is **obtuse.** In a right-angled triangle the side opposite the right

Geometry

☞ PI

Pi (π) is the Greek equivalent of the Roman *p* and is used in math to represent the ratio of the circumference of a circle to its diameter. Depending on how sophisticated you are as a mathematician, you can say that π = 3.142, 3.14159, or 3.14159265358979323846264338327 95, but even then it is not 100 percent exact. Expressed as a fraction, pi is roughly $3\frac{1}{7}$, or $\frac{22}{7}$.

Before we go on, three more quick definitions:
- The **circumference** of a circle is its perimeter, the distance around the outside.
- The **diameter** is the length of a straight line through the middle, from one point on the circumference to another.
- The **radius** is half the diameter; that is, the distance from the center of the circle to the circumference.

So to calculate the circumference of a circle, you multiply the diameter by π: a circle that is, say, 7 inches in diameter has a circumference of 7 x $\frac{22}{7}$ = approximately 22 inches. The formula for this can be expressed as πd, but is usually given as 2(πr).

Area is $πr^2$—that is, π times the radius squared. So a circle of 6 inches radius has an area of $\frac{22}{7}$ x (6 x 6) = approximately 113 square inches.

The three-dimensional equivalent to a circle is a **sphere**, and its volume is calculated by the formula $\frac{4}{3}πr^3$—that is, four thirds (or one and one third) of the product of π and the radius cubed (multiplied by itself and then by itself again). So a sphere with a radius of 6 inches has a volume of $\frac{4}{3}$ x π x (6 x 6 x 6) = approximately 905 cubic inches.

Geometry

Geometry is about measuring lines and angles and assessing the relationship between them, so let's start with some ways of measuring.

- The **perimeter** of a two-dimensional object is the total length of all its sides. For example, if these sides are straight, it's a matter of simple addition: A rectangle measuring 4 inches by 5 inches has two sides 4 inches long and two sides 5 inches long, so its perimeter is 4 + 5 + 4 + 5 = 18 inches.
- The **area** of a four-sided figure is calculated by multiplying the length by the width: In the above example 4 x 5 = 20 square inches (in.²).
- **Volume** is calculated in the same way, by multiplying the length by the width by the height (or, if you prefer, the area by the height). For instance, a box that is 6 inches high, whose base measures 4 inches by 5 inches, has a volume of 4 x 5 x 6 = 120 cubed inches (in³).

The volume of a pyramid is the area of the base multiplied by the height, divided by 3:

$$\frac{h \times b}{3}.$$

It's when you get to circles that it all becomes more complicated, because then you have to start dealing with…

you first simplify the equation by getting rid of the 14. Subtract it from both sides to leave:

$$a^2 + 12a = 33 - 14 = 19.$$

Square the 12 to give 144, divide by 4 to give 36, and—as always—add that to both sides:

$$a^2 + 12a + 36 = 19 + 36 = 55.$$

The square root of that gives you

$$a + 6 = 55 = \text{(approximately)} \; 7.4, \text{ or, of course, } -7.4.$$

Deduct 6 from each side to leave the simple statement $a = 1.4$ or -13.4.

You can check that this is right by going back to the original equation and putting in $a = 1.4$:

$$a^2 + 12a + 14 = 33$$
$$\text{becomes}$$
$$(1.4 \times 1.4) + (12 \times 1.4) + 14 = 1.96 + 16.8 + 14$$
$$\text{(near enough for the purposes of this exercise)}$$
$$= 2 + 17 + 14 = 33.$$

QED, as they say in math (or essentially, problem solved). You'll find it also works out with $a = -13.4$.

angle (also always the longest side) is called the **hypotenuse,** which brings us neatly to…

☞ THE PYTHAGOREAN THEOREM

This theorem states that the square on the hypotenuse is equal to the sum of the squares on the other two sides. The simplest example of this is what is called a 3:4:5 triangle, in which the hypotenuse is 5 inches (or centimeters or miles, it doesn't matter) and the other two sides are 3 inches and 4 inches.

The square on the side that is 3 inches long is 9 in.² (3 × 3), the square on the 4-inch side is 16 in.² (4 × 4), and when you add them together, you get 25 in.², which is the square of the hypotenuse (5 × 5).

This can also be remembered using the formula $a^2 + b^2 = c^2$, where c is the hypotenuse.

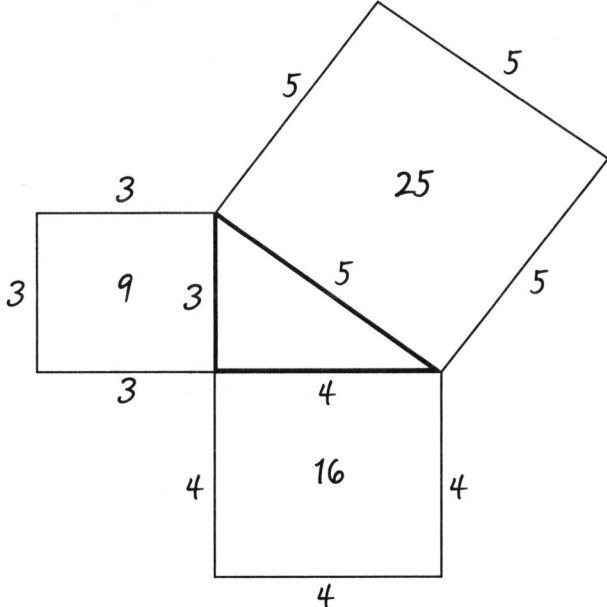

The burning question, of course, is, Why does it matter? Well, it *could* have had some practical value in the ancient world. It has been suggested, for example, that the Egyptians could have used ropes in the proportion 3:4:5 to produce right angles when building the pyramids. Unfortunately, there isn't the remotest scrap of evidence that they did any such thing. In fact, the Pythagorean theorem matters most to mathematicians because it is fundamental to our next topic.

Trigonometry

Trigonometry is "the branch of mathematics that deals with the relations between the sides and angles of a triangle," and a **trigonometric function** is "any function of an angle that is defined by the relationship between the sides and angles of a right-angled triangle."

There are six basic trigonometric functions: sine, cosine, tangent, cotangent, secant, and cosecant, and they are calculated as follows. In a right-angled triangle where the other two angles are valued at x and y degrees, the side opposite x is a, the side opposite y is b, and the hypotenuse is c:

$$\sin x = a/c$$
$$\cos x = b/c$$
$$\tan x = a/b$$
$$\cot x = b/a$$
$$\sec x = c/b$$
$$\csc x = c/a$$

Trigonometry

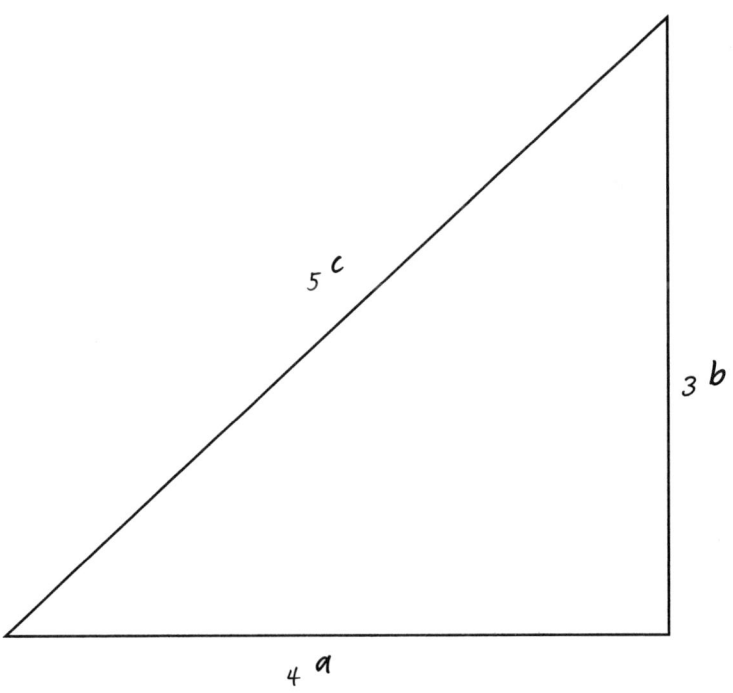

Why do we care? Well, the point is that the functions or ratios remain the same whatever the size of the triangle. So if you know the sine of a 90° angle in a triangle whose sides measure 3, 4, and 5 inches, you can extrapolate all sorts of measurements for a much larger triangle with the same proportions.

The trigonometric version of the Pythagorean theorem tells us that for any angle x,

$$\sin^2 x + \cos^2 x = 1,$$

where $\sin^2 x$ is a conventional way of writing $(\sin x)^2$ without the need for brackets. If you know the sine of an angle, you can use this formula to calculate all the rest of the trigonometric functions given above.

Trigonometry is vital to the study of higher mathematics and the sciences. At a more comprehensible and practical level, it is used in land surveying, mapmaking, engineering, astronomy, geography, satellite navigation systems, and so on.

SCIENCE

The world of science is so vast and expanding that to condense it into 30 pages seems like a futile experiment. Every school system teaches the topic differently, so what may seem familiar and commonplace to one person can remain a mystery to others. Consider this chapter the foundation on which you can build.

Biology

The term biology comes from the Greek, meaning *study of life;* therefore, this field of learning concerns plants and animals and how the human body works.

☞ PHOTOSYNTHESIS

This is the process by which plants convert carbon dioxide and water into the carbohydrates they need for growth, using energy that they absorb from light (hence, the photo element). Light is absorbed into the plant by the green pigment called chlorophyll, stored mainly in the leaves, which provides the green color of so many plants. In fact, plants need only the hydrogen element from water (H_2O), so photosynthesis releases oxygen back into the atmosphere, enabling the rest of us to breathe.

☞ THE STRUCTURE OF A PLANT

The **flower** contains the plant's reproductive organs. The stigma, style, and ovary make up the carpel, which contains the female cells; if a flower has more than one carpel, these combine to form the pistil. The male organ is called the stamen and consists of an anther that contains the pollen sacs and is supported on a filament. Most plants self-pollinate, but some, such as certain hollies and the kiwifruit, require a male and female plant of the same species in order to reproduce.

The **leaves** enable the plant to feed and breathe. They contain the chlorophyll that is essential to photosynthesis, which absorbs light. Leaves also contain pores (stoma), through which gases and water are absorbed and released back into the atmosphere. The shape of the leaf reflects the plant's needs: big, broad leaves are designed to absorb maximum light; the fleshy, succulent leaves of a cactus store water in case of drought.

The **stem** is the plant's support and the conduit between roots, leaves, and plants. It contains phloem, a tissue that transports food within the plant; and xylem, which principally transports water. It is the xylem that hardens to form the trunks of trees and shrubs.

The **roots** anchor the plant in the ground and absorb nutrients and water from the soil. A tap root system has a single main root; a fibrous system has—well, lots of fibers. In root vegetables, such as turnips and carrots, the vegetable part is, in fact, a swollen root. Adventitious roots are less common; the name means *coming from the outside,* and these roots grow in unusual places, such as from the stem.

☞ THE CARBON CYCLE

The process by which carbon (in the form of carbon dioxide) is absorbed from the atmosphere during photosynthesis and is then transferred from one organism to another and eventually released back into the atmosphere is known as the carbon cycle. For example, a plant takes in carbon dioxide; the plant

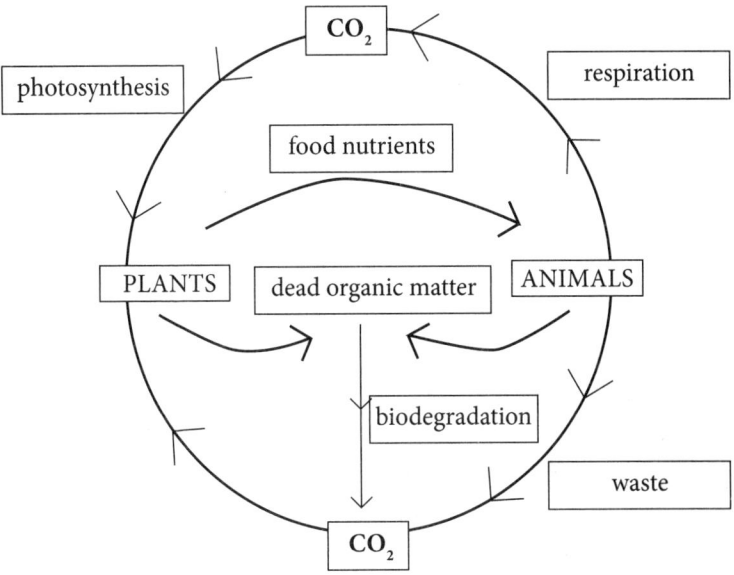

is eaten by a herbivorous animal, which is in turn eaten by a carnivore; when the animal dies, its rotting body releases carbon dioxide. Alternatively, the herbivorous animal excretes its waste, which also degrades to give off carbon dioxide.

This provides a smooth transition from plants to the human body.

☞ CHROMOSOMES

A normal human body has 46 chromosomes composed of 22 matched pairs and two sex chromosomes. Half of each pair, along with a single sex chromosome, is found in the sperm. The other half is in the egg. Fusion of the two creates the human embryo. Sex chromosomes are of two types, called X (female) and Y (male). The egg always contains an X chromosome, so the sex of the embryo is determined by whether a sperm is carrying an X or Y chromosome. Other chromosomes dictate other genetic factors, such as hair and eye color.

Chromosomes are made up of DNA, RNA, and protein.

DNA stands for deoxyribonucleic acid and is fundamental to the organization and functioning of living cells. It consists of the famous "double helix" (identified by the scientists Crick and Watson in 1953), with two strands coiled around each other. When the strands of a helix separate, each provides a template for the synthesis of an identical strand, containing the same genetic information. This enables normal growth, cell repair, and the production of cells that will turn into the next generation—which is why humans produce babies rather than tiger cubs, and why tigers produce tiger cubs rather than roses.

RNA stands for ribonucleic acid, which occurs as a single strand and contains different sugars and bases but is otherwise structurally similar to DNA. It's vital to the synthesis of…

Proteins, which fulfill many important roles in a living organism—they are involved in the makeup of tissue; the properties of muscles; and the functioning of hormones, the immune system, and the digestive system, to name a few. They are manufactured within cells using information conveyed by the DNA and RNA.

☞ THE SKELETAL SYSTEM

The human skeleton is made up of more than 200 bones, held together by fibrous tissue called **ligaments,** and linked at the **joints.** Joints allow varying degrees of movement from none (between the bones that make up the skull) through some (the hinge joints at the elbow and knee) to lots (the ball-and-socket joints at the hip and shoulder).

The principal bones of the body, starting at the top and working down, are:
- **cranium:** skull
- **spine:** made up of 26 smaller bones called vertebrae
- **clavicle:** collar bone
- **scapula:** shoulder blade
- **humerus:** upper arm
- **radius** and **ulna:** lower arm—the radius is the broader one on the thumb side, the ulna the narrower one on the little finger side
- **carpus:** a collective name for the bones of the wrist, individually known as carpals
- **metacarpus:** ditto for the five long bones of the hand
- **phalanges:** fingers
- **sacrum:** actually a fusion of five vertebrae attached to the
- **hip bone**
- **coccyx:** tail bone, a fusion of the lowest four vertebrae
- **femur:** thigh bone
- **patella:** knee cap
- **tibia** and **fibula:** lower leg—the tibia is the broader one that runs down toward the big toe; the fibula the narrower one that runs toward the little toe

- **tarsus:** a collective name for the bones of the ankle and heel, individually known as tarsals
- **metatarsus:** ditto for the five long bones of the foot
- **phalanges:** toes

☞ THE CIRCULATORY SYSTEM

Blood is the body's transportation system—everything from oxygen to hormones is transported around the body in the bloodstream, and its waste products, from carbon dioxide to urea, are carried away for disposal.

In order for blood to do its job, it needs to be pumped around, and that is the primary purpose of the **heart**. The heart is two pumps, each consisting of two chambers—an auricle and a ventricle—with a valve in between. The left side of the heart receives oxygen-rich blood from the lungs and forces it throughout the body; the right side receives the oxygen-depleted blood and returns it to the lungs to be re-oxygenated. (Oxygen, of course, comes into the lungs in the air that we breathe, and without it the cells in the body would die.)

All this requires a well-organized system of blood vessels. These are divided into **arteries,** which are strong and muscular and carry fast-flowing blood *away* from the heart, and **veins**, which are weaker and more sluggish and bring it back. The principal artery, the **aorta,** divides into smaller arteries and arterioles. Smaller veins are called venules, and really tiny blood vessels—whether veins or arteries—are called capillaries.

The exception to the useful mnemonia—*arteries go away*—is the pulmonary artery—the one that goes from the lung to the heart. The pulmonary vein runs from the heart to the lungs. Therefore, the truth is that the arteries simply carry the oxygen-rich blood.

Blood has four major components:
- **red blood cells,** which carry hemoglobin, made up of heme (an iron-containing pigment) and globin (a protein) (This combines with oxygen to form oxyhemoglobin, the means by which oxygen is transported throughout the body. Oxyhemoglobin also gives the blood its red color, which is why arterial blood is bright red; venous blood, having deposited oxygen in cells all over the body, has a bluish tinge.)
- **white blood cells,** or leukocytes, which fight infection
- **platelets,** which are necessary for the clotting process
- **plasma,** the liquid that makes the blood... well, liquid

☞ THE DIGESTIVE SYSTEM

The digestive process is divided into four parts:
- **ingestion:** eating food
- **digestion:** breaking the food down into constituent parts
- **absorption:** extracting nutrients from the food
- **elimination:** disposing of waste

Once you swallow food or drink, it enters the **esophagus,** or gullet, and passes (through a process of muscular contraction called **peristalsis**) into the stomach. From there it continues into the **small intestine** (comprising the duodenum, jejunum, and ileum), where digested food is absorbed into the bloodstream. The whole process is helped by the secretion of **enzymes.** One of the effects of the digestion of protein (which enters the body via meat, fish, eggs, etc.) is the release of **amino acids,** which are the building blocks of the protein the body needs for all sorts of different purposes.

Anything undigested after this stage passes into the **colon** (the beginning of the large intestine), where water is extracted from it. What remains are the feces, which pass through the rectum and out of the body via the anus.

Organs encountered along the way include:
- the **liver,** which in adult life often copes with our alcohol intake, but which has many more functions to do with digestion and keeping the blood healthy
- the **gall bladder,** which stores bile, needed in the digestion of fats
- the **pancreas,** which secretes various enzymes and the hormones insulin and glucagon, which regulate levels of blood sugar
- the **kidneys,** which control the amount of salt and water in the blood. (Excess fluid containing waste products is filtered through the kidneys down to the bladder and leaves the body in the form of urine.)

☞ THE RESPIRATORY SYSTEM

Air passes into the body through the **trachea** or windpipe via the mouth and nose. With the help of contractions from the **diaphragm,** which is a large muscle extending across the bottom of the rib cage, it is carried down into the lungs via two smaller tubes, called **bronchi,** which then split into even smaller bronchioles. Inside the lungs are lots of little air sacs, or **alveoli.** Within the alveoli oxygen is extracted from the air, absorbed into the bloodstream, and carried off to the heart via the pulmonary artery. The pulmonary vein brings "used" blood back to the alveoli, and the process is reversed as we breathe out air that now has a high carbon dioxide content.

☞ THE NERVOUS SYSTEM

The brain, spinal cord, and nerves make up perhaps the most

important and intricately complex system in the human body. The nervous system essentially controls all the other systems in your body. It is what allows you to remember things, or at least remember that you used to know something. It tells your muscles and organs what to do and how to do it. The three interconnected parts of the nervous system are:

- the **central nervous system,** composed of the brain and spinal cord, which sends nerve impulses and analyzes information from the sense organs (eyes, ears, nose, mouth, skin, etc.). These organs enable you to see, touch, taste, hear, and feel.
- the **peripheral nervous system,** which includes the craniospinal nerves, a vast network of nerves that extends from your brain and spinal cord to all parts of your body and carries signals back and forth. It carries nerve impulses from the central nervous system to the muscles and glands.
- the **autonomic nervous system (ANS),** which regulates involuntary actions, such as pulse rate and digestion. The ANS is broken into the sympathetic nervous system (fight or flight), the parasympathetic nervous system (rest so you can digest), and the enteric nervous system (the digestive system's personal messenger).

However, no discussion of the nervous system is complete without those trusty **neurons,** the nerve cells that send and carry the signals throughout your body. A neuron consists of a main cell body with a long nerve fiber, called an **axon,** branching from it. Electrical signals pass from axon to axon through small gaps called **synapses.** In order to do this, these electrical signals turn into chemical ones, called **neurotransmitters.** In fact, right now the neurons in the temporal lobe of your brain (which interprets language), your frontal lobe (which involves reasoning), and your occipital lobe (which controls sight) are firing away!

Chemistry

This is the study of elements and compounds and the reactions they undergo—which is a definition that surely cries out for a few more definitions.

atom: the smallest particle in an element that can take part in a chemical reaction, made up of a **nucleus,** which is containing positively charged **protons** and neutral **neutrons;** and a number of **electrons,** which are negatively charged particles that orbit the nucleus. Each atom normally has the same number of protons and electrons, leaving it with a neutral charge. The movement of electrons is responsible for most commonly observed chemical, electrical, or magnetic reactions. If an atom loses or gains an electron, it becomes either positively or negatively charged and is known as an **ion.**

element: a substance that cannot be decomposed into a simpler substance by a chemical process. Groups of elements come together to form a compound. So, for example, a combination of the element hydrogen (H) and the element oxygen (O) can form the compound water (H_2O).

mole: also known as Avogadro's number or Avogadro's constant, a mole contains the same number of particles as there are in 12 g of carbon-12 atoms—that is, 6.022×10^{23} particles.

Carbon has three naturally occurring isotopes (forms of the same substance with different numbers of neutrons), and one of these is carbon-12.

molecule: the smallest particle of a compound that can exist independently and retain its properties. So in the previous example, the smallest imaginable quantity of hydrogen and oxygen joined together in the right conditions and right proportions will still produce a molecule of water. Only when the hydrogen and oxygen are chemically separated again do they lose the properties that make them water and return to being atoms of hydrogen and oxygen.

☞ THE PERIODIC TABLE OF THE ELEMENTS

The periodic table was first devised in 1889 by the Russian chemist Dmitri Mendeleev. When putting the table together, Mendeleev realized there were gaps between some of the elements. Based on this, he predicted that some elements had yet to be discovered.

The table arranges the elements in ascending order of **atomic number** (the number of protons that each possesses) in such a way that the vertical columns contain groups or families with similar chemical properties. The horizontal rows represent periods, with the most electropositive (an alkali metal) on the left and the so-called inert gases on the right, and the whole thing proves that "the chemical properties of the elements are periodic functions of their atomic weights"—or, in other words, that similar properties in an element recur at regular intervals.

PERIODIC TABLE OF THE ELEMENTS

1A																	
1 **H** 1.00794 Hydrogen	2A																
3 **Li** 6.341 Lithium	4 **Be** 9.012182 Beryllium																
11 **Na** 22.989769 Sodium	12 **Mg** 24.3050 Magnesium	3B	4B	5B	6B	7B		8B									
19 **K** 39.0983 Potassium	20 **Ca** 40.078 Calcium	21 **Sc** 44.955912 Scandium	22 **Ti** 47.867 Titanium	23 **V** 50.9415 Vanadium	24 **Cr** 51.9961 Chromium	25 **Mn** 54.938045 Manganese	26 **Fe** 55.845 Iron	27 **Co** 58.933195 Cobalt	28 **Ni** 58.6934 Nickel								
37 **Rb** 85.4678 Rubidium	38 **Sr** 87.62 Strontium	39 **Y** 88.90585 Yttrium	40 **Zr** 91.224 Zirconium	41 **Nb** 92.90638 Niobium	42 **Mo** 95.96 Molybdenum	43 **Tc** [98] Technetium	44 **Ru** 101.07 Ruthenium	45 **Rh** 102.90550 Rhodium	46 **Pd** 106.42 Palladium								
55 **Cs** 132.9054519 Cesium	56 **Ba** 137.327 Barium	57-71 *Lanthanides	72 **Hf** 178.49 Hafnium	73 **Ta** 180.94788 Tantalum	74 **W** 183.84 Tungsten	75 **Re** 186.207 Rhenium	76 **Os** 190.23 Osmium	77 **Ir** 192.217 Iridium	78 **Pt** 195.084 Platinum								
87 **Fr** [223] Francium	88 **Ra** [226] Radium	89-103 **Actinides	104 **Rf** [267] Rutherfordium	105 **Db** [268] Dubnium	106 **Sg** [271] Seaborgium	107 **Bh** [272] Bohrium	108 **Hs** [270] Hassium	109 **Mt** [276] Meitnerium	110 **Ds** [281] Darmstadtium								

	57 **La** 138.90547 Lanthanum	58 **Ce** 140.116 Cerium	59 **Pr** 140.90765 Praseodymium	60 **Nd** 144.242 Neodymium	61 **Pm** [145] Promethium	62 **Sm** 150.36 Samarium	63 **Eu** 151.964 Europium
*Lanthanides							
**Actinides	89 **Ac** [227] Actinium	90 **Th** 232.03806 Thorium	91 **Pa** 231.03588 Protactinium	92 **U** 238.02891 Uranium	93 **Np** [237] Neptunium	94 **Pu** [244] Plutonium	95 **Am** [243] Americium

The elements are traditionally designated by a one-, two-, or three-letter abbreviation, as you can see in the table, and there are 118 of them. The table above lists 103; listed below them are elements 104 through 118. From 93 upward the elements don't occur naturally but have been synthesized in particle accelerators. The last few are recent achievements, and they have temporary names based on their atomic numbers. Element 117, which will be called Ununseptium, hasn't been synthesized yet, but scientists are working on it. The lanthanides and actinides are usually separated from the rest of the table, as shown above, because—unlike the other rows—they have similar properties as you read across.

		3A	4A	5A	6A	7A	8A
							2 **He** 4.002602 Helium
		5 **B** 10.811 Boron	6 **C** 12.0107 Carbon	7 **N** 14.0067 Nitrogen	8 **O** 15.9994 Oxygen	9 **F** 18.9984032 Fluorine	10 **Ne** 20.1797 Neon
		13 **Al** 26.9815386 Aluminum	14 **Si** 28.0855 Silicon	15 **P** 30.973762 Phosphorus	16 **S** 32.065 Sulfur	17 **Cl** 35.453 Chlorine	18 **Ar** 39.948 Argon
1B	2B						
29 **Cu** 63.546 Copper	30 **Zn** 65.38 Zinc	31 **Ga** 69.723 Gallium	32 **Ge** 72.64 Germanium	33 **As** 74.92160 Arsenic	34 **Se** 78.96 Selenium	35 **Br** 79.904 Bromine	36 **Kr** 83.798 Krypton
47 **Ag** 107.8682 Silver	48 **Cd** 112.411 Cadmium	49 **In** 114.818 Indium	50 **Sn** 118.710 Tin	51 **Sb** 121.760 Antimony	52 **Te** 127.60 Tellurium	53 **I** 126.90447 Iodine	54 **Xe** 131.293 Xenon
79 **Au** 196.966569 Gold	80 **Hg** 200.59 Mercury	81 **Tl** 204.3833 Thallium	82 **Pb** 207.2 Lead	83 **Bi** 208.98040 Bismuth	84 **Po** [209] Polonium	85 **At** [210] Astatine	86 **Rn** [222] Radon
111 **Rg** [280] Roentgenium	112 **Uub** [285] Ununbium	113 **Uut** [284] Ununtrium	114 **Uuq** [289] Ununquadium	115 **Uup** [288] Ununpentium	116 **Uuh** [293] Ununhexium	117 **Uus** [294] Ununseptium	118 **Uuo** [294] Ununoctium

64 **Gd** 157.25 Gadolinium	65 **Tb** 158.92535 Terbium	66 **Dy** 162.500 Dysprosium	67 **Ho** 164.93032 Holmium	68 **Er** 167.259 Erbium	69 **Tm** 168.93421 Thulium	70 **Yb** 173.054 Ytterbium	71 **Lu** 174.9668 Lutetium
96 **Cm** [247] Curium	97 **Bk** [247] Berkelium	98 **Cf** [251] Californium	99 **Es** [252] Einsteinium	100 **Fm** [257] Fermium	101 **Md** [258] Mendelevium	102 **No** [259] Nobelium	103 **Lr** [262] Lawrencium

104	Rutherfordium	Rf	112	Ununbium	Uun
105	Dubnium	Db	113	Ununtrium	Uut
106	Seaborgium	Sg	114	Ununquadium	Uuq
107	Bohrium	Bh	115	Ununpentium	Uup
108	Hassium	Hs	116	Ununhexium	Uuh
109	Meitnerium	Mt	117	Ununseptium	Uus
110	Darmstadtium	Ds	118	Ununoctium	Uuo
111	Roentgenium	Rg			

☞ ACIDS, BASES, AND SALTS

An **acid** is a substance (often sour and corrosive) that contains hydrogen atoms that, when dissolved in water, dissociate into ions and may be replaced by metals to form a salt.

A **base** is a compound that combines with an acid to form a salt plus water. Bases that are soluble in water are called **alkalis.** Many bases are oxides (so their formula ends in O, possibly with a little number after it) or hydroxides (OH).

A **salt** is a (usually crystalline) solid compound formed from the combination of an acid and a base by the replacement of hydrogen ions in the acid by positive ions in the base.

For example, combine sulphuric acid with the base cupric oxide in the right conditions and you have copper sulphate (that lovely bright blue stuff) and water:

$$H_2SO_4 + CuO \longrightarrow CuSO_4 + H_2O.$$

In a school lab you test whether a substance is an acid or a base with litmus paper. Acids turn litmus red; bases turn it blue. Serious scientists use the **pH**—potential of hydrogen—which is measured by sensors and electrodes and such. Pure water has a pH of 7, with anything less considered acidic and anything higher alkaline. Gardeners use this as a way of testing soil; you also sometimes see the pH listed on shampoo bottles.

Another term you might remember—and one worth mentioning here—is **valency**, which means the number of atoms of hydrogen that an atom or group displaces when forming a compound. Hydrogen has a valency of 1 and oxygen a valency of 2, which is why the formula for water is H_2O and not just

HO—because you need two atoms of hydrogen to "match" one of oxygen. Copper can have either of two valencies, which is why the one mentioned a moment ago is called cupric oxide, not just copper oxide. There's also cuprous oxide, CuO_2.

☞ OXIDATION

Oxidation is a commonly quoted chemical reaction, and the most common example of it is rust. In fact, anything that reacts when it comes into contact with oxygen is being subjected to oxidation: The green coating on an old copper coin is the result of oxidation; the browning of fruit is caused by oxygen burning away at the stuff that is released when you peel off the protective skin. Rust is, strictly speaking, the oxide that forms on iron or steel. Stainless steel doesn't rust, because it is protected by a layer of chromium, which doesn't react to oxygen in the same way.

☞ DIFFUSION AND OSMOSIS

Molecules are constantly in motion and tend to move from regions where they are in higher concentration to regions where they are less concentrated—a process known as **diffusion.** Diffusion can occur in gases, in liquids, or through solids.

Osmosis is a form of diffusion that is specific to the movement of water. Water moves through a selectively permeable membrane (that is, one that lets some types of molecules through but not others) from a place where there is a higher concentration of water to one where it is lower.

In any form of diffusion, when the molecules are evenly distributed throughout a space, they have reached **equilibrium.**

☞ BOILING AND FREEZING POINTS

If the temperature is low enough, every known substance except helium becomes a solid. The temperature at which this happens is called its **freezing point.** Above its freezing point a substance is a liquid. At the other end of the scale, if the temperature is high enough, it becomes a gas, and this is called the **boiling point.**

Solid is the only state in which a substance retains its shape; a liquid assumes the shape of its container but does not necessarily fill it; a gas expands to fill the space available.

Take water, for instance. In its solid state, it is ice and retains its shape—whether ice cube, icicle, or iceberg—until the temperature rises sufficiently for it to melt and become liquid (water). If you take a tray of melted ice cubes and pour the water into a pan, it will take the shape of the container—that is, spread out to cover the bottom—but it may only come a certain distance up the side. If, however, you then turn on the heat under the pan, put a lid on it, and boil the water, it will turn into gas (steam), fill the pan completely, and probably seep out under the lid as well.

Nonscientists commonly measure temperature according to one of two scales: Celsius and Fahrenheit, both named after the people who invented them. Celsius was also once called centigrade, from the Latin for *one hundred degrees.*

The freezing point of water is 0°C, and its boiling point is 100°C. The equivalent in Fahrenheit is 32°F and 212°F. This means that the difference between freezing and boiling is 100°C and 180°F (212 − 32).

To convert Celsius to Fahrenheit, you need to divide by 100 and multiply by 180, which can also be expressed as multiplying by 1.8, or 9/5. Then, because the freezing point of water is 32°F, not 0°F, you need to add 32:

15°C x 1.8 = 27; 27 + 32 = 59°F.

To reverse the process, first deduct 32 from your Fahrenheit temperature, then divide by 9/5 (or multiply by 5/9; it's the same thing):

104°F − 32 = 72; 72 x 5/9 = 40°C.

This works for any temperature above freezing.

There are two other scales used by scientists—the Réaumur and the Kelvin. According to René Antoine Ferchault de Réaumur, water freezes at 0° and boils at 80°. Kelvin is interesting because he invented the concept of absolute zero, a temperature at which particles cease to have any energy—so a scientific impossibility, although in the laboratory, scientists have achieved temperatures within a millionth of a degree of it. Absolute zero is 0°K, or −273.15°C, which is very, very cold. Imagine how much energy you would have at that temperature.

Physics

Physics deals with the properties and interactions of matter and energy, but its theories are constantly being redefined as physicists discover new things.

☞ OPTICS

Optics is all about light and there are several terms that may ring a bell.

Remember "The angle of incidence equals the angle of reflection"? You probably do. But do you remember what it means? Well, the **angle of incidence** is the angle at which light hits a surface; with **specular** (mirrorlike) reflection the light is reflected at the same angle. If the surface is rough, you get **diffuse** reflection, which means that the light bounces off in all directions.

Light may also pass through a medium—such as glass or water—and be **refracted** (change direction). This is because of the difference in the velocity with which light passes through the two different media (say, air and water), which is measured by the **refractive index**.

☞ CONDUCTION, CONVECTION, AND RADIATION

There are three ways in which heat is transferred:

Conduction can occur in solids, liquids, or gases and means (more or less) that a cool thing is warmed up by coming into contact with a hot thing. The different levels of conductivity in metals are reflected in their uses in anything from the science lab to kitchenware: Copper, for example, is highly conductive, and therefore it works well for fast cooking (although it may react with certain foods, which is why copper-bottomed pans are often lined with tin); whereas cast iron heats slowly but then cooks evenly.

Convection occurs in liquids and gases and is the basis of the principle that hot air rises. A hot liquid or gas is generally less dense than a cool one; as the hot particles rise, cooler ones rush in underneath to take their place. As the hot particles rise, they cool and come down again, and so on.

Radiation involves the energy that all objects, hot or cold, emit. It is the only one of the three that works in a vacuum and is how the sun's rays manage to warm the Earth from such a far distance away.

Heat is not the only commodity that is transferred in these ways. There is also electrical conduction, mass convection (of which evaporation is an example), and electromagnetic radiation. So, strictly speaking, you should insert the words "heat" or "therma" in front of conduction, convection, and radiation if that is what you mean.

☞ PHYSICAL LAWS

Physics is based on properties that explain what matter and energy can or can't do; without these interactions the universe would probably fall apart. From the observation of the interactions, laws were developed. Some of the physical processes and phenomena are revealed in this section. But a few definitions might help first.

Mass is the quantity of matter a body contains. Newton defined it more precisely by bringing in inertia, which is "a property of matter by which it continues in its existing state of rest or uniform motion in a straight line, unless that state is changed by an external force." All this means is that a thing will sit still until you push it.

Force is calculated by multiplying mass by acceleration and concerns producing motion in a stationary body or changing the direction of a moving one.

Velocity is speed (the dictionary says, "measure of the rate of movement," but most people call that speed) in a given direction.

Acceleration is the rate of increase in velocity.

Work is the exertion of force overcoming resistance (which might be electrical resistance, or it could be physical resistance, such as friction).

And, regardless of what anyone else may tell you, in this context a **body** is a thing. The dictionary says, "an object or substance that has three dimensions, a mass, and is distinguishable from surrounding objects."

☞ THE LAWS OF THERMODYNAMICS

Thermodynamics is the study of heat and its relationship with other forms of energy, and it is important in the study of heat engines such as gas-driven motors and gas turbines.

The other key term here is **entropy,** which is defined as "a measure of the disorder of a system." A solid has less entropy than a liquid, since the constituent particles in a solid are in a more ordered state. The flow of energy maintatins order and life. Entropy states the opposite. Entropy takes over when energy ceases.

If you have managed to follow along this far, then you are ready for the three laws of thermodynamics:

1. Energy can change from one form to another, but it can never be created or destroyed.
2. In all energy exchanges, if no energy enters or leaves the system, the potential energy of the state will be less than that of the initial state.
3. As the thermodynamic temperature of a system approaches absolute zero, its entropy approaches zero.

The British scientist and author C. P. Snow came up with a great way of remembering the three laws:

1. You cannot win (you cannot get something for nothing, because matter and energy are conserved).
2. You cannot break even (you cannot return to the same energy state, because there is always an increase in disorder).
3. You cannot get out of the game (because absolute zero is unattainable).

Moving swiftly on.

☞ THE LAWS OF CONSERVATION OF ENERGY AND MASS

The most common of these laws states that energy in a closed system cannot be created or destroyed (it's similar to the first law of thermodynamics), and nor can mass. At a more advanced level, similar laws apply to electric charge, linear momentum, and angular momentum, but most people never get that far.

☞ NEWTON'S THREE LAWS OF MOTION

1. A body remains at rest or moves with constant velocity in a straight line unless acted upon by a force.
2. The acceleration (a) of a body is proportional to the force (f) causing it: $f = ma$, where m is the mass of the body in question.
3. The action of a force always produces a reaction in the body, which is of equal magnitude but opposite in direction to the action.

Newton also came up with a **law of gravity,** which states that the force between two bodies is directly proportional to the product of their masses and inversely proportional to the square of the distance between them. The universal gravitational constant that makes this equation work is called G, and its value is 6.673×10^{-11} newton m² per kg².

However, Einstein's general theory of relativity describes gravity more accurately.

☞ EINSTEIN'S THEORIES OF RELATIVITY

Before reviewing Einstein's general theory of relativity, take a look at his *special* theory of relativity. Before Einstein—that is, until the start of the 20th century—it was believed that the speed of light relative to an observer could be calculated in the same way as the relative speed of any other two objects (such as two cars driving at different speeds). Einstein's theory is based on the assumption that the speed of light in a vacuum is a constant (186,000 miles—or 2.998×10^8 m—per second), regardless if the observer is moving or at what speed. Furthermore, he suggested that as bodies increase in speed, they increase in mass and decrease in length (relative to the observer)—although this effect became noticeable only as objects neared the speed of light.

Relative to each observer, time moves at a slower rate. All this led him to the conclusion that mass and energy are two different aspects of the same thing, which led to the famous equation

$$E = mc^2,$$

where E is energy, m is mass, and c is the velocity of light.

So, back to gravity. The special theory of relativity concerned motion in which there was no acceleration—that is, a constant speed. The general theory extended this to consider accelerated motion. According to this, gravity is a property of space and time that is "curved" by the presence of a mass. Einstein posited that the motion of the stars and planets was controlled by this curvature of space in the vicinity of matter, and that light was also bent by the gravitational field of a massive body. Subsequent experiments have shown him to be correct.

☞ ELECTRIC CURRENT

There are also a handful of laws to do with electricity. Here's one of the more familiar:

Ohm's law states that the current *(I)* flowing through an element in a circuit is directly proportional to the voltage drop or potential difference *(V)* across it: $V = IR$, where R means resistance—anything that gets in the way of the flow of current. What this means, more or less, is that the greater the resistance (measured in ohms), the greater the voltage (measured in volts) required to push the current (measured in amps) through it.

☞ EQUATIONS OF MOTION

These are basic equations that describe the motion of a body moving with constant acceleration.

A body moving with constant acceleration (a) starts with an initial velocity (u) and achieves a final velocity (v) in a time of t seconds, covering a total distance s. If you know any three of these components, you can decipher the other two.

Acceleration can be expressed as

$$a = \frac{v - u}{t}.$$

Distance traveled (s) is simply time multiplied by average speed:

$$s = t\frac{(u + v)}{2}.$$

These two equations—one for calculating acceleration and the other for calculating distance—are essentially all that is known here, but some other equations can be obtained by combining them.

For example, eliminate v from both of them. The first equation can be recast as

$$v = u + at$$

(multiply everything by t, then add u to both sides) and the second as:

$$v = \frac{2s}{t} - u$$

(multiply everything by 2, divide by t, and deduct u from both sides).

This may sound complicated, but the point is to produce an equation that defines v. Just in case you want to calculate v, you understand.... But you also now have two equations beginning "v=," so you can put them together and deduce that:

$$u + at = \frac{2s}{t} - u,$$

which, after a bit of rearranging, is equivalent to

$$s = ut + \tfrac{1}{2}at^2.$$

This looks a bit more impressive, but it's not really telling you anything new.

Similarly, you could eliminate u from each of our original equations, yielding:

$$s = vt - \tfrac{1}{2}at^2.$$

Or eliminate t from them both to show that:

$$v^2 = u^2 + 2as.$$

So, to give an example, if a body traveling at 30 m/sec (u) accelerates at 2 m/sec/sec (a) for 10 sec (t), it reaches a velocity (v):

$$v = at + u = (2 \times 10) + 30 = 50 \text{ meters per second}$$

$$s = ut + \tfrac{1}{2}at^2 = (30 \times 10) + (\tfrac{1}{2} \times 2 \times 10^2)$$
$$= 300 + 100 = 400 \text{ meters.}$$

Average speed is distance traveled (s) divided by t, which in this instance is $400/10 = 40$ m/sec. Which sounds reasonable, because it starts at 30 and ends up at 50.

Apparently, this isn't rocket science, unless you have a rate of acceleration equal to the force of gravity, in which case you are into the realm of projectiles and ballistics, which is, um, rocket science.

HISTORY

High-school history books are typically gargantuan tomes of no fewer than 1,500 pages. You probably never covered more than 10 chapters or so, but you still had to lug those monstrous compilations onto the bus each day. Today, with history just a click away, students can quickly locate a specific historical tidbit or surf for hours (or even days) collecting information on major historical events.

With thousands of years to cover, and many choices and opinions regarding the proper texts, this chapter can only scratch the surface. But one thing most people agree upon regarding history is the importance of its study. As writer and philosopher George Santayana stressed so insightfully, "Those who cannot remember the past are condemned to repeat it."

Notable U.S. Presidents

At the time of publication, there have been 44 presidents of the United States. Since there is not enough room to include a compete list, what follows are facts about some of the most notable ones, with their time in office noted following their name. (D = Democrat, R = Republican—parties that came into being around 1828 and 1854, respectively.)

George Washington (1789–97): commander-in-chief of the forces that rebelled against British rule in the 1770s, and president of the Constitutional Convention of 1787, which produced the blueprint of today's Constitution. Unanimously elected first President of the United States two years later. Probably didn't chop down a cherry tree or tell his father that he couldn't tell a lie, but the legend persists.

John Adams (1797–1801): another major figure in the War of Independence, known as the "colossus of the debate" over the Declaration of Independence. Became America's first vice president, then president after Washington's resignation.

Thomas Jefferson (1801–09): credited with drafting the Declaration of Independence and something of a polymath, with an interest in architecture, science, and gardening, to name but a few. Lived for 17 years after ceasing to be president and became a respected elder statesman.

James Madison (1809–17): "the father of the Constitution," having played a major role in the Constitutional Convention of 1787.

James Monroe (1817–25): promulgator of the Monroe Doctrine, which stated that "the European powers could no longer colonize or interfere with the American continents."

John Quincy Adams (1825–29): the son of John Adams. Secretary of State under Monroe, he may actually have written the Monroe Doctrine. Also an antislavery campaigner.

Abraham Lincoln (R, 1861–65): really *was* born in a log cabin. Gained national stature from his stance against slavery. His election to the presidency caused the Southern states to secede from the Union, thus beginning the Civil War. His famous Gettysburg Address—"Four score and seven years ago our fathers brought forth upon this continent a new nation, conceived in Liberty..."—further expressed his antislavery views, as did his campaign for reelection in 1864. He was shot by John Wilkes Booth five days after the surrender of the Confederate general Robert E. Lee, which effectively ended the Civil War.

Ulysses S. Grant (R, 1869–77): the leader of the Union army during the Civil War; presided over the reconstruction of the South.

James Garfield (R, 1881): assassinated by a disgruntled office-seeker after only four months in office.

William McKinley (R, 1897–1901): president during the Spanish-American War that saw the United States acquire Cuba and the Philippines. Assassinated by an anarchist in Buffalo.

Theodore Roosevelt (R, 1901–09): one of four U.S. presidents to be awarded a Nobel Peace Prize (for his role in ending the Russo-Japanese War). Expansionist policies included promoting the growth of the U.S. Navy and the building of the Panama Canal. A great advocate of the United States, entering the First World War.

Woodrow Wilson (D, 1913–21): avoided joining the war for several years, but in the end was forced "to make the world safe for democracy." His Fourteen-Point plan to prevent future wars formed the basis of the League of Nations (the forerunner of the United Nations).

Warren Harding (R, 1921–23): campaigned on the issue of opposing U.S. membership of the League of Nations during Wilson's tenure; died in office under mysterious circumstances.

Calvin Coolidge (R, 1923–29): notoriously taciturn president whose economic policies were blamed for the 1929 Wall Street crash. Apparently, a woman who sat next to him at a dinner party bet him that she would get at least three words out of him in the course of the evening. "You lose" was the president's reply—and she did; he didn't say another word for the rest of the night.

Franklin D. Roosevelt (D, 1933–45): the longest-serving president in U.S. history. Stricken with polio and confined to a wheelchair throughout his presidency, he came to power at the height of the Great Depression and instituted the New Deal for economic recovery. He was president during most of World War II and died in office three weeks before Germany surrendered. His wife, Eleanor, was a noted diplomat and political adviser.

Harry S Truman (D, 1945–53): Roosevelt's vice president, who succeeded him in the last months of World War II and was responsible for the decision to drop atomic bombs on Nagasaki and Hiroshima. Also popularized the expression "The buck stops here."

Dwight D. Eisenhower (R, 1953–61): Nicknamed Ike, he was the Supreme Commander of the Allied forces during the 1944 Normandy landing. His presidency coincided with the height of the Cold War and the birth of the civil rights movement.

John F. Kennedy (D, 1961–63): the first Catholic to be elected president. He and his glamorous wife, Jackie, changed the image of the presidency. President during the Cuban Missile Crisis, which may be the nearest the world has ever come to nuclear war. Assassinated in Dallas by Lee Harvey Oswald, who was himself shot and killed by Jack Ruby two days later. The conspiracy theorists are still working on it.

Lyndon B. Johnson (D, 1963–69): Known as LBJ, he was Kennedy's vice president. The Civil Rights Act and the Voting Rights Act, which extended the voting rights of African Americans, were passed during his presidency, but Johnson is mostly remembered for his escalation of the Vietnam War and the subsequent protests.

Richard Nixon (R, 1969–74): the only U.S. president to resign under the threat of impeachment, following the scandal known as Watergate: The Democratic Party's headquarters at the Watergate Hotel had been robbed during the 1972 elections, and it became apparent that Nixon knew all about it and the subsequent cover-up. *Washington Post* journalists Bob Woodward and Carl Bernstein led the exposure—the story is told in their book *All the President's Men,* and a film based on the book was made.

Gerald Ford (R, 1974–77): the only president not to have been elected, even as vice president: Nixon appointed him after the elected vice president, Spiro Agnew, resigned over a tax scandal. Ford granted Nixon a presidential pardon for his role in Watergate.

Jimmy Carter (D, 1977–81): the peanut farmer from Georgia who brought social reform at home and was instrumental in arranging a peace treaty between Israel and Egypt. He will be most remembered for the chaos surrounding the taking of U.S. hostages in the American embassy in Iran. Carter won the Nobel Peace Prize in 2002 for his international peacekeeping efforts, work in human rights, and economic development.

Ronald Reagan (R, 1981–89): former Hollywood film star and long-term governor of California before becoming president. Introduced the anti-Russian Strategic Defense Initiative (known as Star Wars) but later reached an arms-reduction agreement with the USSR. Reagan ordered military action in Granada, an island north of Venezuela. His administration is also remembered for the Iran-Contra affair. In 1981 there was an unsuccessful assassination attempt against him that provoked his remark, "Honey, I forgot to duck."

George H. W. Bush (R, 1989–93): a former West Texas oil executive before becoming president, his political posts included director of the Central Intelligence Agency and vice president in Ronald Reagan's administration. He took the world into the first Gulf War and ordered military action in Panama, and was in office when the Berlin Wall fell and the Soviet Union collapsed. His popularity at home declined when he broke a campaign promise to lower taxes. Bush is the father of the forty-third president George W. Bush and Jeb Bush, former governor of Florida.

Bill Clinton (D, 1993–2001): young, charismatic, Clinton spent a lot of time in the headlines because of his alleged affair with a White House intern. Married to Hillary, who ran, unsuccessfully, for the 2008 democratic presidential nomination.

George W. Bush (R, 2001–2009): a former partner of the Texas Rangers baseball team and governor of Texas, Bush was elected president in 2000, receiving a majority of the electoral votes, but narrowly losing the popular vote. In his first term he enacted "No Child Left Behind," a measure later signed into law that aimed to close the gap between rich and poor student performance. After the September 11, 2001 attacks on the United States, he initiated a global war on terrorism and launched attacks on Afghanistan and Iraq.

Canadian Prime Ministers

Prime Minister Pierre Trudeau once said: "Living next to the Americans is like sleeping next to an elephant—no matter how friendly and even-tempered the elephant, one is affected by every twitch!" It takes a certain kind of character to cope with such sleeping arrangements, as well as the challenges that come with running the second largest (in area) country in the world. Here are the top politicians that Canadians voted in and out.

Sir John A. Macdonald (1867–73; 1878–91): a Scottish-born lawyer with a soft spot for hard drink, he shepherded the country from being a rump of four tiny provinces into a vast nation linked from sea to sea by a brand-new transcontinental railway. A champion of Canadian autonomy within the British Empire as well as the status of the French in public institutions, the Conservative PM is also remembered for the binge drinking that dogged him during his time in office.

Alexander Mackenzie (1873–78): emigrated from his native Scotland at age 20 in pursuit of the girl he loved. As the country's first Liberal head of government, Mackenzie established the Supreme Court and founded the Royal Military College. A staunch democrat proud of his working-class roots, the former stonemason turned down an offer of knighthood three times.

Sir John Abbott (1891–92) son of an Anglican priest and two-term mayor of Montreal. The Conservative also happened to be the great-grandfather of Hollywood actor Christopher Plummer.

John Thompson (1892–94): Conservative PM who suffered a stroke and promptly died during a visit to Windsor Castle. Queen Victoria was not amused.

Mackenzie Bowell (1894-96): forced to resign by his own cabinet ministers, this prominent Orangeman lived long and prospered, dying in his 95th year.

Sir Charles Tupper (1896): Conservative who served the shortest period in office of any prime minister: 69 days. On the other hand, his marriage to wife Frances Morse lasted the longest: 66 years.

Sir Wilfrid Laurier (1896–1911): once decreed: "The nineteenth century was the century of the United States. I think we can claim that Canada will fill the twentieth century." During the Liberal's 15 years as head of government, Laurier witnessed an era of unprecedented immigration, infrastructure expansion, and the creation of two new western provinces.

Robert Borden (1911–20): last prime minister to be born before Confederation, whose bold commitment to the war effort precipitated the Conscription Crisis. This cost the Conservative the support of many French-speaking Canadians. His face adorns the Canadian $100 bill.

Arthur Meighen (1920–21; 1926): the Ontario-born prime minister. The son of a farmer, he studied mathematics and physics at the University of Toronto. The Conservative was instrumental in creating the Canadian National Railways system.

Mackenzie King (1921–26; 1926–30; 1935–48): grandson of William Lyon Mackenzie, leader of the 1837 Rebellion in Upper Canada. As Canada's longest-serving prime minister, this Liberal led the country for 22 years. King was a bachelor who had a penchant for holding séances and talking to his dog. But he was also a capable politician and statesman. He steered the country through much of the Depression as well as World War II. A social reformer, his government brought in unemployment insurance and family allowances.

Richard Bennett (1930–35): elected on the eve of the Great Depression, he was Canada's only prime minister to be buried abroad. It took the Conservative several years to implement radical economic reforms, but by then it was too late for his government. After his defeat he moved to England, where he died.

Louis St. Laurent (1948–57): dubbed Uncle Louis for his folksy and avuncular campaigning style, he staked Canada's global role as an important middle power. His Liberal administration got the ball rolling on the Trans-Canada Highway and St. Lawrence Seaway, welcomed Newfoundland into Confederation, and oversaw Canadian participation in the Korean War.

John Diefenbaker (1957–63): set out to make Canadian citizenship more inclusive to people of diverse origins, with an emphasis on aboriginal peoples. The Progressive Conservative appointed the first female federal cabinet minister, Ellen Fairclough, and was an outspoken opponent of apartheid in South Africa. But economic and fiscal woes, as well as his decision to scrap the Avro Arrow jet project, led to his government's demise.

Lester Pearson (1963–68): considered to be the "inventor" of U.N. peacekeeping, for which he won the 1957 Nobel Peace Prize, his Liberal government initiated federal bilingualism, established a national pension plan, signed the Auto Pact with the United States, introduced universal Medicare, and unveiled a new national flag. A well-rounded athlete, Pearson played semipro baseball in Ontario and hockey while studying at Oxford.

Pierre Elliott Trudeau (1968–79; 1980–84): not only a swinging playboy, but also a no-nonsense gunslinger. When rioters hurled objects at him during a 1968 ceremony, he refused to withdraw to safety. When separatist terrorists took hostages in Quebec, he sent in the army. He stuck it to the Alberta oil barons during the energy crisis of the 1970s. He made mincemeat of his main opponent during the 1980 referendum on Quebec sovereignty. A Liberal, he brought in official bilingualism, the metric system, and—in his proudest moment—repatriated the Constitution, to which he added the Charter of Rights and Freedoms. Fidel Castro, his good friend, was among the pallbearers at his funeral.

Joe Clark (1979–80): dismissed as "Joe Who?" during his early years on the national stage, this Progressive Conservative politician astounded the pundits when he was elected Canada's youngest-ever prime minister at age 39.

John Turner (1984): dashing, dapper, and athletic, he inherited the prime minister's job after Pierre Trudeau retired. The Liberal is remembered for his tooth-and-nails crusade against the proposed free-trade deal with the United States.

Brian Mulroney (1984–93): won the largest majority government in Canadian history in 1994. The Progressive Conservative soon came under fire for his cozy friendship with U.S. president Bush, a revolving door of scandals, and ill-advised tinkering with the Constitution. Nevertheless, his administration hammered out the 1988 Free Trade Agreement with the United States and the 1992 North American Free Trade Agreement.

Kim Campbell (1993): Canada's first female prime minister, who voters never actually gave a mandate to rule. Instead, she briefly inherited the reigns of power, only to go down to a prompt and decisive defeat.

Jean Chrétien (1993–2003): eighteenth child of a paper-mill worker, he was a seasoned veteran of Liberal cabinets dating back to the 1960s. A brilliant, if rustic, campaigner, his long experience and political instincts won him three consecutive majority governments.

Paul Martin (2003–6): as a Liberal three-time finance minister, he has been credited with getting Canada's fiscal health into shape. The scion of a wealthy shipping family, he faced the electorate, but once as prime minister won a short-lived minority mandate.

Stephen Harper (2006–present): the current prime minister, he represents a Conservative party that removed the word Progressive from its official name. An influential back-room player whose survival skills brought him to the fore, Harper has consolidated power in the prime minister's office as rarely seen before.

Notable Kings and Queens of England

House	Name	Known for
Normandy	William I (1066–87)	Won Battle of Hastings, created the feudal system.
Plantagenet	Henry II (1154–89)	Son of Matilda, the one who conflicted with Thomas à Becket.
	Richard I (1189–99)	The Lionheart, fought the Crusades. Depicted as good king in Robin Hood stories.
	John (1199–1216)	Richard's brother, the wicked Prince John in Robin Hood. Forced to sign Magna Carta.
	Edward I (1272–1307)	Conquered most of Wales, built many castles, son was titled Prince of Wales. Died fighting the Scottish.
Lancaster	Henry IV (1399–1413)	Richard's cousin Henry Bolingbroke. Battled Welsh prince Owen Glendower and Henry Percy of Northumberland.
	Henry V (1413–22)	Shakespeare's Prince Hal, has merry dealings with Falstaff but grows up to win the battle of Agincourt.
York	Edward IV (1461–83, briefly deposed 1470–71)	Great-great grandson of Edward III; brought back with help of cousin Richard Neville, who later betrayed him.
	Richard III (1483-85)	Uncle of Ed V; depicted by Shakespeare and others as wicked hunchback/mass murderer. Defeated at battle of Bosworth.
Tudor	Henry VII (1485–1509)	Defeated Richard III, taking the throne more by force than by lineage, effectively ending the War of the Roses.
	Henry VIII (1509–47)	Six wives: Catherine, Anne, Jane, Anne, Catherine, Catherine; often remembered as divorced, beheaded, died, divorced, beheaded, survived.

House	Name	Known for
Tudor (continued)	Mary I (1553–58)	Older sister of Edward VI, daughter of Catherine of Aragon. Overthrew Lady Jane Grey and had her beheaded.
	Elizabeth I (1558–1603)	Mary's sister, daughter of Anne Boleyn. Defeated the Spanish Armada. Beheaded Mary Queen of Scots, but since Liz had no heir, Mary's son became king.
Stuart	James I (1603–25)	Already James VI of Scotland, Mary's son. Oversaw the translation of the Bible.
	Charles I (1625–49)	Believed in the Divine Right of Kings. Did whatever he wanted and was beheaded as a result.
Stuarts, Restored	Charles II (1660–85)	The Merry Monarch, reintroduced theater. Ruled during the Great Plague and the Great Fire of London.
	Anne (1702–14)	First sovereign under a unified England and Scotland. Died without living children. Throne went to the Hanoverians.
Hanover	George I (1714–27)	Never really mastered English, lived in Hanover most of his life.
	George III (1760–1820)	The mad one who lost the American colonies after the Revolutionary War.
Saxe–Coburg–Gotha	Victoria (1837–1901)	Longest-reigning monarch. Her children married diplomatically; most royal houses of Europe are, in some way, descended from her.
Windsor	George V (1910–36)	King during WWI, the General Strike and Great Depression. Valuable political advisor.
	George VI (1936–52)	Brother of edward VIII. Ruled during WWII, wife Elizabeth known as Queen Mother.
	Elizabeth II (1952–)	The present queen. Mother of Prince Charles; former mother-in-law to Lady Di.

Major World Conflicts

Times may change, but the issues that incite wars among people around the world remain the same: Power, territory, religion, and resources are usually at the heart of the matter.

☞ 1066: BATTLE OF HASTINGS

The year 1066 was a busy one. King Edward the Confessor died on January 5, leaving four claimants to the throne. The legitimate heir, Edward's son Edgar, was a child and no one took much notice of him. Military expediency preferred the successful Saxon general Harold Godwin, but there was also the Norwegian king, Harald Hardrada, who invaded northern England and, on September 25, was defeated by Harold at Stamford Bridge, near York. Three days later an army led by William of Normandy (to whom Harold Godwin may or may not have promised allegiance in a visit to Normandy the previous year) landed at Pevensey in Sussex, some 249 miles (400 km) away. Harold marched to meet him, and the battle now known as Hastings took place on October 14. Harold was killed (tradition has it by an arrow in his eye), and on Christmas Day, William the Conqueror was crowned King William I.

☞ 1337–1453: HUNDRED YEARS WAR

A war between England and France. Primarily a dispute over territory because parts of France, notably the prosperous wine-growing areas of Gascony and Aquitaine, had come into English possession through a succession of strategic marriages. The battles include: Crécy (1346), at which Edward III's son, the Black Prince, "won his spurs;" Poitiers (1356), when the French king, John II, was captured and held for ransom; and Harfleur and Agincourt (both 1415), when English archers won the day. After Henry V's early death in 1422, a French resurgence inspired by Joan of Arc gradually pushed the English back, until in 1453 the French won a decisive victory at Castillon and reclaimed all of the southwest part of the country. Only Calais remained in English possession.

☞ 1455–85: WARS OF THE ROSES

A series of civil wars between the English royal houses of York and Lancaster. In a nutshell, Edward III had far too many descendants who thought they ought to be in charge. Key battles were, Wakefield (1460), in which Richard, Duke of York, leader of the opposition to the Lancastrian Henry VI, was killed; and Tewkesbury (1471), a Yorkist victory, shortly after which Henry VI died—probably murdered—in the Tower of London. Rivalry between the in-laws of the new (Yorkist) king, Edward IV, the numerous and opportunistic Woodvilles, and other members of the aristocracy ensured that conflict continued. It culminated in the Battle of Bosworth (1485), when Henry Tudor, a Lancastrian descended from an illegitimate son of Edward III's son, John of Gaunt, defeated and killed the Yorkist Richard III and became Henry VII.

☞ 1622-1917: THE AMERICAN INDIAN WARS

In the past, American history books have conveniently skimmed over or skipped the Indian wars altogether. A few early proprietors, such as William Penn, formed alliances with the Native American people, even learning to speak their language, but a large number of the early settlers encroached upon Indian territory, defied treaties, monopolized game, and practiced outright slaughter of the Native Americans. In some cases the Native Americans attacked first, but most often they felt threatened. The Pequot War of 1637, one of the earliest skirmishes, essentially eliminated the power of the Pequot tribe in present-day New England; most were killed, others were sold into slavery. The Indian wars were eventually fought in other parts of the East, the Great Plains, the Southwest, and in California. Some of the wars include Tecumseh (the Creek War), the Texas-Indian Wars, the Battle of Little Big Horn (Custer's Last Stand), the Wounded Knee Massacre, the Navajo and Apache conflicts, the California Indian wars, and many more. Native Americans were killed, relocated, or escaped to Canada. The 10th Cavalry Regiment, an African-American unit that the Native Americans termed Buffalo Soldiers, fought one of the last battles in 1917.

☞ 1759: THE BATTLE OF THE PLAINS OF ABRAHAM

A significant turning point in North American history, the British rout over French forces at the Battle of the Plains of Abraham near Quebec City on September 13 was an important milestone for the ascendant British Empire. This battle by land and sea that cost the lives of the commanding generals on both sides all but eradicated France's colonial role in the New World. It also helped set the stage for the American War of Independence less than two decades later.

☞ 1775–83: AMERICAN WAR OF INDEPENDENCE, OR THE REVOLUTIONARY WAR

The clue is in the title, really. The thirteen British colonies in North America revolted against British rule, specifically against taxation without representation. The Boston Tea Party (1773) was an act of direct action, which helped spark the American Revolution. Late on the night of April 18, 1775, a silversmith named Paul Revere recieved word that the British posed an imminent threat, which Longfellow preserved in the infamous poem *Paul Revere's Ride* ("Listen my children and you shall hear..."). Early battles at Lexington and Concord (the shot heard 'round the world) were followed by the Battle of Bunker Hill, which was really fought on Breed's Hill. The Declaration of Independence was signed in 1776, and battles followed across what are now the northeastern United States and eastern Canada. George Washington, the American commander-in-chief, led troops across the Delaware River to mount an attack upon the British and Hessian troops. This success at the Battle of Trenton (1776) marked the turning point of the war. France, Spain, and Holland all sided with the Americans—the Dutch gained control of the English Channel and threatened to invade Britain. Britain finally acknowledged American independence by the Treaty of Paris (1783).

☞ 1789: FRENCH REVOLUTION

The French finally had enough of the Bourbon kings and overthrew them, storming the state prison, the Bastille, on July 14, mobbing the palace of Versailles and eventually beheading King Louis XVI and his queen, Marie Antoinette. The revolutionaries proclaimed a republic, but the moderate

Girondins were ousted by the more extreme Jacobins. Power passed to the hands of the Committee of Public Safety (one of those names that you can just tell is going to lead to trouble). Georges Danton, initially one of the most important members of the committee, was superceded by a lawyer named Maximilien Robespierre, and the ensuing Reign of Terror saw the execution of thousands of alleged antirevolutionaries. Perhaps inevitably, Danton and Robespierre both also ended up on the guillotine.

☞ 1792–1815: NAPOLEONIC WARS

Napoleon Bonaparte rose to prominence in the aftermath of the French Revolution, and was in charge of the French army fighting the Austrians in Italy by 1796. Next he decided to break down the British Empire by conquering Egypt. Defeated by the British admiral Horatio Nelson at the Battle of the Nile (1799), he returned to France, overthrew the Executive Directory (the post-revolutionary government), became consul and then emperor in 1804—and he was 35 years old. The following year, he was again defeated by Nelson (at Trafalgar, where Nelson was killed) but did better on land, winning victories at Austerlitz, Jena–Averstedt, and Friedland and more or less conquering continental Europe. The British Duke of Wellington, Arthur Wellesley, defeated him in the Iberian Peninsula—a subsection of the Napoleonic wars known as the Peninsular War (1808–14), in the course of which Napoleon also found time to march on Moscow, losing about 400,000 of his 500,000-strong army in the harsh Russian winter. He was defeated again at Leipzig in 1813, forced to abdicate, and exiled to Elba, an island off the coast of Italy. He escaped, resumed power for the

☞ 1812–15: THE WAR OF 1812

Contrary to its name, this war lasted almost three years. The British were invading American ships and putting its sailors into servitude. And a British sea blockade on France during the Napoleonic Wars made trade difficult (although New England opposed the war and was trading with Britain and Canada). The British also didn't appreciate that forces within the United States were moving into the Northwest Territories and the Canadian border. However, British and Mohawk forces stood ready for a U.S. advance and many American soldiers were taken prisoner at the Battle of Beaver Dams. This war ended with the conclusion of the Napoleonic War when the British fleet pulled out of its blockade, and the Treaty of Ghent took effect in 1815. Since, technically, the United States was not defeated (although it took a beating), the war was considered a stalemate, with both sides going back to their corners and calling it a day. The United States considered the war a confirmation of its independence because they stuck together, once again, and fought bravely.

☞ 1846–48: THE MEXICAN-AMERICAN WAR

The bankrupt Mexican government had a loose hold on Texas and its northern and western provinces (the West) after it won its own independence from Spain. American settlers in the Texas region, such as a group led by Colonel Davy Crockett, fought a war of independence from Mexican forces in the area (remember the Alamo?). With many losses the Texas settlers eventually won this war and proclaimed annexation from Mexico in 1845, but Mexico did not recognize this secession. The Texans and Western states obtained support from the U.S. government. Although many Whigs in the United States opposed the war, many southern Democrats, who wished to gain territory and expand slavery, held the belief of Manifest Destiny, proclaiming that the United States was somehow divinely destined to expand from the Atlantic seaboard to the Pacific Ocean. Mexico and the United States disagreed regarding borders, and after more skirmishes and battles the United States declared war on Mexico in May 1846. Author Henry David Thoreau refused to pay his taxes as a protest to the war and was put in jail for a night as a result—an incident that inspired him to write an essay that was later dubbed "Civil Disobedience," which stated that individuals should not allow the government to sway or overrule their own sense of conscience, especially in true matters of injustice. Ultimately, the United States won the war and signed the Treaty of Guadalupe Hidalgo, which required Mexico to secede not only Texas but also parts of Colorado, Arizona, New Mexico, and Wyoming as well as all of California, Nevada, and Utah in return for $15 million.

☞ 1861–65: AMERICAN CIVIL WAR

Eleven breakaway Confederate states objected to the antislavery sentiments of the North. These sentiments (and eventual policies) had their roots in the Abolitionist Movement, which was spearheaded by Northern Transcendentalists such as

Ralph Waldo Emerson, Henry David Thoreau, and Louisa May Alcott, and in large part by Harriet Beecher Stowe's novel, *Uncle Tom's Cabin*.

The Southern plantations had become well off from the extremely profitable combination of slavery and the Cotton Gin (Eli Whitney's then recent invention). This fact, combined with Southern fears regarding the North's control of the banking system, would lead to the idea of states' rights, from which was born the Confederacy of the Southern states.

A few decades earlier, a geographic border divided the North from South, and it became known as the Mason-Dixon Line. The Confederate secession was led by Jefferson Davis, and the war began with a Confederate attack on Fort Sumter, South Carolina (the first state to secede from the Union). Later key encounters included the Confederate victory at Bull Run, Confederate General Stonewall Jackson's campaign in Shenandoah, and the Union victories in the Seven Days' Battle and at Gettysburg (where Lincoln delivered the famous Gettysburg Address).

The Battle of Gettysburg lasted for three days and is still considered the largest battle in the history of the Western Hemisphere. The casualties of the war were horrific, with as many as 23,000 dead and wounded at the Battle of Antietam alone, which to this day remains the single bloodiest day in American history. After this battle, President Lincoln announced the Emancipation Proclamation, which freed "all people." After Union general William T. Sherman's brutal march through the South in 1864 and the capture of Atlanta and Savannah, much of the South would soon be in Union control. Within months Confederate general Robert E. Lee (who commanded the feared army of Northern Virginia), would surrender to future president Ulysses S. Grant at Appomattox Court House. Following the Union victory and the assassination of Abraham Lincoln, there was a painful reconstruction period in the South, where some cities, such as Vicksburg, would not celebrate the Fourth of July until 1938.

☞ 1880–81 and 1899–1902: BOER WARS

These were revolutionary wars fought by the Afrikaners (Boers, descended from Dutch settlers) of South Africa against British rule. The first, in which the Boers were led by Paul Kruger, gained a degree of independence for Transvaal, which became known as the South African Republic. The second involved lengthy Boer sieges of Ladysmith and Mafeking. Lord Horatio Kitchener was one of the leaders of the British forces; Robert Baden-Powell, who went on to found the Boy Scouts, distinguished himself in the siege of Mafeking. British public and political opinion was polarized by the second Boer War, and it led to a lot of rising and falling of governments.

☞ 1914–18: WORLD WAR I

The principal players were an alliance of Britain, France, Russia, and others (the Allied Powers, united by the Entente Cordiale and later the Triple Entente), against Germany, Austro-Hungary, and Turkey (the Central Powers); the United States joined in 1917. The complicated causes included the Allies' fear of German expansion in Europe and various colonies, particularly in Africa; and a conflict of interest between Russia and Austro-Hungary in the Balkans.

Although war was looming for years, it was sparked by the assassination of the Archduke Franz Ferdinand, heir to the Austro-Hungarian throne, by a Serb nationalist, Gabriel Princip. Austro-Hungary declared war on Serbia, Russia backed the Serbs, and you can guess the rest. Much of "The Great War" took place on what is known as the Western Front in the trenches of northeastern France and Belgium after Germany's thwarted attempt to invade France and take over Paris. It is most notable for the horrific loss of life: over a million men in the Battle of the Somme alone, with Ypres and Passchendaele not much better. On the Eastern Front the Gallipoli Campaign in Turkey killed many Australians and New Zealanders. The Central powers not only suffered great loss of life but were losing resources and support on the homefront, which led them to agree to the armistice treaty and subsequently the Treaty of Versailles, which ended the fighting.

Some of the provisions of the treaty required Germany and its allies take full responsibility for the war, pay reparations, and essentially redraw the map of Europe. Austria-Hungary was sliced into Austria, Hungary, Czechoslavakia, and Yugoslavia. The Ottoman Empire was distributed among the Allied Powers (with the Turkish core remaining as the Republic of Turkey). The western frontier of the Russian Empire became Estonia, Finland, Latvia, Lithuania, and Poland. As a result of the treaty, the League of Nations (later replaced by the United Nations) was founded to help countries settle disputes through negotiation, diplomacy, and the global improvement of the quality of life.

☞ 1917: RUSSIAN REVOLUTION

Actually two revolutions—one in February and one in October of the same year. The first, sparked by a shortage of food, led to the abdication of the Romanov czar Nicholas II; the second involved the Bolsheviks (led by Vladimir Lenin and Trotsky) seizing power, executing most of the royal family, and establishing the first communist state. A civil war between the "Red" Bolsheviks and the anticommunist "White" Russians lasted until 1921. After Lenin died in 1924, Trotsky lost a power struggle with Stalin, went into exile in Mexico, and was murdered there.

☞ 1939–45: WORLD WAR II

Hitler rose to power in Germany in the early 1930s and proceeded to take over various parts of Europe. Britain and France had promised to protect Polish neutrality, so they were forced to declare war when Germany invaded Poland. The Berlin, Rome, Tokyo pact bound Germany, Italy, and Japan together, known as the Axis powers.

Hitler's invasion of France led to the evacuation of hundreds of thousands of Allied forces, many of them in small boats, from Dunkirk, in 1940; Britain now faced the threat of invasion and months of bombing (the Blitz). The war in the air that followed (1940–41) is known as the Battle of Britain. The previously neutral United States began selling arms and goods to Great Britain, provided it sent its own ships to U.S. ports for "cash and carry."

In 1940 the United States implemented a series of embargoes against Japan, and in September of that same year, the United

States agreed to swap American destroyers for British bases. In December 1941 the Japanese bombed the Hawaiian naval base at Pearl Harbor, bringing the United States into the war and opening up a whole new theater of conflict in the Pacific.

Exactly six months after Pearl Harbor, the U.S. Navy defeated a Japanese attack of the Midway Islands, sinking four Japanese carriers and a warship. This defense severely weakened Japanese Naval power, turning the tide in the United State's favor. The Battle of the Japanese island, Iwo Jima, constituted another hard-fought victory for the Allied forces and was a stepping-stone toward the Japanese heartland. The Japanese had built an elaborate bunker and tunnel system on the island through Mount Suribachi. Allied forces used flamethrowers and grenades to clear them out. Eventually the Japanese ran out of water, food, and supplies. Most of the 21,000 Japanese soldiers fought to their deaths, and one in four U.S. soldiers died during the attack—over 26,500. One of the most reproduced photographs in history is the flag raising by U.S. soldiers on the top of the mountain, which was converted into a statue at Arlington Cemetery and a war memorial in Harlingen, Texas. Three of the six flag raisers would die soon after the photograph was taken.

After Iwo Jima, another major win for the Allied forces—the Battle of Okinawa—took more lives than the atomic bombs later dropped on Hiroshima and Nagasaki. Kamikazes, or suicide aviation bombers, sunk almost 34 Allied ships and crafts of all kind, damaging 368; the fleet lost 763 aircraft. The cost of this battle in lives, time, and material weighed heavily on the decision to drop the atomic bombs six weeks later, which forced the Japanese to surrender.

Far away, Germany made the mistake of attacking western Russia in July of 1942. The Russians held out in Stalingrad and launched a counteroffensive in the bloodiest battle in human history, with combined casualties of over 1.5 million. The Nazis were held up in the winter on their way to Moscow, some freezing to death. The Germans were ill-equipped and ill-prepared for winter conflict. Stalingrad continued until February 1943, when the last German forces surrendered. This paved the way for the Normandy (D-Day) landings in June 1944, the turning point for Germany, which surrendered in May 1945.

The Holocaust. Prior to and during the war, the German country became involved in state-supported genocide of Jewish people (the Holocaust or Shoah). Many German nationalists held deep-seated resentment, hatred, and prejudice against the Jewish people. Before World War II the Depression hit Germany hard, especially because of reparations required after World War I. Germans blamed communists for WW I, calling it a Judeo-Bolshevist conspiracy and even went so far as to blame Jewish Bankers for the Treaty of Versailles. Many Germans resented Jewish successes and felt that the Jewish people were taking German jobs. Hitler believed in supremacy of the German/Aryan race and considered Jewish, Polish, gay, Gypsies, Slavs, Russian, and mentally challenged people as subhuman. Hitler preached hatred, and the ignorant masses followed, looking for a scapegoat for their desperate situation. Some believed the propaganda that the Jews were being jailed for their "crimes," whereas others simply went along in fear of the Nazis as they essentially brutally beat up or killed anyone who opposed their power.

☞ 1950–53: THE KOREAN WAR

After WWII Korea was divided into the communist Northern half and the American-occupied South, with the dividing line at the 38th parallel. This war began when the North Korean communist army, armed with Soviet tanks, invaded South Korea. Although the territory was not strategically important to the United States, a deep-seated fear of communism led to the country's involvement in what was termed a police action, so Congress did not need to make an official declaration of war. General Douglas MacArthur and his U.S. and U.N. troops orchestrated an invasion of Inchon and then recaptured Seoul, passing the 38th parallel to the Northern side, which prompted China to send in troops to protect its interests in Manchuria. MacArthur continued to push northward until he was relieved of his duties by President Truman, a politically unpopular move since MacArthur was a WWII war hero. Both sides tried to negotiate a peace treaty but disagreed over many of the provisions, so fighting continued. In 1953 at Panmunjom, a treaty was signed that brought about a cease-fire and returned the divided line to its prewar coordinates. The war would later inspire the novel and subsequent film and television series *M*A*S*H*, about the doctors and support staff stationed at the 4077th Mobile Army Surgical Hospital, which was located near Ouijongbu during the war.

☞ THE COLD WAR

Difficult to date because it wasn't really a war, but a period of intense mutual distrust between former World War II Allies—the United States, U.K., and France on the one hand and the

USSR on the other—at its height during the 1950s. Winston Churchill coined the term "iron curtain" for the ideological and political barrier that separated east from west. Tensions began to diminish during the 1970s and 1980s, especially with the introduction by Mikhail Gorbachev of the policies of *glasnost* (openness) and *perestroika* (reconstruction—specifically of the economy), which led to the breakup of the USSR.

☞ 1959–75: THE VIETNAM WAR

Much of the fighting occurred between 1964 and 1975 in South Vietnam and bordering areas of Cambodia and Laos. Several bombing runs over North Vietnam also occurred.

The United States, Australia, New Zealand, and South Korea all joined forces with the Republic of Vietnam to fight the North, with its communist-led South Vietnamese guerrilla movement and the National Liberation Front backed by USSR-supplied weaponry.

The seeds of the Vietnam War were planted during the First Indochinese War, when the communists, under Ho Chi Minh, fought the French for independence. After a socialist state was established in the North, mass killings of "class enemies" followed. Eventually, a U.S.-backed government in the South launched its own anticommunist campaign. However, the South's autocratic and nepotistic president, Ngo Dinh Diem, had trouble with insurgencies. The CIA apparently alerted generals in the South that the United States would support a coup, and Diem was eventually assassinated. This caused chaos in the South, and the Viet Cong gained ground.

At this point U.S. president John F. Kennedy increased U.S. forces in the area to help train troops. Three weeks after Diem's death, Kennedy was also assassinated. The Vietnamese War was fraught with controversy; some Americans strongly feared a communist scourge, whereas others did not feel that the United States should police the world, toppling regimes out of fear, causing even more unrest. President Nixon ordered a suspension of the action in 1973 and soon afterward signed the Paris Peace Accords, which ended U.S. involvement in the conflict. After that, the North ignored the cease-fire agreement, invaded the South, taking Saigon (being renamed Ho Chi Minh City), and forming the Socialist Republic of Vietnam. Many supporters of the South were jailed or executed.

☞ 1991: THE GULF WAR

The Gulf War involved the high-tech conflict between Kuwait and U.N.-led forces against Iraq in order to remove Iraq forces that overran Kuwait in a surprise assault. The Iraqis had several claims for the attack, including that the Kuwaitis were stealing their oil through slant drilling on the border, and that Kuwait had been part of the Ottoman Empire's province of Basra. This war was largely fought from the air and from tanks, with U.N. forces grossly outnumbering the Iraqi forces. U.N. forces liberated Kuwait and attacked southern Iraq. The troops pulled out after Iraq agreed to a U.N. resolution requiring the Middle Eastern country to destroy major weapons, not develop new ones, and cease its support of terrorists groups.

☞ 2003–PRESENT: THE IRAQ WAR

The U.S. sought to remove the corrupt Iraqi government and military establishment from power. The American government claimed that the Iraqis were hiding weapons of mass destruction. And it also hoped to protect and secure U.S. interests in the Middle East, which many people believe to be oil. Many U.N. allies opposed the war, especially the Arab countries, but an abbreviated coalition was sent into Iraq nonetheless, toppling the Saddam Hussein regime. Through the years, a long and continued war in Iraq has lost popularity with most U.S. citizens, but the plan to exit the country was not as well executed as the plan to enter, and many fear the inevitable civil unrest that may ensue upon U.S. departure. Others fear that pouring manpower and trillions of dollars into a war that could last for many years could have futile and catastrophic consequences to a nation that needs to concentrate its money and human resources into conservation and clean and renewable energy.

African American History

Another scantly covered period in American history involves the mass atrocities committed against Africans; they were kidnapped, captured, and sold into slavery. Revolts ensued but were quashed. African Americans persisted and held strong against their persecutors, eventually gaining freedom after the Civil War and affecting major positive changes in the United States and Canada. This small section cannot do justice to the major obstacles that were overcome and the progressive advances made by the African American community. Slavery was finally abolished in 1865 by the 13th Amendment of the

Constitution, and less than 150 years later Barack Obama, of half-Kenyan ancestry, announced his candidacy for president of the United States.

☞ SLAVERY

In 1619 a Dutch trader exchanged Africans for food in the marketplace of Jamestown, Virginia. By the 1660s a race-based slave system became popular with tobacco planters in the American South, who at the time also enslaved Native Americans; slavery soon spread among the colonies. Slaves were not treated as people but as property; they were mistreated, punished harshly, and killed. In the 1700s England's abolitionists, and later the Quakers, within the colonies sought to petition government against slavery. The American abolitionist movement began to gain ground. In 1793 Eli Whitney patented his invention, the cotton gin, increasing demand and production of U.S.-grown cotton. Although this proved positive for the economy, it caused a resurge in slavery trade, especially in the cotton-growing South, since farmers needed more workers to glean the cotton. In the North small progress was being made, and in 1830 the first National Negro Convention was held in Philadelphia, where one point of discussion involved emigration to Canada.

☞ THE UNDERGROUND RAILROAD

The date marking the start of this movement remains unknown. During the 19th century Canada played a key role in the battle to abolish slavery, with at least 30,000 slaves escaping by secret routes to flee enslavement in the American South.

This political movement crossed the racial and geographic borders and exemplified Thoreau's concept of civil disobedience, which also planted the seeds for the women's suffrage movement. In 1790, Philadelphia became Underground-Railroad Central for the Northern states, since it contained a large number of emancipated black individuals and Quakers. In fact, Harriet Tubman originally escaped to Philadelphia before conducting 13 missions for the Underground Railroad to free slaves; she would later serve as a Union spy in the Civil War, and then struggled for the women's suffrage.

As a youngster, a man named John Brown traveled northeastern Ohio guiding fugitives and vowed to dedicate his life to the freedom of slaves. In 1847 he laid out his plans to raid slave plantations and route the freed people through the Appalachian Mountains to a safe haven near Lake Placid, New York. Brown would free slaves by any means necessary. He met violence with more violence, meeting his own brutal fate during an unsuccessful raid at Harper's Ferry in 1859.

A year later the Southern States seceded from the Union, followed by the American Civil War, where emancipated blacks fought bravely in the Union Army for their own freedom.

Other Important Historical Dates

This small section just didn't fit anywhere else, but most of us will remember at least something about these notable events:

☞ 1215: MAGNA CARTA, OR THE GREAT CHARTER
Signed by King John at Runnymede, this was the first successful attempt to control the power of the English monarchy.

☞ 1453: FALL OF CONSTANTINOPLE

You might not think it was a big deal (after all, cities were falling all over the place all of the time), but this was when the Muslim Ottoman Empire took over the Byzantine, or Christian, capital of the Eastern Roman Empire, and all those scholarly monks fled into Western Europe, taking their books with them. In other words, it marked the start of the Renaissance—which, in its narrowest sense, means a rebirth in interest in classic literature, art, and architecture.

☞ 1605: GUNPOWDER PLOT

A failed attempt by a group of provincial English Catholics to blow up the Protestant king, James I, and the Houses of Parliament. Somebody let it be known, and Guy Fawkes was caught in the cellars under the Palace of Westminster with a load of gunpowder.

☞ 1620: PILGRIM FATHERS

A group of Puritans, persecuted in England because of their religion, set sail from Southampton in the *Mayflower* and in due course established a colony in Plymouth, Massachusetts.

☞ EARLY 18TH CENTURY ONWARD: AGRICULTURAL REVOLUTION

Larger, enclosed fields, inventions such as Jethro Tull's planting drill, and the concept of crop rotation pioneered by Viscount "Turnip" Townshend improved agricultural methods and increased food yield, which made it possible to feed the increasing numbers of people not working on the land following the Industrial Revolution.

☞ 1750 ONWARD: INDUSTRIAL REVOLUTION

The invention of Arkwright's water-powered spinning frame, Hargreaves's spinning jenny, and Crompton's mule revolutionized the production of yarn and therefore cloth, leading to the development of factories and mass production.

Explorers

Since this chapter has been talking about fighting over many regions of the world, here is a quick rundown of people who discovered some of them.

Eric the Red and **Leif Eriksson** (late 10th–11th century, Norwegian): father and son. Eric, brought up in Iceland, was the first European to settle in Greenland; Leif, blown (a long way) off course on his way from Iceland to Greenland, became the first European to reach America. He landed at a place he called Vinland, which may have been modern-day Newfoundland or Nova Scotia.

Bartolomeu Dias (*c*. 1450–*c*. 1500, Portuguese): trade routes to India were the big thing after the Turks blocked off the land route. Dias made an attempt at doing it by sea, being the first to round the Cape of Good Hope at the bottom of Africa. But he named it the Cape of Storms, which may suggest why his crew made him turn back before they got farther than Mozambique.

Christopher Columbus (1451–1506, Italian): born in Genoa but had his voyages sponsored by Ferdinand and Isabella of Spain. The idea was to reach the East (that is, Asia) by sailing west, thus proving beyond all doubt that the Earth was round. Of course, America got in the way. Columbus never actually reached mainland North America, but he did discover the Bahamas, Hispaniola, Guadeloupe, Jamaica, and Puerto Rico, among others. His ships were the *Niña,* the *Pinta,* and the *Santa Maria.*

Amerigo Vespucci (1454–1512, Italian): discovered the mouth of the Amazon and the River Plate, which made him important enough to have a continent or two named after him.

Vasco da Gama (*c.* 1469–1525, Portuguese): persisted where Dias had failed and made it to Calicut in India.

Francisco Pizarro (*c.* 1478–1541, Spanish): the conqueror (or *conquistador*) of Peru and destroyer of the Incan Empire.

Ferdinand Magellan (*c.* 1480–1521, Portuguese): leader of the first expedition to sail around the world, although he was murdered in the East Indies. Like Columbus, he was trying to reach the East by sailing west, and this took him through the Straits of Magellan at the southern tip of South America.

Hernán Cortés (1485–1547, Spanish): did for the Aztecs in Mexico (whose emperor was Montezuma) much the same as Pizarro had done in Peru.

Francis Drake (1540–96, English): best known of the Elizabethan seafarers who were in constant battle with the Spaniards over control of the Caribbean (the Spanish Main) and its riches. Drake—in a ship called the *Pelican,* later renamed the *Golden Hind*—was the first Englishman to sail around the world. He was also pivotal in the English defeat of the Spanish Armada.

James Cook (1728–79, British): one of the great navigators of all time, made three expeditions to the Pacific in an attempt to discover the supposed great southern continent. He became the first European to land in New Zealand and also charted parts of Australia and Antarctica. His famous ships were the *Endeavour* and the *Resolution*. He is also remembered for devising a diet of limes—high in vitamin C, which protected his men against scurvy (the source of the nickname "limey" for the British). He was murdered in Hawaii.

Robert Falcon Scott (1868–1912, British): failed by a matter of days to become the first person to reach the South Pole, and died, with the rest of his party, in the course of the return journey. One of his companions was Captain Oates, who—knowing that his weakness was endangering the lives of the others—went out into the blizzard saying, "I may be some time."

Roald Amundsen (1872–1928, Norwegian): the one who made it to the South Pole—and back again. He was also the first to sail through the Northwest Passage, the sea route from Pacific to Atlantic along the north coast of North America.

GEOGRAPHY

"Geography is about maps," said E. Clerihew Bentley, and although geographers would take offense to that definition, a lot of what we learned as a kid was about the stuff that filled maps. The last section of this chapter should really be classed as paleontology, but nobody told us that at the time.

The Countries of the World

The world is divided into seven continents: Europe, Asia, North America, South America, Africa, Australia, and Antarctica. It's a matter of debate to which continent you assign various island nations, because a continent is by definition a continuous landmass. The islands of the Pacific are usually grouped together as Oceania, so for the purpose of this list, I am going to use that convention and place Australia under that heading, too. And I'm going to create a continent called Central America and include in it all the islands of the Caribbean, as well as the stretch of mainland south of Mexico.

Antarctica contains no countries—instead, it is a stateless territory protected from exploitation by an international treaty.

The countries listed here (with their capitals, continents, and any change of name since 1945) are the 192 members of the United Nations, the most recent being Montenegro, which split from Serbia in 2006; Switzerland, that long-term bastion of neutrality, finally succumbed in 2002. And they are given in the alphabetical order used by the United Nations, which provides such delights as The Former Yugoslav Republic of Macedonia, coming under T. SU or Y after a country's name means that it was formerly part of the Soviet Union or Yugoslavia.

Country	**Capital**	**Continent**
Afghanistan	Kabul	Asia
Albania	Tirana	Europe
Algeria	Algiers	Africa
Andorra	Andorra la Vella	Europe
Angola	Luanda	Africa
Antigua & Barbuda	St. John's	N. America
Argentina	Buenos Aires	S. America
Armenia (SU)	Yerevan	Asia
Australia	Canberra	Oceania
Austria	Vienna	Europe
Azerbaijan (SU)	Baku	Asia
Bahamas	Nassau	C. America
Bahrain	Manama	Asia
Bangladesh *formerly East Pakistan*	Dhaka	Asia
Barbados	Bridgetown	C. America
Belarus (SU)	Minsk	Europe
Belgium	Brussels	Europe
Belize	Belmopan	C. America
Benin *formerly Dahomey*	Porto Novo	Africa
Bhutan	Thimphu	Asia
Bolivia	La Paz	S. America

Country	Capital	Continent
Bosnia & Herzegovina (Y)	Sarajevo	Europe
Botswana *formerly Bechuanaland*	Gaborone	Africa
Brazil	Brasilia	S. America
Brunei Darussalam	Bandar Seri Begawan	Asia
Bulgaria	Sofia	Europe
Burkina Faso *formerly Upper Volta*	Ouagadougou	Africa
Burundi *formerly joined with Rwanda to form Ruanda-Urundi*	Bujumbura	Africa
Cambodia *known as Kampuchea from 1976–89*	Phnom Penh	Asia
Cameroon	Yaoundé	Africa
Canada	Ottawa	N. America
Cape Verde	Praia	Africa
Central African Republic	Bangui	Africa
Chad	N'Djamena	Africa
Chile	Santiago	S. America
China	Beijing	Asia
Colombia	Bogota	S. America
Comoros	Moroni	Africa
Congo, Republic of the *formerly the French Congo*	Brazzaville	Africa
Costa Rica	San José	C. America
Côte d'Ivoire *formerly the Ivory Coast*	Yamoussoukro	Africa
Croatia (Y)	Zagreb	Europe
Cuba	Havana	C. America
Cyprus	Nicosia	Europe

Country	Capital	Continent
Czech Republic *used to be joined to Slovakia to form Czechoslovakia*	Prague	Europe
Democratic People's Republic of Korea *(North Korea to you and me)*	Pyongyang	Asia
Democratic Republic of the Congo	Kinshasa	Africa
Denmark	Copenhagen	Europe
Djibouti *formerly the French Territory of the Afars and the Issas*	Djibouti City	Africa
Dominica	Roseau	C. America
Dominican Republic*	Santo Domingo	C. America
Ecuador	Quito	S. America
Egypt	Cairo	Africa
El Salvador	San Salvador	C. America
Equatorial Guinea	Malabo	Africa
Eritrea *gained independence from Ethiopia in 1993*	Asmara	Africa
Estonia (SU)	Tallinn	Europe
Ethiopia	Addis Ababa	Africa
Fiji	Suva	Oceania
Finland	Helsinki	Europe
France	Paris	Europe
Gabon	Libreville	Africa
Gambia	Banjul	Africa
Georgia (SU)	Tbilisi	Asia

* Easily confused: Dominica is one of the Lesser Antilles islands in the southeastern Caribbean; the Dominican Republic, farther north but still in the Caribbean, shares the island of Hispaniola with Haiti and forms part of the Greater Antilles.

Country	**Capital**	**Continent**
Germany *from 1949-90 was divided into West (Federal Republic) and east (Democratic Republic) with capitals Bonn and Berlin respectively*	Berlin	Europe
Ghana	Accra	Africa
Greece	Athens	Europe
Grenada	St. George's	C. America
Guatemala	Guatemala City	C. America
Guinea *formerly French Guinea*	Conakry	Africa
Guinea-Bissau *formerly Portuguese Guinea*	Bissau	Africa
Guyana *formerly British Guiana*	Georgetown	S. America
Haiti	Port-au-Prince	C. America
Honduras	Tegucigalpa	C. America
Hungary	Budapest	Europe
Iceland	Reykjavik	Europe
India	New Delhi	Asia
Indonesia	Djakarta	Asia
Iran	Tehran	Asia
Iraq	Baghdad	Asia
Ireland	Dublin	Europe
Israel	**	Asia
Italy	Rome	Europe
Jamaica	Kingston	C. America

** Israel proclaimed Jerusalem as its capital in 1950, but the U.S., like nearly all other countries, maintains its embassy in Tel Aviv.

Country	Capital	Continent
Japan	Tokyo	Asia
Jordan	Amman	Asia
Kazakhstan (SU)	Astana	Asia
Kenya	Nairobi	Africa
Kiribati *formerly Gilbert Islands*	Tarawa	Oceania
Kuwait	Kuwait City	Asia
Kyrgyzstan (SU)	Bishkek	Asia
Laos	Vientiane	Asia
Latvia (SU)	Riga	Europe
Lebanon	Beirut	Asia
Lesotho *formerly Basutoland*	Maseru	Africa
Liberia	Monrovia	Africa
Libya	Tripoli	Africa
Liechtenstein	Vaduz	Europe
Lithuania (SU)	Vilnius	Europe
Luxembourg	Luxembourg City	Europe
Madagascar	Antananarivo	Africa
Malawi *formerly Nyasaland*	Lilongwe	Africa
Malaysia *created in 1963 from the Federation of Malaya, the states of Sarawak and Sabah in Borneo, and briefly, Singapore*	Kuala Lumpur	Asia
Maldives	Malé	Asia
Mali	Bamako	Africa
Malta	Valletta	Europe
Marshall Islands	Delap-Uliga-Darrit	Oceania
Mauritania	Nouakchott	Africa

Country	**Capital**	**Continent**
Mauritius	Port Louis	Africa
Mexico	Mexico City	N. America
Micronesia, Federated States of	Palikir	Oceania
Moldova (SU)	Chisinau	Europe
Monaco	Monaco	Europe
Mongolia	Ulan Bator	Asia
Montenegro (Y)	Podgorica	Europe
Morocco	Rabat	Africa
Mozambique	Maputo	Africa
Myanmar *formerly Burma; the capital until 2006 was Rangoon/Yangon*	Nay Pyi Daw	Asia
Namibia *formerly South West Africa*	Windhoek	Africa
Nauru *formerly Pleasant Island*	Yaren	Oceania
Nepal	Kathmandu	Asia
Netherlands	Amsterdam	Europe
New Zealand	Wellington	Oceania
Nicaragua	Managua	C. America
Niger	Niamey	Africa
Nigeria	Abuja	Africa
Norway	Oslo	Europe
Oman	Muscat	Asia
Pakistan	Islamabad	Asia
Palau *formerly Belau*	Koror	Oceania
Panama	Panama City	C. America
Papua New Guinea	Port Moresby	Oceania

Country	**Capital**	**Continent**
Paraguay	Asunción	S. America
Peru	Lima	S. America
Philippines	Manila	Asia
Poland	Warsaw	Europe
Portugal	Lisbon	Europe
Qatar	Doha	Asia
Republic of Korea *(the South)*	Seoul	Asia
Romania	Bucharest	Europe
Russian Federation (SU)	Moscow	Europe/Asia
Rwanda *formerly joined with Burundi to form Ruanda-Urundi*	Kigali	Africa
Saint Kitts & Nevis	Basseterre	C. America
Saint Lucia	Castries	C. America
Saint Vincent & the Grenadines	Kingstown	C. America
Samoa	Apia & Pago Pago	Oceania
San Marino	San Marino	Europe
São Tomé & Príncipe	São Tomé	Africa
Saudi Arabia	Riyadh	Asia
Senegal	Dakar	Africa
Serbia (Y)	Belgrade	Europe
Seychelles	Victoria	Africa
Sierra Leone	Freetown	Africa
Singapore *became independent of the Malaysian Federation in 1965*	Singapore	Asia

Country	**Capital**	**Continent**
Slovakia *used to be joined to the Czech Republic to form Czechoslovakia*	Bratislava	Europe
Slovenia (Y)	Ljubljana	Europe
Solomon Islands	Honiara	Oceania
Somalia	Mogadishu	Africa
South Africa	Pretoria	Africa
Spain	Madrid	Europe
Sri Lanka *formerly Ceylon*	Colombo	Asia
Sudan	Khartoum	Africa
Suriname *formerly Dutch Guiana*	Paramaribo	S. America
Swaziland	Mbabane	Africa
Sweden	Stockholm	Europe
Switzerland	Berne	Europe
Syria	Damascus	Asia
Tajikistan (SU)	Dushanbe	Asia
Thailand	Bangkok	Asia
The Former Yugoslav Republic of Macedonia	Skopje	Europe
Timor-Leste (East Timor)	Dili	Asia
Togo	Lomé	Africa
Tonga	Nuku'alofa	Oceania
Trinidad & Tobago	Port-of-Spain	C. America
Tunisia	Tunis	Africa
Turkey	Ankara	Europe/Asia
Turkmenistan (SU)	Ashgabat	Asia
Tuvalu *formerly Ellice Islands*	Funafuti	Oceania

Country	Capital	Continent
Uganda	Kampala	Africa
Ukraine (SU)	Kiev	Europe
United Arab Emirates	Abu Dhabi	Asia
United Kingdom of Great Britain & Northern Ireland	London	Europe
United Republic of Tanzania *formed in 1964 from a union of Tanganyika and Zanzibar*	Dodoma	Africa
United States of America	Washington	N. America
Uruguay	Montevideo	S. America
Uzbekistan (SU)	Tashkent	Asia
Vanuatu *formerly New Hebrides*	Port Vila	Oceania
Venezuela	Caracas	S. America
Vietnam *from 1954–76 divided into North and South, with Hanoi the capital of the North and Saigon (now Ho Chi Minh City) of the South*	Hanoi	Asia
Yemen	San'a	Asia
Zambia *formerly Northern Rhodesia*	Lusaka	Africa
Zimbabwe *formerly Southern Rhodesia, then from 1964–79 Rhodesia; until 1979 the capital was called Salisbury*	Harare	Africa

The 50 United States of America

Listed below are the 50 states with their nicknames, their capitals, and the date they entered the Union. Those marked with an asterisk are the original 13 colonies that declared themselves independent from British rule in 1776. Those marked with two asterisks seceded from the Union during the Civil War and formed the Confederate States of America; all had been readmitted by 1870.

State	Nickname	Capital	Date
Alabama **	Yellowhammer State	Montgomery	1819
Alaska	The Last Frontier	Juneau	1959
Arizona	Grand Canyon State	Phoenix	1912
Arkansas **	Natural State	Little Rock	1836
California	Golden State	Sacramento	1850
Colorado	Centennial State	Denver	1876
Connecticut *	Constitution State	Hartford	1788
Delaware*	First State	Dover	1787
Florida **	Sunshine State	Tallahassee	1845
Georgia * **	Peach State	Atlanta	1788
Hawaii	Aloha State	Honolulu	1959
Idaho	Gem State	Boise	1890
Illinois	Prairie State	Springfield	1818
Indiana	Hoosier State	Indianapolis	1816

State	Nickname	Capital	Date
Iowa	Hawkeye State	Des Moines	1846
Kansas	Sunflower State	Topeka	1861
Kentucky	Bluegrass State	Frankfort	1792
Louisiana **	Pelican State	Baton Rouge	1812
Maine	Pine Tree State	Augusta	1820
Maryland *	Old Line State	Annapolis	1788
Massachusetts *	Bay State	Boston	1788
Michigan	Great Lakes State	Lansing	1837
Minnesota	North Star State	St. Paul	1858
Mississippi **	Magnolia State	Jackson	1817
Missouri	Show-me State	Jefferson City	1821
Montana	Treasure State	Helena	1889
Nebraska	Cornhusker State	Lincoln	1867
Nevada	Silver State	Carson City	1864
New Hampshire *	Granite State	Concord	1788
New Jersey *	Garden State	Trenton	1787
New Mexico	Land of Enchantment	Santa Fe	1912
New York *	Empire State	Albany	1788
N. Carolina * **	Tar Heel State	Raleigh	1789
North Dakota	Peace Garden State	Bismarck	1889
Ohio	Buckeye State	Columbus	1803
Oklahoma	Sooner State	Oklahoma City	1907
Oregon	Beaver State	Salem	1859
Pennsylvania *	Keystone State	Harrisburg	1787

State	Nickname	Capital	Date
Rhode Island *	Ocean State	Providence	1790
S. Carolina * **	Palmetto State	Columbia	1788
South Dakota	Mount Rushmore State	Pierre	1889
Tennessee **	Volunteer State	Nashville	1796
Texas **	Lone Star State	Austin	1845
Utah	Beehive State	Salt Lake City	1896
Vermont	Green Mountain State	Montpelier	1791
Virginia * **	The Old Dominion	Richmond	1788
Washington	Evergreen State	Olympia	1889
West Virginia	Mountain State	Charleston	1863
Wisconsin	Badger State	Madison	1848
Wyoming	Equality State	Cheyenne	1890

The District of Columbia is a federal district, not a state, sharing its boundaries with the city of Washington, D.C.

The Canadian Provinces and its Territories

In 1867 Canada became a self-governing dominion. The country is made up of seven provinces and three territories, the difference being that the provinces receive their power from the Monarchy, and the territories from the federal government. The territories are marked with an asterisk.

Province	Nickname	Capitol	Year
Alberta	The Princess Province	Edmonton	1905

Province	Nickname	Capitol	Year
British Columbia	The Pacific Province	Victoria	1871
Manitoba	The Keystone Province	Winnipeg	1870
New Brunswick	The Loyalist Province	Fredericton	1867
Newfoundland and Labrador	The Rock	St. John's	1949
Northwest Territories*		Yellowknife	1870
Nova Scotia	Canada's Ocean Playground	Halifax	1867
Nunavit*		Iquluit	1999
Ontario		Toronto	1867
Prince Edward Island	The Garden Province	Charlottetown	1873
Quebec	The Beautiful Province	Quebec	1867
Saskatchewan	The Wheat Province	Regina	1905
Yukon*	Land of the Midnight Sun	Whitehorse	1898

The World's Highest Mountains

All the mountains in the world that top 26,244 feet (8,000 m) are in the Himalayas, which is frankly a bit boring for a book like this, but what can you do?

Mountain	Country	Feet	Meters
Everest	China/Nepal	29,029	8,848

The World's Highest Mountains

Mountain	Country	Feet	Meters
K2 (Godley Austen)	China/Kashmir	28,251	8,611
Kanchenjunga	India/Nepal	28,209	8,598
Lhotse	China/Nepal	27,940	8,516
Makalu	China/Nepal	27,825	8,481
Cho Oyu	China/Nepal	26,906	8,201
Dhaulagiri	Nepal	26,811	8,172
Manaslu	Nepal	26,759	8,156
Nanga Parbut	Kashmir	26,660	8,126
Annapurna	Nepal	26,503	8,078
Gasherbrum	China/Kashmir	26,470	8,068
Broad Peak	China/Kashmir	26,414	8,051
Xixabangma	China	26,286	8,012

There are another 20 that are above 22,966 feet (7,000 m), all still in Asia; then we shift to South America for Aconagua in Argentina, which is 22,835 feet (6,960 m).

And 19 more above 20,341 feet (6,200 m), all in the Andes, before it is worth even glancing elsewhere.

Here is a list of the top three from the other continents:

Mountain	Country	Feet	Meters
NORTH AMERICA			
McKinley	U.S. (Alaska)	20,322	6,194

Mountain	Country	Feet	Meters
Logan	U.S.	19,551	5,959
Citlaltepetl	Mexico	18,701	5,700 |//
AFRICA			
Kilimanjaro	Tanzania	19,341	5,895
Mount Kenya	Kenya	17,057	5,199
Ruwenzori	Uganda/Zaire	16,762	5,109
ANTARCTICA			
Vinson Massif		16,066	4,897
Mount Kirkpatrick		14,856	4,528
Mount Markham		14,268	4,349
EUROPE			
Mont Blanc	France/Italy	15,771	4,807
Monte Rosa	Italy/Switzerland	15,203	4,634
Dom	Switzerland	14,911	4,545
OCEANIA			
Mount Wilhelm	Papua New Guinea	14,790	4,508
Aoraki *(formerly Mount Cook)*	New Zealand	12,313	3,753
Mount Balbi	Solomon Islands	8,002	2,439

The World's Largest Bodies of Water

The four principal oceans of the world with areas in square miles (sq km) are:

OCEANS

Ocean	Square miles	Sq km
Pacific	69,374	179,679
Atlantic	35,665	92,373
Indian	28,539	73,917
Arctic	5,440	14,090

SEAS

Sea	Location	Square miles	Sq km
South China	between mainland Asia & the Philippines	1,149	2,975
Caribbean	east of Central America	1,068	2,766
Mediterranean	between Europe and Africa	971	2,516
Bering	at the very north of the Pacific, between Alaska and Russia	875	2,268
Gulf of Mexico	south of the eastern U.S., east of Mexico	596	1,543
Sea of Okhotsk	south of eastern Russia, north of Japan	590	1,528

Sea	Location	Square miles	Sq km
East China & Yellow	east of mainland China, north of South China, and south of the Okhotsk	482	1,249
Hudson Bay	Canada	475	1,232
Sea of Japan	between Japan and eastern Asia	389	1,008
North	east of the UK, bounded on the east by Denmark	222	575

The deepest point in the world is the Mariana Trench (in the Pacific, east of the Philippines), at 36,161 feet (11,022 m).

The World's Longest Rivers

The world's longest rivers are more fairly divided than its mountains, so here are the 17 that are longer than 2,175 miles (3,500 km), with the countries they mostly flow through:

River	Location	Miles	Km
Nile	Egypt	4,145	6,670
Amazon	Brazil	4,008	6,450
Yangtze	China	3,964	6,380
Mississippi–Missouri	U.S.	3,748	6,020
Yenisey–Angara	Russia	3,448	5,550
Huang He	China	3,395	5,464
Ob–Irtysh	Russia	3,361	5,410

River	Location	Miles	Km
Zaire/Congo	Zaire/Congo	2,901	4,670
Mekong	Vietnam/Cambodia	2,796	4,500
Paraná–Plate	Argentina	2,796	4,500
Amur	Russia	2,734	4,400
Lena	Russia	2,734	4,400
Mackenzie	Canada	2,634	4,240
Niger	Nigeria/Niger/Mali	2,597	4,180
Murray–Darling	Australia	2,330	3,750
Volga	Russia	2,299	3,700
Zambezi	Mozambique/Zimbabwe/Zambia	2,199	3,540

If you counted the Mississippi and Missouri as two separate rivers, they would both still find a place on this list, as would the Ob and Irtysh. The Yenisey on its own would also qualify.

Geological Time

The largest subdivision of geological time is an **era**, which can be divided into **periods** and then into **epochs**. The major divisions tend to be marked by mass extinctions, with smaller ones indicated by smaller extinctions and/or climate change. There have been three main eras; anything earlier than this was referred to as Precambrian.

☞ PALEOZOIC ERA, FROM ABOUT 600–250 MYA (MILLION YEARS AGO)

Paleozoic literally means *ancient life*. Life on Earth had existed for perhaps 4,000 million years before this, but it consisted largely of single-celled creatures such as algae and bacteria. The Cambrian period, the first part of the Paleozoic, is when bigger creatures—some of them with backbones—began to emerge, although they were still living in the sea. The Paleozoic was followed by the Permian extinction, when 95 percent of all life on Earth—plants and animals on both land and sea—died. Just like that. Just when they were beginning to get the hang of it. (To be fair, the period of extinction lasted millions of years, so "just like that" is an exaggeration, but scientists still don't know for sure why it happened.)

Anyway, it paved the way for...

☞ MESOZOIC ERA, FROM ABOUT 250–65 MYA

Mesozoic means *middle life*. This was the age of the dinosaurs, and it was divided into three periods:

- **Triassic** (*c.* 250–220 mya): the time of the first dinosaurs, small and agile to start with but poised to take over the world.
- **Jurassic** (*c.* 220–155 mya): when giant herbivores such as *Apatosaurus* (which used to be called Brontosaurus) and *Diplodocus* ruled.
- **Cretaceous** (*c.* 150–65 mya): dominated by *Tyrannosaurus rex*, but also the time when plants first produced flowers.

Then along came the Cretaceous–Tertiary (known as the KT) extinction, when the Earth may or may not have been hit by a meteorite. Nothing quite as bad as the Permian but still enough to wipe out the dinosaurs, and following that...

☞ CENOZOIC ERA, FROM ABOUT 65 MYA TO THE PRESENT

Cenozoic means *recent life*. This is when mammals and birds took over. It is sometimes divided into the Tertiary and Quaternary periods and then subdivided into these epochs:

- **Palaeocene** (65–55 mya): when the first large mammals emerged to fill the gaps left by the dinosaurs.
- **Eocene** (55–35 mya): a period of great warmth, when the first grasses started to grow.
- **Oligocene** (35–25 mya): when mammals and flowering plants began to greatly diversify.
- **Miocene** (25–5.5 mya): when the common ancestor of human beings and primates emerged.
- **Pliocene** (5.5–2 mya): when that same common ancestor came down from the trees.
- **Pleistocene** (2 million–11,750 years ago—this is where you enter the Quaternary period if you belong to that school of thought.): mammoths and Neanderthal man came and went, but *Homo sapiens* may be here to stay.
- **Holocene** (11,750 years ago–present, but see below): the emergence of agriculture and thus of the first civilizations.

There is a suggestion that the Holocene period finished in the year 1800 and that human impact since the time of the Industrial Revolution justifies us designating a new period, the Anthropocene.

GENERAL STUDIES

This chapter covers various subjects that didn't fit elsewhere in the book: mythology, art, music—all the subjects that weren't included in the exams but you had to learn a bit of anyway.

World Religions

There are, of course, lots of them and lots of subdivisions within them, but here is a little about the five really big ones, starting with the oldest.

☞ JUDAISM
Monotheistic religion whose beginnings are lost in the mists of time. Its adherents are called Jews, their god is eternal and invisible, and trusting in God's will is a fundamental tenet. Jewish law as revealed by God is contained in the Torah, which comprises the first five books of the Christian Old Testament. The Wailing Wall in Jerusalem is a sacred site.

☞ HINDUISM
Polytheistic, about 5,000 years old, and followed primarily in India. One of its tenets is that one's actions lead to the reward or punishment of being reincarnated in a higher or lower form of life. The aim is to be freed from this cycle and attain the state of unchanging reality known as Brahman. The three principal creator gods are Brahma, Vishnu, and Shiva, but

Krishna (an incarnation of Vishnu) is also widely worshipped. The main scriptures are the Vedas. The Ganges River is seen as a goddess of purity and pilgrims come to the holy city of Varanesi (Benares) to bathe in the river. The cow is a sacred symbol of fertility.

☞ BUDDHISM

Founded in the 6th century B.C. by Gautama Siddhartha, known as the Buddha or "Awakened One." There are no gods in Buddhism; its adherents follow the philosophy expressed in the Buddha's Four Noble Truths—that existence is characterized by suffering, that suffering is caused by desire, that to end desire is therefore to end suffering, and that this may be achieved by following the Eightfold Path to the ideal state of nirvana.

☞ CHRISTIANITY

Monotheistic religion that grew out of Judaism 2,000 years ago and is based on the belief that Jesus Christ is the son of God. The holy book is the Bible, divided into the Old and New testaments; the New Testament is the one concerned with the teachings of Christ and his apostles. The church divided initially into Eastern (Orthodox) and Western (Roman Catholic) branches. The Catholic Church still recognizes the Pope as leader and Rome as a holy city, but a major rift beginning in the 16th century led to the emergence of the Protestants and many subsequent subdivisions. Jerusalem is the traditional site of Christ's burial and resurrection.

☞ ISLAM

Monotheistic religion whose god is called Allah, founded in the 7th century A.D. by the one prophet, Mohammed. The holy book—the Koran or Qur'an—contains the revelations that Allah made to Mohammed. The holy cities are Mecca, birthplace of Mohammed, and Medina, where he is buried. All able-bodied Muslims who can afford it are expected to make a pilgrimage (*hadj*) to Medina at least once in their lives. The Dome of the Rock in Jerusalem is the oldest intact Muslim temple in the world and is built over the point from which Mohammed traditionally ascended to heaven.

☞ THE TEN COMMANDMENTS

Given to Moses by God on Mount Sinai (remember Charlton Heston and those massive tablets?), these are a basic code of conduct for both Jews and Christians.

1. Thou shalt have no other gods before me.
2. Thou shalt not make unto thee any graven image, or any likeness of any thing that is in heaven above or that is in the earth beneath, or that is in the water under the earth.
3. Thou shalt not take the name of the Lord thy God in vain.
4. Remember the Sabbath day and keep it holy.
5. Honor thy father and thy mother.
6. Thou shalt not kill.
7. Thou shalt not commit adultery.
8. Thou shalt not steal.
9. Thou shalt not bear false witness against thy neighbor.
10. Thou shalt not covet thy neighbor's house, thou shalt not covet thy neighbor's wife, nor his manservant, nor his maidservant, nor his ox, nor his ass, nor any thing that is thy neighbor's.

Roman Numerals

I = 1	C = 100
V = 5	D = 500
X = 10	M = 1,000
L = 50	

From there, the Romans could make up any number they wanted—except, interestingly enough, zero, because they didn't have a symbol for it. They made the other numbers by adding (putting letters at the end) or subtracting (putting them at the beginning).

For example:

$$I = 1$$
$$II = 2$$
$$III = 3 \quad \text{but IV (for example, 1 before 5)} = 4$$

Similarly,

$$V = 5$$
$$VI = 6$$
$$VII = 7$$
$$VIII = 8 \quad \text{but IX (1 before 10)} = 9$$

The same principle applies with the big numbers, so you end up with something like XLIV (44, because it is 10 before 50 and 1 before 5) and CDXCIX (499, made up of 100 before 500, 10 before 100, and 1 before 10). You would have thought 499 might be ID (1 before 500), but it isn't.

The Seven Wonders of the World

The Seven Wonders of the Ancient World, described in an old encyclopedia as "remarkable for their splendor or magnitude," were:

- The Hanging Gardens of Babylon
- The Mausoleum at Halicarnassus
- The Lighthouse of Alexandria
- The Colossus of Rhodes
- The Temple of Artemis at Ephesus
- The Statue of Zeus at Olympia
- The Great Pyramid of Giza

Of the seven, only the Great Pyramid is still in existence.

A Bit of Classical Mythology

There are lots of Greek and Roman gods, as well as enough mythological characters and demigods to fill a book on their own, but these are some you might remember:

Greek Name	Roman Equivalent	God of…
Zeus	Jupiter	father of the gods, also god of thunder
Hera	Juno	his wife and sister, goddess of marriage
Apollo	Apollo	god of hunting and of healing, who was consulted at the Oracle of Delphi
Ares	Mars	god of war
Aphrodite	Venus	goddess of love
Artemis	Diana	goddess of hunting and the moon

Greek Name	Roman Equivalent	God of...
Hermes	Mercury	messenger of the gods, who wore the winged sandals and helmet
Athena	Minerva	goddess of war and wisdom
Hephaestus	Vulcan	god of fire
Poseidon	Neptune	god of the sea
Demeter	Ceres	goddess of corn and the harvest
Dis	Pluto	god of the underworld

Famous Artists

This was meant to be a Top 20, but the list kept growing. There are so many artists that have contributed to the wonderful world of art we know today that I found I couldn't leave any of these names out.

Sandro Botticelli (1445–1510, Italian): best known for *The Birth of Venus* (Venus with flowing hair, standing in a shell).

Leonardo da Vinci (1452–1519, Italian): painter, sculptor, inventor, and all-around polymath—one of the great figures of the Renaissance. Among many of his celebrated works are *Mona Lisa* and *The Last Supper*.

Michelangelo Buonarotti (1475–1564, Italian): painter—most famous for the ceiling of the Sistine Chapel in the Vatican—and sculptor of the statue of *David* in Florence.

Raphael (1483–1520, Italian): painter of many versions of the Madonna and Child; and of frescoes, notably *The School of Athens* for the Sistine Chapel.

Titian (*c.* 1490–1576, Italian): greatest painter of the Venetian school. His religious and mythological subjects include *Assumption of the Virgin* and *Bacchus and Ariadne.*

Hans Holbein the Younger (*c.* 1497–1543, German, latterly in England): court painter to Henry VIII, responsible for the flattering portrait of Anne of Cleves, which encouraged the king to marry her.

Pieter Brueghel the Elder (1525–69, Flemish): famous for scenes of peasant life and landscapes.

El Greco (Domenikos Theotokopoulos, 1541–1614, Greek living in Spain): used distinctive elongated figures in his paintings of saints and in *The Burial of Count Orgaz.*

Peter Paul Rubens (1577–1640, Flemish): greatest of the Baroque artists, based mainly in Antwerp. Painted the ceiling of the Banqueting Hall in Whitehall, London, but is best remembered for depictions of abundantly fleshy women.

Frans Hals (*c.* 1581–1666, Dutch): best known for portraiture. Painter of *The Laughing Cavalier.*

Diego de Velázquez (1599–1660, Spanish): court painter to Philip IV, producing many portraits of his patron and his family, notably *Las Meninas.* Also *The Rokeby Venus*, painted where the goddess is lying naked on a bed, facing away from the viewer, and looking at herself in a mirror.

Rembrandt van Rijn (1606–69, Dutch): prolific portraitist and self-portraitist; creator of *The Night Watch*, the most famous painting in the Rijksmuseum in Amsterdam.

Jan Vermeer (1632–75, Dutch): based in Delft and noted for his skillful use of light; painted everyday scenes of women reading or writing letters or playing musical instruments. Best known for his oil on canvas, *Girl with a Pearl Earring*.

Canaletto (Giovanni Canal, 1697–1768, Italian): famous for his views of Venice, but also spent time in London and painted scenes of the Thames.

William Hogarth (1697–1764, British): engraver; hard-hitting social satires such as *The Rake's Progress* and *Gin Lane*.

Francisco de Goya (1746–1828, Spanish): painter, notably of the portraits *Maja Clothed* and *Maja Nude*, and the dramatic *Shootings of May 3rd 1808*, inspired by Spanish resistance to French occupation.

J(ohn) M(allord) W(illiam) Turner (1775–1851, British): prolific painter of landscapes and maritime scenes, most famously *The Fighting Téméraire*. His use of color and light and his portrayal of weather inspired the French Impressionists Monet and Renoir.

John Constable (1776–1837, British): painter of landscapes, notably *The Haywain*.

Edouard Manet (1832–83, French): established before the Impressionists, he adopted some of their techniques but was never quite one of that school. Famous works include *Déjeuner sur l'Herbe* (the one where the men are fully dressed and the women are not) and *A Bar at the Folies-Bergère*.

James McNeill Whistler (1834–1903, American, working in England): painter, notably of *The Artist's Mother*; also known as a wit. When Oscar Wilde remarked, "How I wish I'd said that," Whistler responded, "You will, Oscar, you will."

Edgar Degas (1834–1917, French): Impressionist who painted all those ballet dancers.

Paul Cézanne (1839–1906, French): post-Impressionist and precursor of cubism, based in Provence. In addition to landscapes, famous works include *The Card Players* and various groups of women bathing.

Claude Monet (1840–1926, French): most important painter of the Impressionist movement, famous for the "series" paintings that studied the effect of light at different times of day and year on the same subject: Rouen cathedral, haystacks and poplars. Lived latterly at Giverny, outside Paris, now a much visited garden, and painted a series of the waterlilies (*nymphéas*) there.

Auguste Rodin (1840–1917, French): sculptor, most famously of *The Kiss*, *The Thinker,* and *The Burghers of Calais*.

Pierre-Auguste Renoir (1841–1919, French): Impressionist, best known for *Les Parapluies* and *Le Moulin de la Galette* (a bar in Montmartre).

Paul Gauguin (1848–1903, French): the one who went to Tahiti and painted the people there.

Vincent van Gogh (1853–90, Dutch, working mainly in France): cut off part of his ear and subsequently committed suicide. Self-portraits, *The Potato Eaters*, *Sunflowers*, *The Starry Night*.

John Singer Sargent (1856–1925, American): portrait painter of the stars, including Ellen Terry, John D. Rockefeller, and various young ladies of fashion.

Henri de Toulouse-Lautrec (1864–1901, French): the little one. Lived in Montmartre and painted music halls, cafés, and their habitués. Works include *At the Moulin Rouge* and *La Toilette*.

Pablo Picasso (1881–1973, Spanish, working mostly in France): arguably the greatest and certainly the most versatile painter of the 20th century. After the famous "rose" and "blue" periods of his early years, he was fundamental to the development of cubism, expanded the technique of collage, became involved with the surrealists, designed ballet costumes, and did a bit of pottery. His greatest painting is probably *Guernica*, a nightmarish portrayal of the horrors of the Spanish Civil War.

Salvador Dalí (1914–89, Spanish): surrealist and notable egomaniac. Studied abnormal psychology and dream symbolism and reproduced its imagery in his paintings. Also worked with the surrealist film director Luis Buñuel (*Le Chien Andalou*) and designed the dream sequence in Alfred Hitchcock's *Spellbound*. His painting of the Last Supper is the one that shows the arms and torso of Christ floating above the disciples at the table.

Jackson Pollock (1912–56, American): abstract expressionist painter who believed that the act of painting was more important than the finished product. His paintings are therefore highly colorful and chaotic to the point of frenzy. And often huge.

Famous Composers

I was much more disciplined with this list—my Top 20 actually has 20 people in it.

Antonio Vivaldi (1678–1741, Italian): composed operas and church music galore but is now mostly remembered for *The Four Seasons*, a suite of violin concertos.

Johann Sebastian Bach (1685–1750, German): highly esteemed and vastly influential composer—without him there might have been no Haydn, no Mozart, and no Beethoven. Wrote mostly organ music, church music, and orchestral music, such as the *Brandenburg Concertos*, the *St. Matthew Passion*, *The Well-Tempered Clavier*, and *Jesu Joy of Man's Desiring*. Came from a famous musical family and had many children, including the composers Carl Philip Emmanuel and Johann Christian; the latter moved to London and became known as the English Bach.

George Frideric Handel (1685–1759, German, working in England): successful in Germany before moving to England when George I became king; wrote the *Water Music* for him. Also wrote a number of operas and developed the English oratorio, of which *Messiah* (which contains the *Hallelujah Chorus*) is the best known; composed the anthem *Zadok the Priest* for the coronation of George II.

Franz Josef Haydn (1732–1809, Austrian): "Papa Haydn," another vastly prolific composer, credited with the development of the classical symphony (he wrote 104 of them, including the *London* and the *Clock*) and the four-movement string quartet.

Wolfgang Amadeus Mozart (1756–91, Austrian): infant prodigy and all-around genius. Composer of 41 symphonies, including the *Jupiter;* operas, including *Don Giovanni* and *The Magic Flute*; innumerable concertos, sonatas, solo piano pieces, and chamber music. Not bad for someone who died at 35.

Ludwig van Beethoven (1770–1827, German): wrote nine symphonies, but the ones we all know are the Fifth (da-da-da-DAH) and the Ninth (the *Choral Symphony*, whose last movement includes the glorious *Song of Joy*—amazing to think that he was already deaf by this time and never heard it performed). Also wrote *Für Elise*, a piano piece studied laboriously by generations of budding pianists. And lots of other stuff, including one opera, called *Fidelio*.

Gioachino Rossini (1792–1868, Italian): known mostly for operas, including *La Cenerentola*, *The Barber of Seville*, and *William Tell*, which boasts the world's most famous overture.

Franz Schubert (1797–1828, Austrian): wrote about 600 songs (*lieder*) and *The Trout* piano quintet. This ambitious career seems odd, then, that he would ever leave anything unfinished. But when we talk about the *Unfinished Symphony*, we tend to mean Schubert's Eighth.

Frédéric Chopin (1810–49, Polish): wrote some beautiful tear-jerking stuff for the piano, much of it influenced by Polish folk music: mazurkas, polonaises, waltzes, and short romantic pieces called nocturnes, a term he popularized.

Franz Liszt (1811–86, Hungarian): virtuoso pianist, possibly the best there has ever been, as well as a prolific composer. His best-known works are probably the *Hungarian Rhapsodies*. His daughter Cosima became Mrs. Richard Wagner.

Richard Wagner (1813–83, German): was once said that he had wonderful moments but bad quarters of an hour. Fans of his work use words like "a masterpiece" and "greatest achievement in the history of opera," but given that the four "musical dramas" that comprise the *Ring* cycle run for a total of nearly 16 hours, I am never going to find out firsthand.

Giuseppe Verdi (1813–1901, Italian): wrote rather shorter operas, notably *Rigoletto*, *La Traviata*, *Don Carlos*, and *Aida*.

Pyotr Tchaikovsky (1840–93, Russian): best known as a composer of ballet music (*The Nutcracker Suite*, *Swan Lake*,

The Sleeping Beauty) but also wrote the wonderfully loud and patriotic *1812 Overture* after Napoleon had been forced to retreat from Moscow.

Edward Elgar (1857–1934, English): responsible for the *Enigma Variations*, including *Pomp and Circumstance* ("Land of Hope and Glory").

Giacomo Puccini (1858–1924, Italian): another one for the opera buffs—*La Bohème, Tosca, Madama Butterfly, Turandot.* My reference book says he "lacks the nobility of Verdi" but makes up for it in dramatic flair and skill. And he certainly wrote tunes.

Arnold Schoenberg (1874–1951, Austrian): wrote only a few tunes but invented a form of music called atonality and, later, serialism, which are bywords for "unlistenable" to many people.

Gustav Mahler (1860–1911, Austrian): became widely known after Tom Lehrer wrote a song about his wife, Alma, but he was also a great conductor and wrote some good music, too. This included nine finished symphonies and an unfinished one, all on a grand scale, and a song-symphony called *Das Lied von der Erde* ("The Song of the Earth").

Gustav Holst (1874–1934, English): best known for the *Planets* suite, which has seven parts—Earth was not deemed worthy of inclusion and Pluto was not discovered yet. Which is convenient in light of recent events.

Igor Stravinsky (1882–1971, Russian): composed the *Firebird Suite* specifically for Diaghilev's Ballets Russes and followed this with *Petrushka* and *The Rite of Spring.* His style was always experimental, and he turned to neoclassicism and later to serialism, but he was never in the same league as Schoenberg

My Grammar and I... Or Should That Be "Me"?

How to Speak and Write It Right

CAROLINE TAGGART
J. A. WINES

The Reader's Digest Association
Pleasantville, NY / Montreal

A READER'S DIGEST BOOK

Copyright © 2009 Michael O'Mara Books Limited

All rights reserved. Unauthorized reproduction, in any manner, is prohibited.

Reader's Digest is a registered trademark of
The Reader's Digest Association, Inc.

First published in Great Britain in 2008 by Michael O'Mara Books
Limited, 9 Lion Yard, Tremadoc Road, London SW4 7NQ

FOR READER'S DIGEST

U.S. Project Editors: Sarah Janssen, Abigail Wilentz

Copy Editor: Siobhan Sullivan

Canadian Project Editor: Pamela Johnson

Project Production Coordinator: Wayne Morrison

Senior Art Director: George McKeon

Executive Editor, Trade Publishing: Dolores York

Manufacturing Manager: Elizabeth Dinda

Associate Publisher: Rosanne McManus

President and Publisher, Trade Publishing: Harold Clarke

Taggart, Caroline
  My grammar and I ... or should that be "me"? : how to speak and write it right /
Caroline Taggart, J.A. Wines.
    p. cm.
  ISBN 978-1-60652-026-0
  1. English language--Grammar--Miscellanea. I. Wines, J. A. II. Title.

PE1112.T34 2009
428.2--dc22

2009015349

We are committed to both the quality of our products and the service we provide
to our customers. We value your comments, so please feel free to contact us.

The Reader's Digest Association, Inc.
Adult Trade Publishing
Reader's Digest Road
Pleasantville, NY 10570-7000

For more Reader's Digest products and information, visit our website:

www.rd.com (in the United States)

www.readersdigest.ca (in Canada)

Printed in the United States of America

3 5 7 9 10 8 6 4 2

English usage is sometimes more than mere taste, judgment, and education—sometimes it's sheer luck, like getting across the street.

—E. B. White

CONTENTS

Introduction 9

1. SPELLING AND CONFUSABLES 13
ABC: Easy as 1, 2, 3 (or, Spelling) 15
That Which Comes First (or, Prefixes) 29
Happy Endings (or, Suffixes) 30
Living Large (or, Capitalization) 32
Take a Letter (or, Vowels and Consonants) 34

2. PARTS OF SPEECH 35
Say What? (or, the 8 Parts of Speech) 37
Definitely Indefinite (or, Articles) 39
Demonstrate Your Determination (or, Determiners) 43
What's in a Name? (or, Nouns) 45
One Die, Two Dice (or, Singular and Plural) 53
Thou and Thee (or, Pronouns) 61
What a to-Do (or, Verbs) 68
Kind of Funny Looking (or, Adjectives) 84
Reverently, Discreetly, Advisedly, Soberly...(or, Adverbs) 88
Dangling by a Thread (or, Misplaced Modifiers) 91
May I Compare Thee to a Summer's Day? (or, Comparatives) 93
And Now We'll Move On (or, Conjunctions) 96
It's behind You! (or, Prepositions) 101
Holy Moly! (or, Interjections) 106

3. SENTENCE STRUCTURE 107
Do I Get Time Off for Good Behavior? (or, Sentences) 109
Subject-Verb-Object 111
On the Subject of I and the Object of Me
   (or, Subject and Object) 115
Don't You Agree? (or, Agreement) 121
From Major to Minor (or, Clauses) 125
How Do You Phrase That? (or, Phrases) 129

4. PUNCTUATION 131
Punctuation: The Virtue of the Bored? 133
Stop! (or, Periods) 134
Take a Deep Breath (or, Commas) 136
What Is This, the Spanish Inquisition? (or, Question Marks) 143
Something to Shout about (or, Exclamation Marks) 145
Two Dots (or, Colons) 147
Supercomma to the Rescue (or, Semicolons) 148
Dash Away All (or, Dashes) 149
Joined-Up Writing (or, Hyphens) 150
"Quotation Marks" 152
What's All the Fuss? (or, Apostrophes) 153
What's Not in a Name? (or, Possessive Apostrophes) 155

5. ODDS AND ENDS
(OR, ELEMENTS OF STYLE) 163
Being a Bit Fancy 165
A Big No-No (or, Double Negatives) 165
Pleonasm, Prolixity, and Tautology (or, Wordiness) 168

INTRODUCTION

It is in the nature of a living language to evolve, since new inventions require new words, foreign influences enliven the vocabulary, and social changes give people more or less leisure to write at length. The monks who copied out medieval texts invented short forms to save themselves time, which passed into the language as ligatures in words such as *mediæval*, which we now deem archaic. In our own time great revolutions have occurred because of e-mailing and texting, and who knows: a standard dictionary of 2028 may well contain the word *gr8* (great).

We cannot stop English from changing—and only the most ardent, dyed-in-the-wool pedants waste their time trying—but we can do our best to ensure that it does not become compromised along the way, and to preserve its best features. Since linguistic sloppiness often leads to ambiguity—one of the things that grammar rules try to avoid—a few rules are surely a good thing. And frankly, if you can't bring yourself to agree with that, you might as well stop reading now and get your money back before the book starts to look tattered.

Rules were very much in the minds of the sticklers of the eighteenth century, who, fearing for the health of the English language, decided to impose on it a grammar system that would fix it "good and proper." Unfortunately for us, these scholars were specialists in ancient Greek and Latin—not German, the language from which English is derived—so they imposed a number of Latin rules that didn't fit too comfortably with English, thereby creating all manner of unnecessary complications.

My Grammar and I

GRAMMAR RULES (TO AVOID)

1. Verbs has to agree with their subjects.
2. Remember to never split an infinitive.
3. Parenthetical remarks (however relevant) are (usually) unnecessary.
4. Never use a big word when a diminutive one would suffice.
5. Use words correctly, irregardless of how others elude to them.
6. Use the apostrophe in it's proper place and omit it when its not needed.
7. Eliminate unnecessary references. As Ralph Waldo Emerson once said, "I hate quotations."
8. Who needs rhetorical questions?
9. Exaggeration is a billion times worse than understatement.
10. Last but not least, avoid clichés like the plague.

Ignoring this major flaw in the plan, in 1762, an Oxford professor called Robert Lowth produced a prescriptive text titled *A Short Introduction to English Grammar*, a publication so influential that it dominated grammar teaching into the twentieth century (and indeed is quoted in this book). Over time, one no longer dared to end a sentence with a preposition, to split an infinitive, or to say "between you and I."

Introduction

> ☛ **Teacher's Corner:** When grammar became a required subject in many U.S. schools in the mid-nineteenth century, teachers complained that they knew no more about it than their pupils.

Grammar lessons began to fall out of favor as the twentieth century progressed. This book aims to fill in some of the gaps that the education system may have left you with, but remember that English is a rich and fluid language and that one person's unbreakable rule is another person's insufferable pedantry. Knowing the rules—and breaking them because you feel like it, not because you don't know any better—will make you a more confident, creative, and entertaining writer and speaker.

If your reaction to that is along the lines of "Yeah, right," consider this: When you're chatting among friends, it may not much matter how you express yourself, but what about when you are applying for a job? Language is as much a part of how you present yourself—and how other people react to you—as the way you dress. if we alwez rote howeva we pleazd itd b like showing up 2 an interview in ript jeanz n a scruffy t-shirt, y'know?

1
Spelling *and* Confusables

ABC: Easy as 1, 2, 3 (or, Spelling)

> "My spelling is Wobbly. It's good spelling but it
> Wobbles, and the letters get in the wrong places."
> —A. A. Milne, *Winnie the Pooh*

In the late-1500s, the state of English **spelling** and the "invasion" of foreign words was so troubling to scholars and teachers that some of them took it upon themselves to harness the language by compiling dictionaries. But even if we have the help of education and dictionaries, spelling can still be an uphill climb.

> ✋ **Smart Aleck:** More than one-tenth of English words are not spelled the way they sound.

We have an overwhelming tendency to leave letters in words even though they are no longer pronounced (think of the *g* in *weight* or *daughter*, for example, or the *b* in *subtle*, or the *p* in *pneumonia*). And we are surely the only language to have nine ways to pronounce a single four-letter combination:

A rough-coated, dough-faced, thoughtful ploughman strode through the streets of Scarborough; after falling into a slough, he coughed and hiccoughed.

Spelling and Confusables

Then we have things called **eye rhymes,** which are words that look alike and perhaps used to rhyme but which, due to shifts in pronunciation, no longer do. In Shakespeare's day, for example,

> *Blow, blow thou winter wind*
> *Thou art not so unkind*

would probably have rhymed, as would have

> *I am monarch of all I survey…*
> *From the centre all round to the sea*

when poet William Cowper wrote those lines nearly two hundred years later. Then there is another problem. Many words that sound the same are spelled differently:

aloud/allowed	*fair/fare*	*pale/pail*
beach/beech	*knot/not*	*plane/plain*

which makes English a wonderful language for puns but a nightmare for non-native speakers and for those who aren't confident in their spelling (or who rely on their spellcheckers).

> "They went and told the sexton, and
> The sexton toll'd the bell."
> —Thomas Hood

🖐 **Smart Aleck:** A **homophone** is a word that is pronounced the same as another word but differs in meaning. The words may be spelled the same or differently.

It's My Bizness to Be Definate

Here are the correct spellings of a random selection of commonly misspelled words:

accidentally	*cemetery*	*liaison*
accommodate	*definite*	*millennium*
allege	*diarrhea*	*necessary*
avocado	*ecstasy*	*niece*
association	*embarrass*	*privilege*
broccoli	*grammar*	*separate*
business	*height*	*sincerely*

Take My Advice

In these commonly confused noun/verb pairs, the noun has a *c* and the verb has an *s*.

Noun	**Verb**
advice	*advise*
device	*devise*
prophecy	*prophesy*

Useful mnemonic: *I'd advise you not to give advice.*

> ➤ **Teacher's Corner:** Until the eighteenth century, English spelling was not standardized on either side of the Atlantic. Then, in 1755, Samuel Johnson published his *Dictionary of the English Language*, and in 1828, Noah Webster published *An American Dictionary of the English Language*.

Spelling and Confusables

Webster was an orderly minded man who disapproved of a lot of the spelling that Johnson had recorded. (Indeed, he disapproved of a lot about Johnson, saying that he was "naturally indolent and seldom wrote until he was urged by want. Hence...he was compelled to prepare his manuscripts in haste.")

Webster's dislike of words that weren't pronounced the way they looked led him to decree that words such as *centre* and *theatre* should be spelled *center* and *theater*; he also dropped the silent *u* from words such as *colour*, *favour*, and *honour*. In fact, Webster was singlehandedly responsible for most of the differences between British and American spelling that survive to this day.

Seize the Sieve: A Spelling Rule

The most famous **spelling rule** is *i before e except after c*, although this does not work for *ancient, foreign, neither, protein, science, seize, species, vein* or lots of other words. It really applies only to certain words in which the *ie* or *ei* makes an *ee* sound: *achieve, receive, deceive.*

So even the most famous spelling rule works only in a very limited set of circumstances. There is really no way around this other than reading a lot, taking note of unfamiliar words, and investing in a good dictionary.

One Word or Two?

As a general rule, one word tends to be an adjective, while two words form the noun. Here are some common confusions:

alot/a lot

There is no such word as *alot*. *A lot* of people know that *a lot* should be two words. If you mean to write the verb *allot*, however, you should allot it two *l*s.

alright/all right

According to *Merriam-Webster's Dictionary*, the term *alright* has had its critics since the early twentieth century. Although *alright* is less frequent than *all right*, it is still commonly used.

Useful mnemonic: *don't worry about getting it all right, alright?*

altogether/all together

***Altogether**, it's sixty miles.*
***All together** now: "sixty miles to go…"*

anyone/any one

*Does this bag belong to **anyone**?*
*It could belong to **any one** of those tourists over there.*

always/all ways

*I **always** get lost in Rome.*
***All ways** lead to Rome.*

cannot/can not

Either is acceptable, but *cannot* is more common. Sometimes *can not* may be the better choice if you want to be emphatic: *No, you **can not** speak Swahili.*

everyday/every day

*His **everyday** life is very dull, but at night he's in a cabaret act.*
***Every day** I dream of becoming a showgirl.*

everyone/every one

***Everyone** has a guilty secret.*
***Every one** of you pretends not to like Barry Manilow.*

Spelling and Confusables

into/in to

*I can't seem to get **into** the office.*
*I was hoping to go **in to** use the free Internet.*

maybe/may be

***Maybe** you'll remember what I tell you in the future.*
*Although it **may be** that I forgot to tell you in the first place.*

nobody/no body, somebody/some body, anybody/any body

***Nobody** was at the crime scene, so I assumed they'd all gone home.*
*There was a lot of blood at the crime scene, but **no body**.*
*I think **somebody** is trying to break in.*
*Gosh, that burglar has quite **some body**.*
*Will just **any body** suffice for the bikini advertisement, or does **anybody** here happen to have Pamela Anderson's address?*

sometimes/some times

***Sometimes** trains arrive on time.*
***Some times** on that train schedule I gave you are wrong.*
*I'll give you a call **sometime**.*
*Perhaps we can arrange **some time** for ourselves.*

I'll Get My Coat

When two words are combined to form a single word, the new word is called a **portmanteau.** As Humpty Dumpty tells Alice in *Through the Looking-Glass*, "There are two meanings packed into one word." For example:

breakfast and lunch	*brunch*
French and English	*Franglais*
guess and estimate	*guesstimate*
information and commercial	*infomercial*
motor and hotel	*motel*
smoke and fog	*smog*

> **Smart Aleck:** *Portmanteau* is itself made up of two words, the French *porter* (to carry) and *manteau* (cloak or mantle).

What's the Word I'm Looking for?

abuse/misuse/disabuse

To *abuse* something means "to treat it so badly that you damage it."
To *misuse* something means "to use it wrongly."
To *disabuse* someone of something means "to show them that their thinking is wrong."

acute/chronic

An *acute* illness is one that is sudden and severe but short-lived.
A *chronic* illness persists for a long time.

Useful mnemonics:
acute: children are short, a pain, and not cute for long.
chrOnic = Old (lasting a lOng time).

Spelling and Confusables

affect/effect

Affect is a verb and *effect* is a noun. So you *affect* something by having an *effect* on it. (The exception is if you *effect* a change; that is, cause a change to happen.)

Useful mnemonic: ***RAVEN*, that is:** *Remember Affect-Verb Effect-Noun.*

aggravate/annoy

Aggravate means "to make worse." Therefore, while you can *aggravate* a situation, a problem or a condition, you irritate or *annoy* people.

alternate/alternative

An **alternate** *plan* would be wrong. The verb *alternate* means going back and forth between two things, and thus you have *alternate* letters of the alphabet (a, c, e, g, for example). If you mean "another plan," it should be *alternative.*

among/between

Use *between* for two things; *among* for more than two.
Between *you and me, there's no way we can divide these five loaves and two fishes* **among** *our five thousand guests.*

Useful mnemonics:
beTween = Two
aMong = Many

amount/number

Use *amount* for things involving a unified mass—bulk, weight, or sums. In general it is safe to use *amount* to refer to anything that can be measured. *Number* is used to refer to anything that can be counted in individual units.

*That's a large **amount** of sugar for one cup of tea.*
*What is an acceptable **number** of sugars for one cup of tea?*

Useful mnemonic: *use **amount** for things we **cannot count**.*

as if/like

Something looks *like* something else—they physically resemble one another.

*He looks **like** his mother and she looks **like** Margaret Thatcher.*

However:

*It looks **as if** a storm is coming.*
*Teenagers use words **such as** "like" far too often.*
***As with** all homework, students can now research geography topics online.*

"Dream as if you'll live forever;
live as if you'll die today."
—James Dean

---

complement/compliment

*May I **compliment** you on your new hairstyle? The color **complements** your dress beautifully.*

Useful mnemonics:

*A compl**E**ment adds something to make it **E**nough.*
*A comp**LIME**nt puts you in the **LIME**light.*

continual/continuous

Continual means "happening over and over and over again"; *continuous* means "happening constantly without stopping." You

Spelling and Confusables

---

may *continually* receive unwanted telephone calls from telemarketers. However, if this were happening *continuously*, you would never be able to put the phone down.

Useful mnemonics:

*continuAL = **A**ble to **L**eave off*

*continuouS = never **S**topping*

defuse/diffuse

You *defuse* a situation, by (metaphorically) taking the *fuse* out of it before it catches fire.

Diffuse means "to spread out" if it is a verb, or "already spread out" if it is an adjective.

due to/owing to

Due to means "caused by."

Owing to means "because of."

To determine which to use, decide whether you would replace *due to* or *owing to* by *caused by* or *because of*.

*The collapse of hundreds of buildings was **due to** the earthquake.*

***Owing to** collapsed roads and bridges, it was impossible to get outside help.*

elude/allude

*Your meaning **eludes** me. I do not understand to what you are **alluding**.*

farther/further

This is another example where the difference between words is becoming blurred, but generally speaking *farther* relates to a physical distance, *further* to metaphorical distance.

*Before we travel any **farther**, let's have a **further** look at the map.*

*Before we take this argument any **further**, how much **farther** is it to the hotel?*

Useful mnemonic: ***FAR**ther is about how **FAR**.*

fortuitous/fortunate

Fortuitous means "happening by chance" but not necessarily a *fortunate* chance.

forward/foreword

Useful mnemonics:

*Forw**A**rd means to **A**dvance.*

*Foreword: the **WORD**s that come be**FORE** the main text*

hear/here

Useful mnemonics:

*One h**EAR**s with one's **EAR**s.*

*I want **HER** to come **HER**e.*

hanged/hung

Pictures or jackets are *hung*; criminals used to be *hanged*.

imply/infer

Speakers *imply* something by hinting at it; listeners *infer* something based on the information they hear.

*I **infer** from your tone that you are angry with me.*
*I didn't mean to **imply** that.*

lay/lie/laid

You *lie* in bed but *lay* the book on the table or (if you are a hen) *lay* an egg.

Spelling and Confusables

In the past tense, you *lay* in bed all day yesterday, but you *laid* the book or the egg.

So *lie* is the present tense of an intransitive verb that means "to put oneself or to remain in a more or less horizontal position."*
The present participle is *lying,* the past tense is *lay,* and the past participle is *lain.*

Lay is the present tense of a transitive verb whose basic meaning is "to place something in a more or less horizontal position." The present participle is *laying;* the past tense and the past participle are *laid.*

In the sense of telling an untruth, the forms are *lie, lying,* and *lied.*

lend/loan

Lend is a verb, *loan* is normally a noun.

*If she asks me for a **loan**, I will **lend** her the money.*

Useful mnemonics:

*People will gr**OAN** if you ask them to l**OAN**.*
*People will s**END** if you ask them to l**END**.*

Increasingly *loan* is used as a verb: *the bank will **loan** you the money if you have enough security.* Not everybody likes this, but it's in the dictionaries.

less/fewer

Less means "not as much." *Fewer* means "not as many."

Or, if you prefer, *fewer* is used to denote things that can be counted and *less* to describe things that can't. Never refer to *less people.* People should stand up and be counted!

---

*For more on verbs, see page 68. For more on tenses, see page 76.

loose/lose

Count the *o*s and remember: *if I **lose** any more weight, my clothes will be too **loose**.*

older/elder

An *elder* is a person in old age or a tree. As an adjective, it means *older*, but it is sometimes used to denote respect: *an **elder** statesman* or even *my **elder** sister* may be assumed to have attained a certain amount of wisdom.

Older just means "more old," the way you sometimes feel in the morning, or when you are talking to someone who's never heard of Bob Dylan.

oral/aural/verbal

Oral pertains to the mouth, *aural* to the ears, *verbal* to words. An *oral statement* means one that is not written down. An *oral examination* may be one that is not written down, or it may be performed by a dentist. An *oral/aural examination* may be in a foreign language to test how well you understand what you are hearing as well as how well you speak. A *verbal statement* is a tautology (unnecessary repetition of meaning): how would you make it without using words?

principal/principle

> Useful mnemonic: *the princip**AL** is your **PAL**; she makes ru**LE**s called princip**LE**s.*

rob/steal

You *rob* a person and *steal* a thing, but not the other way round.

> Useful mnemonic: *you can **rob** Rob, and you can **steal** steel, but you can't **steal** Rob and you can't **rob** steel.*

Spelling and Confusables

stationary/stationery

Stationery is sold at the bookstore. The store is likely to be *stationary*.

their/there/they're

Their means "belonging to them."
There means "in that place."
They're means "they are."

> Useful mnemonic:
> *They left t**HEIR** money to their son and **HEIR**.*
> *W**HERE** shall we place ourselves, **HERE** or t**HERE**?*
> ***THEY'RE** mad at **THEIR** son, who is standing over **THERE**.*

weather/whether

*I do not know **whether** he is **weather**-wise.*

"Whether the weather be fine,
Whether the weather be not,
We must weather the weather,
Whatever the weather,
Whether we like it or not."
—Unknown

THAT WHICH COMES FIRST (OR, PREFIXES)

A **prefix** is a group of letters added to the beginning of a word to change its meaning. Common ones include:

anti	*extra*	*mono*	*pseudo*
auto	*hyper*	*multi*	*re*
circum	*inter*	*omni*	*sub*
demi	*intra*	*photo*	*tele*
dis	*mega*	*pre*	*trans*

Rule: Adding a prefix does not change the spelling of the original word, nor usually the spelling of the prefix, even when the last letter of the prefix and the first letter of the original word are the same: *disservice, dissimilar, unnerve, unnecessary.*

> **Smart Aleck:** What of *dispirited*? And *transubstantiation*? **Answer:** There are always exceptions. *Always* being one of them.

All's Well That Starts Well...

Rule: When *all* and *well* are used as prefixes, take away one *l*—*altogether, welfare*. But note that this is not the case with hyphenated words: *all-embracing, well-adjusted, well-bred.*

The prefixes *dis-, il-, im-, in-, ir-, mis-,* or *un-* create words that mean the opposite of the root word (*il-, ir-,* and *im-* are all

Spelling and Confusables

variants of *in-*, used respectively in front of words beginning with *l*, *r*, and *b*, *m*, or *p*): *disobey, illogical, impossible, inapplicable, irresponsible, misunderstood, unattainable.*

But be careful when a root word can take two or more of these prefixes, since the resulting words will have subtly or completely different meanings: *do I **dis**remember or **mis**remember? I can't remember.*

> *The loss of paid overtime left most of the workers **dis**affected. The only ones who were **un**affected by this decision were those who never worked overtime.*
>
> *I collected my children's **dis**used toys, intending to donate them to the fundraiser. However, years of **mis**use had left many of them fit only for the trash.*
>
> *He was a **dis**interested lawyer and therefore **un**interested in taking a bribe.*

HAPPY ENDINGS (OR, SUFFIXES)

Suffixes are added to the *end* of a word to change its meaning. Common ones include:

-ant	*-ise*	*-ful*
-ent	*-ist*	*-ness*
-ible	*-fy*	*-ism*
-ing	*-ly*	*-ment*
-ize	*-able*	*-ation*

Adding a suffix may alter the spelling of the preceding word. If a word ends in a *y* that is preceded by a consonant (*happy, beauty*), the *y* changes to *i*:

happy	*happiness*
beauty	*beautiful*

But if the *y* is preceded by a vowel, the *y* remains: *I envy your enjo**yment** of the situation. It obviously caused you much merr**iment**.* And if the original word ends in an *e*, this is usually dropped: *You are most **lovable** but not at all **sensible**.*

> ✋ **Smart Aleck:** Hold on to the *e* if dropping it would alter pronunciation. *Pronouncable* would be pronounced *pronounkable*, but *pronounceable* is quite *manageable*.
> Actually, both *aging* and *ageing* are correct.
> As are *likable* and *likeable*.

"-able" and "-ible"

It's not easy to remember which words end in *–able* and which in *–ible*, and there certainly isn't a hard and fast rule. Too much of it depends on the Latin root and whether the word comes to us directly from Latin or via French. Wouldn't you rather just invest in a decent dictionary and look each word up as the necessity arises?

Spelling and Confusables

> ☛ **See Me after Class:**
> *She stopped using a curling iron because
> she kept singing her hair.*
> I don't think I know that tune.
>
> *Romeo was dyeing to see Juliet.*
> Did she insist on a new color?
>
> *Toad was carless to wreck his car.*
> He was afterward!

LIVING LARGE
(OR, CAPITALIZATION)

A **capital letter** is the Large Letter that is used at the beginning of a sentence and as the first letter of certain words. The word comes from the Latin *capitalis*, derived from *caput*, a head.

Use a capital letter...

- for the first word of a sentence

- for the first word in a line of poetry (usually)

- for the major words in the titles of books, plays, films, works of art: *Death of a Salesman, The Catcher in the Rye, Casablanca, The English Patient, Starry Night*

- for proper nouns: *James, Dad* (but *my dad*), *the Queen*

- for place names and the names of buildings: *London, Paris, Easy Street, the Taj Mahal, the Sears Tower*

- for adjectives derived from proper nouns: *English, Shakespearean, Victorian*

- for the pronoun *I*
- for personal titles that come before a name: *Mr., Ms., Mrs., Dr., Captain, Reverend, Senator*
- for most letters in words that are acronyms: *NASA, NATO*
- for the months of the year, days of the week, and special occasion days: Christmas, Easter, Thanksgiving, Happy Birthday (but *in the new year* or *his birthday seemed to come around faster each year*)
- for brand names: *Kleenex, Mars, Cadillac*

Do Not Use a Capital...
- after a semicolon
- when talking about kings, queens, presidents, and generals in general, rather than a specific individual
- for the seasons—spring, summer, autumn, winter
- for compass points: *north, south, east, west, going north, heading south.* However do write *the South,* as in *the Civil War was fought between the North and the South* or *the South Pole*

> ☛ **Teacher's Corner:** Capital letters are sometimes referred to as "upper case." This is because manual typesetters kept these letters in the upper drawers of a desk—the upper type case. More frequently used letters were stored on a lower shelf, thus "lower case" letters.

Spelling and Confusables

TAKE A LETTER
(OR, VOWELS AND CONSONANTS)

> "Always end the name of your child with a vowel,
> so that when you yell, the name will carry."
> —*Bill Cosby*

The word *vowel* derives from the Latin word *vox*, meaning "voice." The dictionary definitions of a **vowel** are a bit scary: "a voiced speech sound whose articulation is characterized by the absence of a friction-causing obstruction in the vocal tract, allowing the breath stream free passage" or "a speech sound made with vibration of the vocal cords but without audible friction, more open than a consonant and capable of forming a syllable." But actually, that "capable of forming a syllable" part is what matters. You can't form a syllable—and therefore can't make a word—without a vowel.

There are five vowels in English: *A, E, I, O,* and *U*.

Useful mnemonic: ***A**n **E**lephant **I**n **O**range **U**nderwear*
But the letter *y*, although classified as a consonant and used as one in words such as *yellow, young,* and *beyond,* is often used as a vowel (with an *i* sound) in words such as *cry, fly, lynx,* and *rhythm.*

Consonants, by the way, are all the letters that aren't vowels.

2
Parts of Speech

Say What?
(Or, the 8 Parts of Speech)

Every word in every language can be categorized according to its grammatical function, which is what we mean by **parts of speech**. As with so many other things, this system was invented by the ancient Greeks, copied by the Romans, and later adopted into English by scholars who were well versed in Latin, whether it was appropriate or not. (In many cases it was not appropriate, but we're stuck with it now, and that's what this book is all about.)

In English there are generally considered to be eight parts of speech: *noun, pronoun, adjective, verb, adverb, preposition, conjunction,* and *interjection,* and you may once have learned this useful piece of doggerel to help you remember what each did:

> *Every name is called a NOUN,*
> *As **field** and **fountain**, **street** and **town**;*
>
> *In place of noun the PRONOUN stands*
> *As **he** and **she** can clap **their** hands;*
>
> *The ADJECTIVE describes a thing,*
> *As **magic** wand and **bridal** ring;*
>
> *The VERB means action, something done -*
> ***To read, to write, to jump, to run**;*

Parts of Speech

> *How things are done, the ADVERBS tell,*
> *As **quickly**, **slowly**, **badly**, **well**;*
>
> *The PREPOSITION shows relation,*
> *As **in** the street, or **at** the station;*
>
> *CONJUNCTIONS join, in many ways,*
> *Sentences, words, **or** phrase **and** phrase;*
>
> *The INTERJECTION cries out, "**Hark!***
> *I need an exclamation mark!"*
>
> *Through poetry, we learn how each*
> *of these make up THE PARTS OF SPEECH.*

We say "generally considered" because there are also three little words—*the, a* and *an*—and a few others that are categorized as **articles** or **determiners** and you can't really ignore them. We'll come back to them in a minute (see page 39), but first let's have a quick look at what parts of speech are all about.

It's Just One Thing After Another

Words from each of the parts of speech are used as **building blocks**: they add to meaning by modifying or qualifying one another. Consider this sentence:

> *A brown cow in a great, green field ate grass greedily.*

By painting a more detailed picture, words limit (modify, qualify—you'll come across all these words to describe the same sort of thing) and thus clarify meaning. In the above sentence, for instance, we are not talking about cows in general; the article *a* tells us we are talking about one specific cow. The cow is not any color; it is brown. The cow is not just standing there; it is eating grass. Where is it eating grass? In a field. Not any old field; but a great, green one. How is it eating? Greedily.

In fact, that sentence doesn't cover all the parts of speech, so let's add another few words:

A brown cow in a great, green field ate grass greedily, and gosh it grew fat!

The conjunction *and* tells us that we are joining one thought to another. The interjection *gosh* gives us an excuse to write an exclamation mark at the end of the sentence. And *it*, of course, is a pronoun that refers back to the cow.

So let's now look at each of these building blocks in more detail.

DEFINITELY INDEFINITE (OR, ARTICLES)

"A horse, a horse, my kingdom for a horse."
—Shakespeare, *Richard III*

An **article** is any one of a group of things. *I have lost an article of luggage*, for example, means you have lost only one bag of several. In grammar an article is any one of the words *a*, *an*, and *the*.

A and *an* are known as **indefinite** articles because they describe nouns in general. *The* restricts the meaning of a noun to make it more specific. Or definite. It is therefore known as the **definite article**.

Parts of Speech

A drunk man	any old drunk man (he could be anyone—we haven't mentioned him yet)
The drunk man	a specific drunk man (someone we are already talking about)
A drunk man was lurching down the street.	This implies the man is a stranger to all.
The drunk man was crawling down the street.	This implies the speaker/writer or listener/reader already knows something about this man—he has already cropped up.

Bizarrely, however, when speaking in very general terms, *the* can be used instead of *a* to make something less specific:

There was a tiger in my garden.	an individual animal
The tiger is an endangered species.	that is, all of them
I bought a ukulele.	one specific instrument
I play the ukulele.	I can pick up any ukulele and strum away happily on it.

> **Smart Aleck:** *The* is the most common word in the English language.

Absolute Zero

Another way to make a statement more general is to use no article at all. This is sometimes referred to as the **zero article** and it usually applies to plurals or to mass nouns (see page 46).

Definitely Indefinite

Children *are not good with **maps**.*
Shorts *are not suitable office attire.*
Cats *are thankless creatures.*
Grammar *is hard to learn.*

No Need for Introductions…

Pronouns and proper nouns do not require articles. They stand by themselves.

I am not good at grammar.
*Ms. **Banks** is better at grammar than I am.*

A or *an*?

Rule: Nouns or adjectives beginning with a vowel usually take the article *an*, while nouns or adjectives beginning with a consonant take the article *a*.

For example:

an orange, a peach
an octopus, a squid
an ax, a chopper
an island, a continent
an orange peach, a red apple

However, as usual there are exceptions to the rule, because some vowels are sometimes pronounced as if they were consonants, and some *h*s aren't pronounced at all:

***a** **u**nique event, **an** **u**nusual event*
***a** **h**orrid man, **an** **h**onorable gentleman*
***an** **h**our, **an** **h**our and **a** **h**alf*
***a** **E**uropean, **an** **E**skimo*
***a** **e**ulogy, **an** **e**pigram*

Parts of Speech

We say *a* unique event because we pronounce the letter *u* in *unique* as a hard *y* sound—*yoonique*. We pronounce the *h* in *horrid*, but not in *honorable*.

Similarly, abbreviations such as *MGM* or *SEC*—pronounced respectively *em gee em* and *ess e see*, sound as if they begin with vowels, and so we say *see an MGM film, it was an SEC regulation*.

☞ **See Me after Class:** There is no *h* at the beginning of the word *aitch*.

An Historical Note

Here's a hypothesis—or rather four separate but vaguely related hypotheses—on words beginning with *h* and an unstressed syllable (or why some people say *an history, an hotel*, and *an hypothesis*):

1. Once upon a time all educated English speakers learned French and so pronounced *history*, such as the French word *histoire*, with a silent *h*. Appropriately they gave it the article *an*.

2. Some—less well-educated and therefore non-French-speaking—people spoke badly, were lazy about pronouncing their *aitches*, and so got into the habit of saying *an 'istory*.

3. Educated people disliked dropping aitches, so they began to pronounce them in French words that traditionally used the article *an: an history*.

4. People spoke too quickly, running together the words *a* and *history*, so that it became pronounced *anistory*. When they paused for breath and separated things out a bit, they thought the word must be *an history*.

Note the inherent snobbishness of these hypotheses. It crops up a lot in the study of language. But whatever the origins of the practice may be, the rule is: if the *h* is pronounced (as in *history*, *hotel*, and *hypothesis*), the correct article is *a*; if it is not pronounced (as in *honor* and *hour*), use *an*.

> ☞ **Teacher's Corner:** Some of those old grammarians who decreed that *an* should be used before an *h* did so because we aspirated less in those days. Aspiration is the release of air that comes out of our mouths when we speak. If you try talking to a candle flame, you should notice that the flame definitely flickers when you say *hotel* or *history* (aspirated), but much less so when you say *'otel* or *'istory* (unaspirated).

DEMONSTRATE YOUR DETERMINATION (OR, DETERMINERS)

In fact articles are a subdivision of a class of words called **determiners,** which include **possessive adjectives**, **demonstratives,** and **quantifiers**.

Parts of Speech

Possessive adjectives—*my, his, her, its, our, your, their*—perform the useful task of telling us what belongs to, or is related to, something else.

*The captain stood firm at the bow of **his** ship as **its** deck was consumed in flames.*

*The bemused sailors redoubled **their** efforts and extinguished the blaze without **his** assistance.*

Used carelessly, however, they can cause confusion:

Both the fashion editors liked her new hat. (Whose hat? If you mean that each fashion editor had a new hat that she liked, try, *each of the fashion editors liked her new hat,* and if you mean there was only one new hat, be specific: *both the fashion editors liked Susanna's new hat.*)

Mrs. Jones and Mrs. Brown disliked their neighbors. (Whose neighbors? Did Mrs. Jones and Mrs. Brown cohabit and dislike the same neighbors? Or did each woman dislike her own neighbors? Or possibly her own neighbors and the other woman's neighbors, too?)

Demonstratives are the words *this/that, these/those* (which may also be demonstrative pronouns; see page 65). When used as determiners, they precede the noun in much the same way as *the* or *a* but are used to differentiate between things that are near at hand (*this, these*) and things that are farther away (*that, those*). The nearness or farness may refer to time or space:

*Do I look fat in **this** dress* (the one I have on)*?*

*Ah, do you remember **that** weekend in Paris* (back in the day)*?*

*I have never seen **these** people before* (though they are standing in front of me now).

*If I had known **those** chocolates* (the ones I ate earlier, so they are now in the past) *had nuts in them, I would have left them alone.*

Quantifiers are words such as *no, none of, either, neither, any, both, few, little, half,* and so on. Again, some of these words may serve as other parts of speech—*either* or *neither* as conjunctions, for example (see page 100) or *little* as an adjective (see page 84). In this context, however, they go before the noun and tell us the number or quantity of something:

Which of the candidates will I back? ***None of the*** *above.*
Neither *politician has **any** charisma.*
Every one of the *candidates is a crook.*
*It would be completely hypocritical of me to vote for **any of** those people.*
Half the *problems of modern life can be blamed on people like that.*
*There is **little** chance of anyone decent winning.*

WHAT'S IN A NAME? (OR, NOUNS)

There are various categories of **noun**, but they are all "naming words." They just name different types of things.

Common noun: a word used to name a person, animal, place, thing or abstract idea, such as *book, smell, dog, forest, leg, delight, boredom, success* and *failure.* Common nouns can be further subdivided into:

Concrete noun: used to name something you can identify with one or more of the five senses *(book, leg,* for example*).*

Parts of Speech

Abstract noun: names something that has no physical existence *(delight, failure,* for example*)*.

Proper noun: used to name a specific person, animal, place, or thing. It is usually written with a capital letter to show its importance, such as *President Obama, the Statue of Liberty, Monday, Christmas, Ibiza,* and *Rolls-Royce.*

Compound noun: a noun made up of more than one word, usually (but not always) two nouns or a noun and an adjective, to make something with a meaning of its own, such as *apple tree, lion tamer, feel-good factor, tan line, lawsuit, science fiction* (or indeed *science fiction writer*), and *will-o'-the-wisp.*

Wikipedia says that English has a habit of "creating compounds by concatenating words without case markers," which is a wonderfully nonsensical way of saying that we just put words together to make other words or phrases: thus a *science fiction writer* is a *writer* who writes *fiction* based on *science,* but there is nothing in the form of the words to tell us whether they are adjectives or nouns or whatever. And as you can see, these compounds may end up as a single word, two or more separate words or two or more words with one or more hyphens. But let's not get into hyphens just yet.

The Numbers Game

Another way of categorizing nouns is to divide them into **countable** and **mass** (or **non-countable**) nouns.

Countable nouns are (reasonably enough) used to name something that can be counted, such as *one plate, two eggs, three sausages.* It's countable if you can ask ***how many*** *are there?* or state *there are **a number of** men/chairs/staplers*—because you can easily count the specific number of items.

A **mass** or **non-countable noun** refers to something that cannot reasonably be counted and therefore has no plural, such as *air, art, milk, money, stupidity, sand,* and *wisdom.* Quantities of non-countable nouns are described as **an amount of** *hair/sand/ garbage,* either because they refer to an unspecified *amount* of stuff or because there are too many individual pieces (of hair or sand, for example) to number. We can't ask *how many?* with non-countable nouns (how many milk, how many traffic); it's simply *how much?*

> **Twelve Items or Less (Less What?)**
> A common mistake is the confusion of *less* and *fewer.*
> Supermarkets almost always get it wrong.
> Use *fewer* with countable nouns: *12 items or fewer.*
> Use *less* with non-countable nouns: *less traffic than yesterday.*

We're All in It Together

A **collective noun** is one that refers to a group or number of individuals; common examples include *audience, class, family, flock, group, jury, orchestra, parliament, staff,* and *team,* and there are many more.

Strictly speaking, all of these words are singular and take a singular verb. Straightforward enough, you might think. The problem is that a collective noun can refer to a whole group acting as a single entity and also to all the members of that group, acting as individuals. Are you still with me?

Rule: We use a singular verb with a collective noun when we mean the whole group acting as one; we use the plural verb when we are referring to the actions of the individuals within the group.

Parts of Speech

For example:

The battalion lost all its men in that battle.	All of the men died in the battle.
The battalion lost their lives in that battle.	All of the men died but not necessarily all at once.
The group was waiting in the airport bar.	All members of the group were at the bar.
The group took so long drinking their cocktails that they nearly missed their flight.	But they did not all drink the same cocktail at the same time.
The staff has gone crazy.	All employees are acting strangely.
The staff have locked themselves into their offices.	But they are not all locked in the same office.

Some people call this **formal agreement**—when you say *the staff is*—and **notional agreement**—*the [members of the] team are.*

A related source of confusion lies in the names of sports teams. *The New York Yankees*, for example, is not technically a collective noun. It's a proper noun (hence the capital letters; see page 32), and it should strictly speaking—those words again—be treated as singular. So, bizarrely, should *Manchester United, Toronto Maple Leafs*, and the *Boston Red Sox*. On the other hand, there is no denying that lots of people say *the New York Yankees **are** in the World Series*, and frankly only the most pedantic among us (and Red Sox fans) are likely to be offended.

What's in a Name?

Adjectives treated as collective nouns—*the rich, the homeless, the lonely*—are always plural and require a plural verb: *the rich are getting richer.*

> ➤ **Teacher's Corner:** To avoid confusion with collective nouns, it is often sensible to reword a sentence. Try *The hotel manager is offering members of the wedding party a discount on their rooms* instead of *The hotel is/are offering the wedding party a discount on its/their rooms.*

I'm the Leader of the Pack/smack/shiver

There are scores of collective nouns to describe parts of the animal (and particularly bird) kingdom. Some of them are genuinely useful (a flock of sheep and a herd of elephants, for example, if sheep and elephants crop up in your conversation to any great extent). Others are obscure or just plain silly, but the following pages provide a small sample of them.

What Do You Call a Group of…?

Ants	*A colony*	Dolphins	*A pod*
Apes	*A shrewdness*	Ducks	*A flock, brace (in flight), raft (on water), team, paddling (on water), badling*
Bats	*A colony*		
Bears	*A sloth, sleuth*		
Bees	*A grist, hive, swarm*		
Birds in general	*A flight (in the air); flock (on the ground); volary, brace (generally for gamebirds or waterfowl)*	Eagles	*A convocation*
		Elephants	*A herd*
		Fish in general	*A draft, nest, school, shoal*
		Flamingos	*A stand*
		Flies	*A business*
Buzzards	*A wake*	Frogs	*An army*
Caterpillars	*An army*	Geese	*A flock, gaggle (on the ground), skein (in flight)*
Cattle	*A drove, herd*		
Clams	*A bed*	Giraffes	*A tower*
Cockroaches	*An intrusion*	Goats	*A tribe, trip*
Cranes	*A sedge*	Grasshoppers	*A cloud*
Crocodiles	*A bask*	Gulls	*A colony*
Crows	*A murder, horde*	Hawks	*A cast, kettle (flying in large numbers), boil (two or more spiraling in flight)*
Deer	*A herd*		

Herring	An army	Seals	A pod, herd
Hippopotamuses	A bloat	Sharks	A shiver
Hornets	A nest	Sheep	A drove, flock, herd
Jellyfish	A smack	Snakes, vipers	A nest
Kangaroos	A troop	Sparrows	A host
Lions	A pride	Squirrels	A dray, scurry
Locusts	A plague	Starlings	A murmuration
Mules	A pack, span, barren	Storks	A mustering
		Swallows	A flight
Owls	A parliament	Swans	A bevy, wedge (in flight)
Oysters	A bed		
Peacocks	A muster, an ostentation	Tigers	A streak
		Toads	A knot
Penguins	A colony	Trout	A hover
Pigs	A drift, drove, litter (young)	Turkeys	A rafter, gang
		Turtles	A bale, nest
Porcupines	A prickle	Whales	A pod, gam, herd
Ravens	An unkindness		
Rhinoceroses	A crash	Wolves	A pack
		Woodpeckers	A descent

Parts of Speech

Is It Common or Proper?

Lots of words have come into English because of the man (with the honorable exception of Mrs. Amelia Bloomer, it was usually a man) who invented or popularized the item concerned. At some stage in the evolution of all these words, they would have been proper nouns, and thus spelled with a capital, but as the word became more commonplace and the association with a person was forgotten, the capital tended to be abandoned, too.

The only one on the list below that merits a capital in the dictionary refers back to an inventor who lived in the twentieth century. We give that capital ten years.

boycott	Captain Charles C. Boycott, Irish land agent ostracized by his neighbors in 1880.
cardigan	The 7th Earl of Cardigan (1797–1868), after whom the garment is named. He was clearly a fashion icon of his day.
dunce	The blessed John Duns Scotus (died 1308), one of the most important theologians and philosophers of the Middle Ages, later accused of unsound reasoning. And presumably made to stand in a corner wearing a pointy hat.
leotard	Jules Léotard, nineteenth-century French acrobat after whom the garment is named.
lynch mob	Captain William Lynch (1742–1820), Virginia justice of the peace at the time of the American Revolution; had a fondness for summarily executing people with whom he disagreed.
maudlin	Mary Magdalene, biblical figure often shown weeping in scripture, to describe the excessively sentimental.

mausoleum	King Mausolos of Caria (died 353 B.C.), whose tomb was one of the Seven Wonders of the Ancient World.
shrapnel	Major-General Henry Shrapnel (1761–1842), English artillery officer, who designed a new type of artillery shell.
silhouette	Etienne de Silhouette (1709–67), unpopular finance minister of Louis XV who imposed harsh economic demands upon the French people. His name became associated with anything done cheaply—particularly the simple form of portraiture that became popular at the time and enabled people to joke that the finance minister was saving money on color paints as well as on everything else.
Zamboni	Frank J. Zamboni (1901–88), ice skating-rink owner who invented an ice resurfacing machine.

ONE DIE, TWO DICE (OR, SINGULAR AND PLURAL)

When a noun means only one thing, it is **singular**. When it is more than one, it is **plural**. The rules on how to change a noun from singular to plural start simply but then tend to head out into left field.

1. Most singular nouns are made plural by adding the letter *s*: *book, bell, candle = books, bells, candles.*

2. However, if you add an *s* to such nouns as *church, bus, fox, bush, bench, Jones,* and *waltz,* they become difficult to pronounce. Which is why we add *-es* and create an extra syllable: *churches, buses, Joneses...*

Parts of Speech

---

3. If a noun ends in *y* and the letter before the *y* is a vowel, again just add an *s*: *key = keys*. However, if a noun ends in *y* and the letter before the *y* is a consonant, the *y* must be changed to an *i* and followed by *es*: *lady = ladies, gallery = galleries*. But, wait, there's an exception: This rule does not apply to proper nouns: *one penny, several pennies*, but *Mr. and Mrs. Penny* become *the Pennys*.

4. To form the plurals of nouns ending in *ff*, add that *s*: *cliffs, bailiffs*, and so on. However, words ending in a single *f* or in *fe* need to have these letters replaced with a *v*—oh, and then add *es*: *leaf = leaves, wife = wives*. Got that? Good, because there are exceptions.

Exceptions to Rule 4
Dwarfs and chiefs
Will cause you griefs.
As will proofs, roofs, safes, beliefs.
Hooves and hoofs can either be,
So, too, scarfs and scarves, you see.
To wharfs and wharves, you may refer,
And turfs and turves, as you prefer.

And just when you thought you were getting the hang of it, humans have one *life*, cats have nine *lives*, but artists can paint as many still *lifes* as they like.

5. Many words ending in *o* can be made plural by adding -*s*: *zoos, kangaroos, igloos, solos, sopranos,* *discos, photos, Eskimos, infernos*. Others—seemingly chosen at random—need *-es*: **Buffaloes** *have trampled my* **potatoes** *and* **tomatoes**. *If we sit outside to play* **dominoes,** *we shall be plagued by* **mosquitoes**.

6. A number of nouns have irregular plurals, which is why we do not say *Are you mouses or mans?* and why the plural of *house* is *houses*, but the plural of *louse* is *lice*. Then there's *goose/geese, tooth/teeth, child/children, ox/oxen* (but not *box/boxen*).

> ➤ **Teacher's Corner:** The plural of *talisman* is not *talismen* but *talismans*. Why? Because its origins have nothing to do with *man* or *men*. The word comes to us from Arabic and medieval Greek via French or Spanish.

Rule: The rules always apply, except when they don't. With irregular forms such as *child/children*, sorry, you just have to learn them.

Sorry, Don't Know the Plural...
Dear Sir,
Please send me a mongoose.
Oh, by the way, send me another one, too.

In big-game hunting it appears to be fair game to dispense with the usual plurals. Hence we might shoot *several gazelle, two leopard, three lion, three elephant,* and *six wild pig*. This has a

Parts of Speech

---

slightly old-fashioned feel and does somehow suggest that you are going out to kill the poor beasts and hang their heads on your wall.

And on the Agendum Today

Some nouns have no (or a rarely used) singular form:

alms	*marginalia*	*tidings*
bellows	*oats*	*tongs*
billiards	*pants*	*trousers*
braces	*pliers*	*tweezers*
clothes	*scissors*	*vespers*
dregs	*shorts*	*victuals*
eaves	*thanks*	*vittles*

Note: Nouns such as these require a **measure word**; for example, *a pair* of trousers, *some* thanks. You cannot say *one scissors*. Nor, happily, can you sow *just the one wild oat*.

"Singularity Is Almost Invariably a Clue"

No, it isn't. That was just Sherlock Holmes being a smart aleck. With some nouns, singularity is more trouble than it's worth.

Such nouns have a plural form but do what the dictionaries describe as "functioning as a singular." Others can function as either a singular or a plural. Which is, frankly, no help at all to those of us who like rules. Still others function as a singular in some senses and as a plural in others.

If the rules don't help, let's try a few examples.

Mumps is nasty, measles is measly is perfectly correct. But so too is *mumps **are** nasty, measles **are** measly*.

Sports with a plural form tend to take a singular verb when we mean them generically, but a plural when we mean something more countable, such as *exercises*. So:

*Athletics **is** tiresome.*   meaning the whole concept

*Gymnastics **are** a great way to start the day.*   meaning gymnastic exercises

Pilates, by the way, is the name of the man who invented it, so it is singular. And harder than it looks.

A similar distinction can be made with academic subjects. *Acoustics* is singular when we mean the study of sound, but plural when we mean sound qualities: *the acoustics **were** dreadful*. Similarly, if you study *ethics* or *politics*, it is a singular subject, but if you bring a person's *ethics* into question or complain about company *politics*, they are plural.

One Sheep, Two Sheep...

The following nouns take the same form whether they are singular or plural. What would Sherlock Holmes have to say about that?

aircraft	*kudos*	*shambles*
cannon	*means*	*sheep*
deer	*offspring*	*species*
haddock	*series*	*trout*

Take Your Pick...

All self-respecting pedants know about **Latin plurals**; a smattering (and rapidly diminishing number) of older ones know about Greek, too. But here a little learning can be a dangerous

Parts of Speech

thing, because it is easy to assume that a word ending in *-us* is Latin second declension and therefore has a plural ending in *-i*: *abaci, cacti, incubi, succubi*. Then along comes a word such as *platypus*, whose origins are Greek, and whose plural is strictly speaking *platypuses*, to catch you just when you thought you were being clever. A number of words ending in *-on* are derived from Greek neuter nouns and have a plural form ending in *-a*: *criterion/criteria, phenomenon/phenomena*, and so on.

Some words ending in *-is* are Latin third declension in origin and have a plural form *-es*: *crisis/crises, thesis/theses* (pronounced *-eeze* as in *cheese* or *sneeze*).

And then there are those that have decided to ignore their classical background altogether and allow us to choose between two (or even more) plural forms, some of them rather suspect:

hippopotamus	hippopotamuses, hippopotami
necropolis	necropolises, necropoles, necropoleis, necropoli
octopus	octopi, octopodes, octopuses
oxymoron	oxymorons, oxymora
rhinoceros	rhinoceroses, rhinoceros, rhinoceri, rhinocerotes
syllabus	syllabuses, syllabi
terminus	termini, terminuses
uterus	uteri, uteruses

One Die, Two Dice

> ➤ **Teacher's Corner:** *Octopus* is a one-word minefield, because it is a Latinized form of the Greek word *oktopous*, whose "correct" plural form would be *octopodes*. But according to *Merriam-Webster's Dictionary*, today the correct form of the plural is *octopuses* or *octopi*.

Keeping Up with the Joneses

When we talk about a family in the plural, we need to add an *s* to the **family name**; for example, *the Smiths, the Windsors*. However, if the family name ends in *s*, *x*, *ch*, *sh*, or *z*, we add -*es*: *the Joneses, the Foxes, the Bushes*.

> ➤ **See Me after Class:** *The Venables's came to our house this weekend.*
> Do not make a family name plural by using an apostrophe.

Exceptions: When a name ends in an *s* with a hard *z* sound, we don't add any ending to form the plural. *We have the Morrises and the Richards coming to lunch.*

Compounding the Problem

The rule with **plural compound nouns** is to pluralize the base element of the compound noun—that is, generally, the most important element of the word or phrase:

*We have our **mother-in-laws** staying with us, so we stepped out for a beer* is wrong.

> ***Mothers-in-law*** *and **daughters-in-law** don't always get along* is right.

because the key element of the phrase is *mother* (or *daughter*). Ask yourself *What sort of mother? A mother-in-law.* Similarly:

> *The role of **Secretary of State** varies among countries, and in some cases there are multiple **Secretaries of State**.*

Doctors Payne and Betterman *were speaking at the conference* (there is more than one doctor, but only one called Payne and only one called Betterman).

> *Bert and Benny were both idle but amiable **men-about-town**.*

The Media Is the Message

In addition to those mentioned above, here are a few more words whose origins we seem to have forgotten, but in these cases—because the plural forms don't end in *s*—we are beginning to use them as singulars. Lots of perfectly literate people now say (and some even write) *The data **was** incorrect* or *The media **is** very hostile to government policy*, but the purists still cling to the distinction between singular and plural.

Plural	Singular
bacteria	*bacterium*
candelabra	*candelabrum*
data	*datum*
dice	*die*
formulae	*formula*
genera	*genus*
graffiti	*graffito*
loci	*locus*
media	*medium*
opera	*opus*
paparazzi	*paparazzo*

One plural that has lost the fight is *pease,* which used to be the regular plural of *pea*. Now *peas* is found pretty much everywhere except in the phrase *pease pudding* and the nursery rhyme about whether it is hot or cold.

> **Smart Aleck:** If you add an *s* to the plural words *adventures, bras, cares, cosines, deadlines, millionaires, ogres, princes* and *timelines,* they revert to a singular form: *adventuress, brass, caress, cosiness, deadliness, millionairess, ogress, princess,* and *timeliness.*

By the way, *genie* and *genius* have the same plural: *genii.*

THOU AND THEE (OR, PRONOUNS)

Going back to our poem (see page 37), "In place of noun the pronoun stands," a **pronoun** is used to avoid repeating a noun over and over again. Imagine if you were writing a summary of this book and had to say, *Many people find grammar difficult. Lots of people were never taught grammar at school. Grammar has therefore become a source of anxiety. Indeed, some people might call grammar a minefield.* Just because nobody had thought to invent the words *it* or *them*.

The noun to which a pronoun refers is sometimes called the **antecedent**.

> *Many people find grammar difficult. Lots of them were never taught it at school.*

Parts of Speech

The antecedent of *them* is people and *grammar* is the antecedent of *it*.

> "The masculine pronouns are he, his, and him,
> But imagine the feminine she, shis, and shim."
> —Anonymous

There are various categories of pronoun, depending on the function they perform in a sentence. The **subject pronouns** are *I, you, he, she, it, we, they,* and the equivalent **object pronouns** are *me, you, him, her, it, us, them*. If we've lost you here, see page 115 for an explanation of subject and object. But it boils down to the difference between *I love him* and *He loves me*, which could be quite significant.

> ✋ **Smart Aleck:** Since *pronoun* is a noun,
> why isn't *proverb* a verb?

The Part about Sex

Ahem. The English language does not have a **singular pronoun** that encapsulates both genders. It used to be that "the masculine was deemed to embrace the feminine," but 1960s feminism put a stop to that sort of hanky-panky and has left us with a grammatical problem ever since. Some people meticulously write *he or she, his or hers*, wherever it crops up, but this quickly becomes cumbersome and tedious. Others go for *s/he*, but that still leaves them with the his/her dilemma. Still others go to the opposite extreme and use *she* or *her* throughout (so the feminine is now embracing the masculine, as it were).

Lots of people nowadays fudge this by using *their* as a non-gender-specific singular, as in *the judge* (who may be a man or a woman; we don't know and it would be sexist to assume either) *adjusted their robe.* It isn't pretty, but sometimes being a purist is no oil painting either.

It's All Relative

The **relative pronouns** are *who, what, whom, that, whose,* and *which,* and their role is to introduce subordinate clauses that tell us more about the noun that precedes them. For example:

*The waiter **who** served you may remember what time you left.*
*The girl **whose** name was Sue made a lot of money at her garage sale.*
*He **whom** the gods love dies young.*
*He was disturbed by the email, **which** he received this morning.*
*He was disturbed by the email **that** he received this morning.*

Which can also be used to refer back to an entire clause:

*The sun was shining throughout the rainy season, **which** didn't seem right at all.*

Excellent Reflexes

"And not in me: I am myself alone."
—Shakespeare, *Henry VI*

Reflexive pronouns are formed by adding *self* or *selves* to the basic pronoun: *myself, oneself, yourself, himself, herself, itself, ourselves, yourselves, themselves.* They are used when the subject and object of a verb are the same person or thing:

Parts of Speech

> *I can look after **myself**.*
> *Speak for **yourself**!*
> *We enjoyed **ourselves** immensely.*
> *The kids can never be trusted to behave **themselves** when the babysitter is there.*

They can also be used to avoid ambiguity. Compare these sentences:

> *Tom had done surprisingly well on his exams. The teacher was very pleased with **him** (that is, pleased with Tom).*
>
> *Tom had done surprisingly well on his exams. The teacher was very pleased with **himself** (that is, the teacher was pleased with the teacher).*

These pronouns can also be used for emphasis, or to mean "alone, unaided": *I can't see what anyone sees in* Big Brother, ***myself***. Or: *Did you really do all of the decorating **yourself**?*

Overuse of reflexive pronouns in this emphatic sense is one of the banes of modern speech. *I think* is just as persuasive as *I myself think* (we're sorry to be dogmatic, but please bear with us this once).

"Every one to rest themselves betake."
—Shakespeare, *The Rape of Lucrece*

Let's Reciprocate

The **reciprocal pronouns** are *each other* and *one another*. *Each other* refers to two people or things; *one another* to more than two.

> *The two candidates who were still in contention congratulated **each other**. The others adjourned to the bar to commiserate with **one another**.*

What's Mine Is Yours

The **possessive pronouns** are *my, mine, your(s), his, her(s), our(s), their(s),* and *its* (and note that they never—repeat never—need an apostrophe: see page 158 for some common confusions). *Mine, yours, his, hers, ours, theirs,* and *its* tend to be used after the noun to which they refer and mean "the thing belonging to or associated with me/you/whoever":

*He had forgotten his gloves again, so I gave him **mine**.*
*Put that book back where you found it: it isn't **yours**.*
*We were madly envious because their house was much nicer than **ours**.*

I Don't Want to Be Specific…

There are a number of useful pronouns that we can use when we don't want to or are unable to specify exactly what we are talking about: *all, another, any, anyone, anything, each, everybody, everyone, everything, few, many, no one, nobody, none, nothing, one, several, some, somebody, someone.* These are called **indefinite pronouns**.

*I think **someone** is in the house.*
*You've eaten most of the chocolates; there are only **a few** left.*
*In space, **no one** can hear you scream.*

By the way, there is no difference in grammatical terms between *no one* and *nobody, someone* and *somebody, anyone* and *anybody.* For once you can just use whichever you like.

Talking about This and That

The **demonstrative pronouns** are *this, that, these,* and *those*—the same words as the demonstrative determiners we met earlier but used in a slightly different way.

Parts of Speech

*Please take **this** home with you and study it.*	meaning, perhaps, **this** book
*Take **that** to the cleaners, will you?*	**that** jacket
*I want **these** removed at once.*	**these** dirty dishes
***Those** are no good to anybody.*	**those** old clothes

Let's Investigate...

Interrogative pronouns take the place of a noun in a question.

***Who** is that?*	The answer might be: That is Homer Simpson.
***What** is that?*	That is a picture of Homer Simpson.
***Which** is that?*	Which of the many pictures of Homer Simpson in the world are you talking about?
*To **whom** should I give the doughnuts?*	It's pretty obvious, really.

Some Common Confusions

their/theirs/there/there's/they're

Their is a possessive pronoun, showing ownership. *It was **their** version of the story that was reported on the news.*

Theirs is also a possessive pronoun indicating that something belongs to more than one person. *That version of the story is **theirs.***

There is an adverb that indicates a place or position. *My new car is over **there**. **There** is a monkey in that tree.*

There's means *there is*. ***There's** that ring you were looking for.*

They're means *they are*. ***They're** a very happy couple even though they fight all the time.*

its/it's

Its is a possessive pronoun. *We thought the cat was lost, but it somehow found **its** way home.*

It's means *it is*. ***It's** not fair.*

whose/who's

Whose is a possessive pronoun. *The boy **whose** pants were flown from the flagpole.*

Whose can also be an interrogative pronoun. ***Whose** pants are those?*

Who's means *who is*. *The boy **who's** being told off for putting them there.*

Parts of Speech

Who or That?

Rule: Use *who* to refer to people.

Use *that* to refer to animals or inanimate objects.

*The people **who** matter will be impressed by this. (The people **that** matter is not incorrect, but is less formal.)*

*The tigers **that** come from Siberia have thick fur to protect them against the cold.*

*The house **tha**t we used to live in has been knocked down to make way for a supermarket.*

*The song **that** he wrote never made it onto the charts.*

In the last two examples, the antecedent is the object of the following clause (we used to live in the house, he wrote the song). In these cases, another option is to omit the relative pronoun altogether:

The house we used to live in...

The song he wrote...

And, on the subject of which and that, don't miss the exciting installment on restrictive and non-restrictive clauses later in the book (see page 139).

WHAT A TO-DO (OR, VERBS)

> 🖐 **Smart Aleck:** When somebody greets us with *How do you do?* why don't we ever reply, *Do what?*

A **verb** is an "action word": *I **do**, you **go**, he **runs**, we **sleep**, they **sneeze**.* A verb also expresses a state of being: *I **am**, it **is**, we **live**.*

Verbs have a lot of clout. They make things happen.

I books
You grammar
We money

mean nothing without a verb.

*I **write** books*
*You **learn** grammar*
*We **earn** money*

make perfect sense and are good things—particularly the last one.

To Be or Not to Be

With verbs, we start with the **infinitive**, which is made up of the preposition *to* and the basic form of the verb:

***To be**, or not **to be**, that is the question.*
***To sleep**, perchance **to dream**.*
***To have** and **to hold**.*

These verbs have meaning—we know what *to be, to sleep, to dream, to have, to hold* mean—but they don't tell us anything specific about the action that is being performed, the time it is (or was or will be or may have been) being done, or the number of people doing it. For that, we need either:

to **conjugate** the verb—that is, change the ending to show a change of meaning (*he laughs, I laugh**ed***)

or

to add an **auxiliary** or helping verb to specify time and number (*I **will** laugh, you **are** laughing, he **has** laughed*).

Once you have conjugated a verb and added any auxiliaries you want to make the action complete, you have a **finite verb**. (As in, not an infinitive, you see? Clever, right?)

Parts of Speech

To Boldly Split

The old rule was simple: *never split an infinitive*—that is, on pain of death, never put a word between the *to* and the rest of the verb. The example everyone trundles out at this point is *Star Trek*'s "To boldly go..."

It is, however, probably one of the sillier rules to come out of the old grammarians' insistence on applying Latin rules to English: Latin infinitives are one word—*amare, potare, studere*—so they couldn't be split anyway. Modern scholars believe that splitting an infinitive is perfectly acceptable if the alternative would be clumsy or ambiguous. In the following sentences, for example, we think that the non-split version is more elegant, and the meaning is equally clear, so it is preferable. But it is surely preferable *because it is more elegant*, not because the infinitive is unsplit.

*Many people choose **to incorrectly split** an infinitive in everyday speech.* ☒

*Many people **incorrectly choose to split** an infinitive in everyday speech.* ☑

*They decided **to quickly devour** the pie.* ☒

*They decided **to devour the pie quickly**.* ☑

*She put aside extra time **to closely mark** the exam papers.* ☒

*She put aside extra time **to mark the exam papers closely**.* ☑

On the other hand, this fragment (from the British newspaper the *Daily Telegraph*) scrupulously avoids splitting the infinitive and in so doing sacrifices clarity: *A family doctor who installed a camera **secretly to film** a woman using his bathroom...* What was it that was done secretly? The installation or the filming? (Or, given the context, perhaps both?)

What a to-Do

> "The English-speaking world may be divided into (1) those who neither know nor care what a split infinitive is; (2) those who do not know but care very much; (3) those who know and condemn; (4) those who know and approve; (5) those who know and distinguish… Those who neither know nor care are the vast majority, and are a happy folk, to be envied by most of the minority classes."
> —H. W. Fowler, *Modern English Usage*, 1926

A Few Irregularities

Regular verbs—those that follow the rules—are conjugated as follows:

Present tense: *I love, you love, he loves, we love, they love*

Past tense: *I loved, you loved, he loved, we loved, they loved*

Present participle: *loving, biting.*

(Note that if a verb ends in *e*, we drop the *e* to form the present participle. If not, we just add *-ing*: *wanting, hanging, staggering*, for example.)

Because this is English, however, there are inevitably lots of **irregular verbs**. Some past tenses and past participles are formed by adding *-t* instead of *-ed* (see below). Then we have *to drink*, which becomes *I drank, you drank*, and so on, in the past tense, whereas *to think* becomes *I thought*. *To speak* becomes *I spoke*, but *to squeak* and *to sneak* are regular and become *I squeaked* and *I sneaked*.

Parts of Speech

The most thoroughly irregular verbs of all are the common ones *to be* and *to go*: *I **am**, you **are**, he **is**, we **are**, they **are**, I **was**, you **were**.* *To go* is OK in the present tense, but *I **went**?* What's that all about?

Again, it's the irritating feature of irregular forms; there's no apparent logic to them, and you just have to learn them.

Back Me Up, Will You?

Auxiliary verbs are used "to indicate the tense, voice, mood, and so on, of another verb where this is not indicated by inflection." Don't you just love dictionaries? It means they are the little words you stick in the front of verbs. There are 23 of them, which can be learned by singing them to the tune of *Jingle Bells*.

may, might, must
be, being, been
am, are
is, was, were
do, does, did
should, could, would
have, had, has
will, can
shall

So they can express simple things such as *I **am** coming*, slightly more complicated ones such as *it **will be** done*, or even more complex ones with up to three auxiliaries attached to one main verb: *He **must have been** feeling unhappy for some time.*

Must and *may*, along with *should and ought*, are also called **modal verbs**: they give information about the mood of the verb (see page 79), expressing such things as obligation (*you **must** be home by midnight, he **ought** to pay before leaving the restaurant*), recommendation (*you **should** call and apologize*) or possibility (*I **may** do as you ask, but then again I **may** not*).

May or Might? Can or Could?

Strictly speaking, *may* and *can* operate in the present tense, *might* and *could* in the past or in the conditional (see page 78).

***Can** you lend me 20 dollars?*	Do you have the money?
***Could** you lend me 20 dollars?*	Would you be so very kind as to entrust me with this sum, secure in the knowledge that I will pay it back?

However, this is another distinction that is beginning to be lost in modern-day speech and writing.

Can/could also indicate *capability* or *possibility*, whereas *may/might* grant us *permission* to do something.

***Can** I drive your Rolls-Royce?*	Well, yes, if your feet can reach the pedals and you understand the concept of a steering wheel.
***May** I drive your Rolls-Royce?*	Over my dead body.

Most people in the English-speaking world seem to have had a schoolteacher who, in response to the question *Can I go to the bathroom?* would raise an eyebrow and say, *I don't know—**can** you?*

Parts of Speech

> ☞ **See Me after Class**
> **Could have/could of**
> There is no verb *to of*. *He could've told me* is a short form of *He could **have** told me.*
>
> **Try and/try to**
> *Try and* is wrong. *Try to* get it right.

About Whom Are We Talking?

For the purposes of grammar, there are only three **persons** (not people, there are loads of them) in the world:

first person: the speaker (*I, me, we, us*)
second person: the hearer (*you*)
third person: the person or thing spoken of (*he, she, it, they, him, her, them*)

In modern English, *you* serves as both singular and plural, but always takes a plural verb—***you are*** *my lucky star,* ***you were*** *made for me,* ***you drive*** *me crazy*—even when only one person is being addressed. *Thou* and *thee* were once the singular forms, but they are now never used except as deliberate archaisms, in church and in some dialects.

> ✋ **Smart Aleck:** Many languages have both informal and formal words for *you*: the French *tu* and *vous* and the German *du* and *Sie*, for example. English only has *you*, having done away with *thou* centuries ago. But did you know that *thou* was in fact the more informal of the two? English has preserved the impeccably polite word rather than the chummy one. Now why should that be?

The Voice of Reason

And there are two voices: **active** and **passive**.

Rule: With the active voice the subject acts; with the passive voice the subject is acted upon.

Active: *The teacher reprimanded the boy* because *he spilled milk* on his notebook.

Passive: *The boy was reprimanded* because *milk was spilled* on his notebook.

The two sentences say the same thing but with different emphasis. Using the passive voice too often can make writing dull (let's get on with some action!). However, consider:

*If **it were done** when 'tis done then 'twere well **it were done** quickly.*

*Should auld acquaintance **be forgot**, and never **brought to mind**?*

*Yossarian **was moved** very deeply by the absolute simplicity of this clause of Catch-22.*

*The stars **are not wanted** now.*

The passive should not be ruled out altogether. It may be found to have its uses.

"We have not passed that subtle line between childhood and adulthood until we move from the passive voice to the active voice—that is, until we have stopped saying, "It got lost," and say, "I lost it."
—Sydney J. Harris, *On the Contrary*

Parts of Speech

It's Raining Pronouns

In English we use a little-known thing called the **weather verb** an awful lot.

It is raining.
It is freezing.
It is in the nineties.

What is this nameless, shapeless *it* that is doing all these things? Well, it is known simply as the **dummy subject,** a handy little word that enables us to get to the part we all love: describing the weather. Without it we'd be going around saying, *The sky is raining, the sun is hot,* and so on, which might—perish the thought—make talking about the weather boring.

Getting Tense

> "They said: 'You're Laurie Lee, aren't you? Well just you sit there for the present.' I sat there all day but I never got it. I ain't going back there again."
> —Laurie Lee, *Cider with Rosie*

Tenses add time to verbs. They put actions into the past, present and future, the may-yet-be or the might-have-been.

*I **do** ballet on Tuesdays.*	I do this habitually, and will continue to do this.
*I **am doing** ballet at the moment.*	I am doing this either right at this moment—so I can't come to the phone—or over a longer but current period of time: perhaps I used to do salsa but have changed.

What a to-Do

*I **have done** ballet for years.*	I did ballet in the past and up to and including the present, but I may be getting bored with it now.
*I **have been doing** ballet for years.*	I did ballet in the past and have continued it until the present time and probably will continue in the future. I haven't finished with it yet. Ballet is here for the duration.
*I **did do** ballet once upon a time.*	I did ballet at some indefinite time in the past. It belongs there. I have given it up in the present.
*I **used to do** ballet, but now I do jazz.*	I no longer do ballet.
*I **was doing** ballet on Tuesdays, but now they've changed it to Fridays.*	I was doing ballet on Tuesdays until recently. I may or may not be doing it on Fridays.
*I **would do** ballet if they hadn't changed the class to a Friday.*	If it could be changed to suit me, I would consider doing ballet in the future.
*I **had done** ballet for years, before I switched to jazz.*	I had given up ballet before I took up jazz. There is nothing to suggest whether or not I am still doing jazz.
*I **had been doing** ballet for years before anyone told me I had a crooked spine.*	I was still doing ballet—the action was ongoing—at some time in the past when something else happened.
*I **will do** ballet again one day.*	I intend to/predict that I will do ballet in the future.

*I **will have done** my ballet exam by the time we go on vacation.*	A future action will be completed by or before a specified time in the future.
*I **will be doing** the ballet recital on Saturday.*	It is definitely going to happen at this specific point in the future.

Exactly how many tenses there are in English is arguable. Some grammarians claim that there are only two: the present and the past. (Presumably they let the future take care of itself.) Some say the traditional number is twelve, though others have described as many as thirty and, just to confuse us, some tenses have more than one name. But here are fourteen that should get you through most situations (or ballet positions).

present simple	*I pirouette*
present continuous	*I am pirouetting*
present perfect	*I have pirouetted*
present perfect continuous	*I have been pirouetting*
past simple (also known as **preterite**)	*I did pirouette, I pirouetted*
imperfect	*I used to pirouette*
past continuous	*I was pirouetting*
conditional	*I would pirouette*
pluperfect/past perfect	*I had pirouetted*
past perfect continuous	*I had been pirouetting*
future	*I will pirouette*
future perfect	*I will have pirouetted*
future continuous	*I will be pirouetting*
future perfect continuous	*I will have been pirouetting*

> **Famous Last Words**
> "I am about to—or I am going to—die.
> Either expression is correct."
> —French grammarian Dominique Bouhours,
> who died in 1702

Judging by Your Mood...

Verbs, like the rest of us, act differently depending on which **mood** they are in. There are three moods: **indicative, imperative,** and **subjunctive**.

The **indicative mood** makes a statement or asks a question:

I'm wet, I'm cold, and I'm hungry.

Winter is almost here.

He will come.

Is that the best you can do?

The **imperative mood** gives us a command:

Chill out!

Do as I say!

Don't eat the daisies!

And even the more politely phrased: *Please look after this bear.*

Easy! Unfortunately the **subjunctive mood** is so complicated that it deserves a subheading of its own.

If Only It Were That Easy

The **subjunctive** sounds scarier than it is and has a tendency to fill people with horror. Let's start with a couple of examples:

*I wish it **weren't** going to snow again* (but it is).

*If it **were** to snow* (which it may or may not do, but we don't know yet), *they would not be able to get home.*

Parts of Speech

I were or *it were* may sound odd, but they're right when you are using the subjunctive.

Rule: If you know something for a fact, use *was*. If something is contrary to fact, or if you are imagining a future or different situation to the one you are in, use *were*.

*When I **was** young* (fact: I *was* young once), *I was taught Latin* (it's true, I *was* taught Latin).

*When he **was** young and handsome* (he *was* young and handsome once), *he was also arrogant.*

*I **was** that man* (you *were* indeed).

When I was poor (I once was indeed poor), I wasn't unhappy.

but

*If I **were** you* (but I'm not), *I should teach myself Latin.*

*If I **were** to teach you Latin* (supposing that I taught you Latin), *would you study hard?*

*If I **were** to be young and handsome again* (but I can't be, alas), *I wouldn't be so arrogant about it.*

*If I **were** that sort of man* (but I'm not), *you might find me there.*

*If I **were** rich* (but I might never be rich), *would I be happier than I am now?*

*I wish I **were** taller (but I am currently stuck at this height).*

A number of **set phrases** in English—*come what may, far be it from me, the powers that be*—use the subjunctive, but the joy of set phrases is that you don't have to think about them.

> "If I were reincarnated, I'd want to come back as a buzzard. Nothing hates him or envies him or wants him or needs him. He is never bothered or in danger, and he can eat anything."
> —William Faulkner

Sic Transit Gloria...

A **transitive verb** allows the subject to perform an action on an object (see page 115 for more on subjects and objects):

She slapped his face.   She *slapped* what? His face.

He pulled the communication cord.   He *pulled* what? The cord.

> ✋ **Smart Aleck:** Transitive verbs with one object only are called **monotransitive** (*I corrected my teacher*). Verbs with both a direct object and an indirect object are called **ditransitive** (*The teacher threw me an eraser*).

An **intransitive verb** acts by itself:

I sleep.   I cannot *sleep* something.

I fall.   I cannot *fall* something.

Famous Intransitives
"Jesus wept."
—*Saint John's Gospel*
*
"Thus with a kiss I die."
—Shakespeare, *Romeo and Juliet*

Parts of Speech

Just to confuse things, some verbs can be transitive when used in one sense and intransitive in another. These are known as **ambitransitive verbs**.

Transitive	Intransitive
*He **drank** his coffee.*	*He **drank** like a fish.*
*She **read** the menu.*	*She **read** during dinner.*
*I **gave up** cigarettes.*	*I **give up**.*
*He **kissed** her hand.*	*They **kissed**.*

Tip: To check whether a verb is intransitive, place a period directly after it and see if it makes sense: *He died. You survived.* But *he hit.* (*Hit* what?) *She threw.* (*Threw* what?) A transitive verb needs an object to complete its action.

Verbal Warning

Verbal nouns or **adjectives** are formed from verbs, but they perform the function of nouns or adjectives, and there are three kinds: **participles**, **infinitives,** and **gerunds**. None of these can act on its own as a verb. Instead, each helps a verb to do its job.

Participles

A **participle** is a non-finite form of a verb used with an auxiliary verb to form some compound tenses. It can also be used in **noun, adjectival,** or **adverbial phrases** such as:

***Going to the casino** is a surefire way of losing money.*	**noun phrase**, the subject of the sentence
*The horse **favored by the tipsters** seemed to lose interest at the second fence.*	**adjectival phrase**, describing the horse
*She stormed out, **slamming the door** so hard that the mirror fell off the wall.*	**adverbial phrase**, describing *how* she stormed out

Infinitives

As we saw on page 69, this is the basic form of the verb preceded by *to*, but it is also used in some **compound verb forms** such as:

*I **was going to send** you my address.*
*I **used to go** to a lot of concerts.*

Or following verbs expressing feelings, or to give a reason for an action:

*I **would love to see** her again.*
*Don't **forget to wash** your hands.*
*We **built** a fence around the backyard **to keep** the dog under control.*

Gerunds

> "What are all these **kissings** worth,
> If thou kiss not me?"
> —Percy Bysshe Shelley, *Love's Philosophy*

A **gerund** is a noun formed from a verb by adding *-ing*, so it looks exactly like a present participle, but is used in a different way. *When **the going** gets tough, the tough get going.* The first *going* is a gerund: in this sentence, it performs the same function as a noun. To test this statement, try substituting something you know is a noun:

*When **the exams** get tough…*
*When **the meat** gets tough…*

But in the second part of our original sentence, *going* is the present participle of the verb *to go*, linked to the auxiliary verb *get* to make a complete, finite verb.

Parts of Speech

Here's another example to help you spot the difference:

*I admire the girl **posing** for that photograph.*	**present participle**, referring to the girl who is posing for that photograph
*I admire the girl's **posing** for that photograph.*	**gerund**, referring to the way she is posing, but not necessarily the girl herself

Note the cunning use of the apostrophe here—it carries a wealth of meaning. And guess what? There will be lots more about apostrophes later in the book (see page 168).

KIND OF FUNNY LOOKING (OR, ADJECTIVES)

Most of us were taught the simple rule: an **adjective** is a "describing word." Adjectives modify nouns or pronouns. They tell us what they are like: what they look like, how big they are, and how many of them there are. For example:

An **ugly** bug
A **lovely** girl
A **blue** moon
Thirty people

Adjectives can be derived from proper nouns to describe such things as historical periods (*Elizabethan, Napoleonic*), literary or musical styles (*Shakespearean, Dickensian, Wagnerian*), nationality or geographical location (*French, Parisian*), or other things more loosely associated with people or places (a *Freudian* slip, *Victorian* values, a *Caesarean* section). The suffix *-ian/-ean* means "of or pertaining to (this person/place)"; *-esque* means "in the style of (the person)": so

Dantesque, Kafkaesque, or *Junoesque.* The last of these, intriguingly, is defined as either "of regal beauty" or "large, buxom, and (usually) beautiful," depending on which dictionary you read. Really, if the dictionaries can't agree, what hope is there for the rest of us?

Most of these adjectives are spelled with a capital letter, though *caesarean* has come a long way from Julius Caesar and is now often seen with a lower case *c.* Foods that are named after their place of origin—champagne, parmesan, and the like—are another vague area: strictly speaking they are based on proper nouns, but the more generically they are used, the more it becomes acceptable to drop the capital. It seems bizarre, for example, to insist on using a capital *C* for *New Zealand Cheddar,* on the basis that the cheese is named after a place in Somerset, England.

A Big Bunch of Adjectivals

A group of words can act as an adjective. If they contain a subject and verb, they are known as an **adjectival clause**. If not, they are described as an **adjectival phrase**. (No, we haven't done phrases and clauses yet, but we'll get there—see pages 125 and 129.)

*My colleagues, **who all earn more than I do,** never work overtime.*	**adjectival clause**, describing my colleagues
*He is the one person in the department **earning less than I do**.*	**adjectival phrase**, describing the person in the department

A Fine Piece of Writing—or Not?

It is easy to go overboard with adjectives (and adverbs, too, see page 88). The author Graham Greene once wrote:

> Adjectives are to be avoided unless they are strictly necessary; adverbs too, which is even more important. When I open a book and find that so and so has "answered sharply" or "spoken tenderly," I shut it again: It's the dialogue itself which should express the sharpness or the tenderness without any need to use adverbs to underline them.

Oh dear—what would he have made of this paragraph from *Tess of the D'Urbervilles* by Thomas Hardy?

> The young girls formed, indeed, the majority of the band, and their heads of luxuriant hair reflected in the sunshine every tone of gold, and black, and brown. Some had beautiful eyes, others a beautiful nose, others a beautiful mouth and figure; few, if any, had all... A young member of the band turned her head at the exclamation. She was a fine and handsome girl—not handsomer than some others, possibly—but her mobile peony mouth and large innocent eyes added eloquence to color and shape...

Kind of Funny Looking

Limpet Adjectives (or, Clichés)

Some adjectives are so often attached to certain nouns that they seem permanently stuck together and have become **clichés**. Please do not stick these in your writing:

absolute truth   *new innovation*
close proximity   *original source*
definite decision   *personal friend*
end result   *safe haven*
free gift   *true facts*
local resident   *unexpected surprise*
major breakthrough   *violent explosion*
necessary requisite   *work colleague*

Rule: Verbs and nouns are the bricks of a sentence. They give it structure. Adjectives and adverbs are decorative embellishments. If an adjective or adverb doesn't add anything, don't add it.

☛ **See Me after Class:** *The object is small in size, square in shape, and blue in color.*
Do not waste words on unnecessary description.
The object is small, square, and blue says it all.

Parts of Speech

REVERENTLY, DISCREETLY, ADVISEDLY, SOBERLY... (OR, ADVERBS)

> "When it absolutely, positively has to be there overnight."
> —Federal Express slogan (1978–1983)

An **adverb** describes a verb, adjective, or adverb. Adverbs answer questions such as *how, where, when, how much, how often?*

Many but by no means all adverbs in English end in *-ly* (*almost, once, twice, never, well, hard, fast, soon,* and *there* are all adverbs), and many but by no means all the words that end in *-ly* are adverbs (*manly, beastly,* and *holy* are adjectives and *family, butterfly,* and *barfly* are nouns). But it seems that in everyday speech adverbs are steadily disappearing and the adjectival form is being used instead.

The following are all commonly heard but grammatically incorrect:

*He did the task **clever** and I was **real impressed**.*
*He always drives **careful** so he won't get any points on his license.*
*It rained **so heavy** the roof started to leak.*
*She divided them **fair** but the children still weren't happy.*

They should be:

*He did the task clever**ly** and I was real**ly** impressed.*
*He always drives careful**ly**.*

*It rained so heav**ily**.*
*She divided them fair**ly**.*

Note that in the first example, *cleverly* is an adverb describing the verb *he did* (How did he do the task? Cleverly), and *really* is an adverb describing the adjective *impressed* (How impressed was I? Really impressed).

Ones That Got Away

> *He doesn't play **fair**.*
> *I've got it **bad**.*
> *They're going **steady**.*
> *Go **slow**!!*

All of these are acceptable colloquialisms, but you might think twice about using them in formal writing.

And here's an oddity: *She worked **extremely hard**. Hard* is an adverb qualifying the verb *worked* (How did she work? Hard). And *extremely* is an adverb qualifying the adverb *worked* (How hard did she work? Extremely hard). Despite the fact that *hard* looks like an adjective, we know that it is an adverb because it qualifies the verb. If you invented an adverbial form for it, you would get *she worked hardly*, which just sounds odd, or *she hardly worked*, which means something altogether different. Go figure.

Correctly Placing the Adverb Correctly

Although **word order** is usually important in English (see page 111), the position of the adverb is remarkably flexible. It may go after the verb, *She answered the question **hesitantly***, or it may go before the verb: *She **hesitantly** answered the question.* In fact sometimes it can go just about anywhere in a sentence:

***Scarily**, she must have been dancing too close to the cliff.*
*She **scarily** must have been dancing too close to the cliff.*
*She must **scarily** have been dancing too close to the cliff.*
*She must have **scarily** been dancing too close to the cliff.*
*She must have been **scarily** dancing too close to the cliff.*
*She must have been dancing **scarily** too close to the cliff.*
*She must have been dancing too close to the cliff, **scarily**.*

Time, Manner, and Place

As with adjectives (see page 84), a group of words can serve as an adverb in an **adverbial clause** or **phrase**:

*I'll go to bed **when this TV show has ended**.*	Answering the question *When will you go to bed?*
*I'll pick you up **just up the road from the movie theater**.*	Answering the question *Where?*
*Some people do this **for fun**.*	Answering the question *Why?*—or perhaps *Why, oh why?*

That's a Bit Intense

Extra adverbs, used for emphasis, are called **intensifiers**: *soon **enough**, **very** nicely, **remarkably** good, **clearly** inadequate.*

But don't overuse adverbs too much: while adverbs can be used to great effect—

*He is **tremendously** tiresome. She is **fantastically** daring.*
*He's **disgustingly** rich.*—

it is easy to fall into the trap of using them tautologically (unnecessary repetition of meaning). One way of assessing whether your adverb adds anything is to consider a sentence with the opposite:

*She screamed **loudly**.*	As opposed to screaming quietly, perhaps?
*He clenched his fists **tightly**.*	How else could he clench his fists?

These are the adverbial equivalents of *close proximity* and *free gift* (see page 171).

Likewise, don't fall into the trap of using words such as *fourthly*. Where possible, just keep it simple:

First, I heard a bang.

Second, I switched on the light.

Third, I grabbed a hairbrush.

There is no need for *Fourthly, I checked my make-up… Ninthly, I went back to bed.*

Rule: If in doubt, leave your adverb out.

DANGLING BY A THREAD (OR, MISPLACED MODIFIERS)

> "80 percent of married men cheat in America…"
> (The rest cheat in Europe.)
>
> ✳
>
> "Set against the murky background of gangland London and missing children—buy yours for $14.99…"
> —Radio advertisement for a book

Parts of Speech

Misplaced modifiers, **dangling modifiers**, **dangling participles**, **misrelated participles**—these are all expressions that grammarians toss into the conversation on purpose to confuse and embarrass the rest of us. So what do they mean? Well, consider a sentence such as:

Walking down Main Street, the new shoe store caught her eye.

We probably all know what is *meant*, but grammatically what this sentence *says* is that the shoe store was walking down the street. The participle is dangling (or misplaced or misrelated) because it seems to relate to the wrong part of the sentence. *As she was walking down Main Street, the new shoe store caught her eye* is correct and unambiguous. As is *Walking down Main Street, she was thrilled to notice the new shoe store.*

Rule 1: The (unexpressed) subject of the participle clause—that is, the person or thing that is *walking down Main Street*—should have the same subject as the (expressed) subject of the main clause: *she*. Careless positioning of all sorts of modifiers can cause amusement, confusion or actions for libel:

Rule 2: The modifying clause or phrase (*walking down Main Street*) should always come as near as possible to the noun or pronoun it modifies. Otherwise you'll create unclear sentences like these:

- John still attends his local church where he was married regularly.
- We will continue to sell goods to people in plastic wrapping.
- She was taken to the hospital having been bitten by a spider in a bathing suit.

- American Catholic theologians will have to wait and see the exact wording of a French document permitting the use of condoms before engaging in theological debate.
- The mother of the accused said that God would judge her son in a news conference on Friday.
- The bride was given away by her father wearing her mother's wedding dress.
- Q: Doctor, how many autopsies have you performed on dead people? A: All my autopsies are performed on dead people.

"I once shot an elephant in my pajamas. How he got into my pajamas I'll never know."
—Groucho Marx

May I Compare Thee to a Summer's Day? (or, Comparatives)

"Poets and writers who are in love with the superlative all want to do more than they can."
—Friedrich Nietzsche

Comparatives (which may be adjectives or adverbs) compare two things. We say that one thing is *larger, faster, more lovely,* and *more* *temperate **than** another thing*, or that it runs *more swiftly, more elegantly, less galumphingly **than** another.*

*The African elephant has **larger** ears **than** the Indian elephant.*
*In Aesop's fable, the tortoise was **steadier than** the hare.*
*Shoplifting is **less evil than** murder.*

Comparative adjectives usually employ the suffix *-er* if the original adjective is short enough for it not to become a mouthful. If it doesn't sound right to add *-er* (*beautifuller? temperater?* Don't think so), use the modifier *more: more beautiful, more temperate.* And if we want to say that it is *less* ugly or *less* beautiful—that's how we do it, however short the original adjective is.

Does it sound right? is often a good rule (the proper term is *euphony,* but *does it sound right?* will do just fine). *More big* when we mean *bigger* sounds just as silly as *beautifuller* when we mean *more beautiful.*

Also, there is the question of ambiguity. *The African elephant has **more big ears than** the Indian elephant* sounds as if the elephants have a collection of ears in large and small sizes.

> ☛ **See Me after Class:** Each comparison needs only one comparative suffix or word: *more better* is bad, *more betterer* is even worser.

For Better, for Worse

So often, it is the really common words that have irregular forms.

*The movie he took me to see was **good**, but this one is **better**.*
*The movie he took me to see was **bad**, but this one is **worse**.*

*My father has **many** mansions, but Donald Trump probably has **more**.*

*I have **a lot** of trouble with grammar, but some sports commentators have **more**.*

See also **superlatives,** below.

Comparing Like with Like

Most comparatives say that something is *more* or *less* something *than* the other something, if you see what we mean. But it is also a comparative to say that something is *the same* (or *not the same*) *as* something else:

*He is **as** cunning **as** a fox.*

*This ring is not **as** expensive **as** that one. (I want that one.)*

That's Superlative

*And the **best** and the **worst** of this is*
*That neither is **most** to blame,*
If you have forgotten my kisses
And I have forgotten your name.
—Algernon Charles Swinburne, *An Interlude*

Superlatives are beyond compare. Nothing can be better or worse. They are simply the b**EST**.

*The giraffe is the tall**est** living animal.*

*The Concorde was the fast**est** plane.*

*Churchill was the great**est** prime minister.*

Most superlatives end in *-est*, although not *most*. Nor indeed *worst*. And, as with comparatives, neither do longer words. Where a comparative has *more* or *less*, a superlative has *most* or *least*:

Parts of Speech

Lord of the Rings *is the **most overrated** book of the twentieth century.*

All's Well That Ends Well *is perhaps the **least performed** of Shakespeare's plays.*

Superlatives refer to more than two things: you can't be the *best* of two players; the best you can manage is to be the *better.*

> ☛ **Teacher's Corner:** The Swinburne verse above may be very pretty, but it's another example of poets being allowed to break the rules:
> *neither is **more** to blame*, please, Algernon!

The Most Worstest Thing You Could Say

As with comparatives, you need only one superlative, so all of these are howlers:

*It is **most nicest**.*
*I think that's the **biggest**.*
*She is the **most wonderfullest** cook.*
*He is the **bestest** player the Tampa Bay Rays ever signed.*
*He is the **most best** teacher we've ever had.*

AND NOW WE'LL MOVE ON (OR, CONJUNCTIONS)

Conjunctions are joining words; they are used when we want to join two words, phrases, clauses, or sentences together.

*Friend **or** foe*   *Sad **but** true*
*Old **and** wise*   *Rich **though** poor*

And Now We'll Move On

There are four kinds of conjunctions: **coordinating**, **subordinating, correlative,** and **compound**.

Coordinating conjunctions join sentences (or parts of sentences) of equal importance. They can be remembered by the mnemonic **FANBOYS**:

For
And
Nor
But
Or
Yet
So

I like cats. She likes dogs.

*I like cats **and** she likes dogs.*	I'm doing no more than stating a fact here.
*I like cats **but** she likes dogs.*	…which is perhaps a bit of a shame.
*I like cats **so** she likes dogs.*	She is doing it on purpose, just to be contrary.

When a coordinating conjunction connects two independent clauses, it is often accompanied by a comma: *Should we run through that again, **or** can it wait until tomorrow?* The comma performs no real grammatical function, it simply suggests that you pause for breath. Which is a large part of a comma's job—see page 136.

Subordinating conjunctions link a main clause and a subordinate clause:

*I feel tired **because** I couldn't sleep last night.*
*I feel tired **although** I slept well last night.*
*I hope **that** I have made enough pizza.*
*I wonder **whether** I have bought enough wine.*

Parts of Speech

> ► **Teacher's Corner:** *Asyndeton* is the joining together of two or more complete sentences without the use of a coordinating conjunction—*I came, I saw, I conquered*—whereas *polysyndeton* is the use of multiple conjunctions, usually where they are not strictly necessary: *His hat **and** book **and** pen **and** pencil.*

Correlative conjunctions are used in conjunction with other conjunctions:
> She owns **not only** an apartment in town **but also** a country house.
> She plays **not only** hockey **but also** lacrosse.
> Bob will grow up to be **either** sporty **or** clever.
> Bob grew up to be **neither** sporty **nor** clever.
> Bob's brother is **both** sporty **and** clever.
> I like **both** beer **and** lager.

Rule: In sentences such as these, decide the position of the conjunction by checking on what follows it. They should be the same construction, whether noun, noun phrase, adjective, clause, or whatever. Consider the difference between these sentences:
> She owns **not only** an apartment in town **but also** a country house.
> She **not only** owns an apartment in town, she **also** rents a villa in Tuscany.
> **Not only** does she own an apartment in town, but her parents **also** have a country house.

In each case, the words following *also* balance the words following *not only*. And if you are remotely interested, see the bit about coordination on page 100.

Compound conjunctions is a fancy term for conjunctions made up of several words, often ending with *as* or *that*:

*I don't mind family Christmases **as long as** I am allowed to come home for New Year's Eve.*

*We can go **as soon as** you decide what to wear.*

*He built a shed at the bottom of the garden **so that** he would have somewhere to keep his ferrets.*

A Word on *While* and *Although*

Although some grammarians argue that using *while* in the same way as *although* is perfectly acceptable, there are times when this can lead to confusion, miscommunication, and other bad things that grammar rules strive to avoid.

While she was writing, her pencil broke.	No problem here: her pencil broke at the same time as she was writing.
While I like tea, I would prefer gin.	Fine, but *although* would work equally well in place of *while*.
While Cyprus is hot, you can ski.	You're unlikely to misunderstand this, but replacing *while* with *although* would remove any possibility of ambiguity.
While Sally plays the triangle, Judy sings.	Aha. Now we have genuine ambiguity. Does Sally accompany Judy's singing, or is Judy's specialty singing and Sally's playing the triangle? If the latter, use *although*.

Parts of Speech

> ☛ **See Me after Class:** *While Father was away, Mother seemed to have a lot of fun.* Meaning?

A Bit of Coordination

Some conjunctions have a **coordinating** role between two parts of a sentence, and positioning them correctly can be something of a minefield. Let's start with *both*. *Both* goes directly before the first word of the two to which it refers. So in the sentence *I was **both** unhappy with your work and your time keeping*, the word *both* suggests that there is more than one person involved—which there can't be because there is only *I*.

The correct versions of this sentence are either:

*We were **both** unhappy with your work and your time keeping.*	I and whoever else makes up the *both* were unhappy with two things: your work and your time keeping

or

*I was **both** unhappy with your work and disappointed in your time keeping.*	I experienced two emotions

or

*I was unhappy with **both** your work and your time keeping.*	I was unhappy with two things

The same rule applies in sentences offering a choice of *either/or*.

Not *They had **either** decided to make an offer for the house in the suburbs or the apartment in town;*

nor *They had decided **either** to make an offer for the house in the suburbs **or** the apartment in town*;

but *They had decided to make an offer for **either** the house in the suburbs **or** the apartment in town*;

or *They had decided **either** to make an offer for the house in the suburbs **or** to pay the asking price for the apartment in town.*

IT'S BEHIND YOU!
(OR, PREPOSITIONS)

The word *preposition* means "something that is placed before." **Prepositions** are usually placed before nouns or pronouns. It's their job to show where one thing is in position to another; for example, *The cat is **on** the mat, I was **in front of** you*. Expressions such as *in front of, out of* and the like, made up of more than one word, are known (to the in-crowd) as **complex prepositions**.

If you are unsure what a preposition is, you might like to employ the following sentence:

The squirrel ran ———— the tree.

All you have to do is fill in the missing word. Almost any word you choose will be a preposition. For example:

to	*down*	*under*	*near*
by	*up*	*off*	*along*
around	*past*	*in*	*through*
for	*across*	*behind*	*in front of*
through	*over*	*from*	*out of*

Even *at, with*, and *after* would fit—if this particular squirrel is suicidal or we're in some sort of dream sequence. Others, such as *of, between*, and *before*, do not fit at all here, but you get the point.

Parts of Speech

For non-native speakers prepositions can be tricky. *I get **down off** the bus* tells us exactly what the person is doing, but most native speakers would make do with *I get **off** the bus*. However, even native speakers often think that two prepositions are better than one:

*I get **off of** the bus.* ☒ What's that *of* doing there?

*Put that **back down** on the table.* ☒

*I took a day **off from** work.* ☒

Sometimes even one is too many:
*Where did he go **to**?*
*She admitted **to** her mistakes.*
*All **of** the people present at the rally protested peacefully.*
*I'm going **down** south.*

> ✋ **Smart Aleck:** The use of more words than are necessary is *pleonasm* or *prolixity*.

Let's Not Ask for the Moon

Many prepositions are firmly wedded to other words:

*I **approve of** his choice. They're **discriminating against** us.*

However, others are more loosely connected:

*When I want your opinion I'll **ask for** it*	…but I might **ask after** your health.
*They've **taken in** everything you said to them*	…but she's **taken off** everything except her feather boa.
*You are **good at** what you do*	…which is better than being **good for** nothing.

It's behind You!

absorbed in/by
*I was **absorbed in** my book.*
*All of a sudden I was **absorbed by** a giant sponge.*

agree with/approve of
*I **agree with** your ideas.*
*But I don't **approve of** children being taught grammar.*

aim at/to/for
***Aim at** that target.*
***Aim to** arrive at work before lunchtime.*
***Aim for** Paris and try to fly in a straight line.*

among/between
*I put the cat **among** the (many) pigeons with my thoughtless comment.*
*I placed a pigeon **between** my two cats to see what would happen.*

bored of
Wrong. We should be bored by or bored with something or somebody.

center around/on
How can something center around something else? Presumably it would need to center around another center. Something centers on something—or is based on it.

compare with/to
*You can't **compare** my feet **to** an elephant's: they are too dissimilar to be compared.*
***Compared with** an elephant's, my feet look dainty.*

Parts of Speech

different to/from

Many books claim that *different from* is preferable to *different to* without explaining why. However, Fowler's *Modern English Usage* says "that *different* can only be followed by *from* & not by *to* is a SUPERSTITION. Not only is *to* 'found in writers of all ages' (OED); the principle on which it is rejected (You do not say differ to; therefore you cannot say different to) involves a hasty & ill-defined generalization." All of which is a long-winded way of saying that you can say *different to* if you like.

made of/made from

This one is a bit persnickety, but something is made *from* something that has been transformed; it is made *of* something that is still visible or recognizable:

*This ice cream is **made from** raspberries.*	So if you don't like raspberries, have the chocolate mousse instead.
*This pavlova is **made of** raspberries, cream, and meringue.*	So if you don't like raspberries, you can pick them out, and I'll eat them.

✋ Smart Aleck:

Why does your house burn up as it burns down?
How come you have to fill in a form to fill out a form?
Why can you see stars out but not lights out?

Get Us Out from under This

> "May I end this sentence with a preposition?"
> —Pickup line

Rule: It is wrong to end a sentence with a preposition. This seems to be a rule for a rule's sake. In fact, ending a sentence with a preposition rarely hinders its meaning and often sounds more natural, certainly in speech. Compare:

That's the office in which I work.	*That's the office I work in.*
The choir shown on Songs of Praise *is the one with which I sing.*	*The choir shown on* Songs of Praise *is the one I sing with.*
About what the heck are you talking?	*What the heck are you talking about?*

> "This is the sort of English up with which I will not put."
> —Attributed to Winston Churchill

Parts of Speech

Ha-Ha

Suffering from impotence, a man visits several doctors asking for help, all to no avail. Finally, out of desperation, he visits an herbalist. The herbalist gives him a potion that can only be used once a year and tells him to take it before he is ready to be intimate. Then, when the time is right, he should say "one, two, three" and his impotence will be cured for as long as he likes. The man asks, "How do I make the potion stop working?" "Oh, that's easy," the doctor replies, "You just say, 'one, two, three, four.'" That evening before he enters the house, the man drinks the potion. He surprises his wife by immediately leading her to the bedroom. Things are going well and the man whispers, "One, two, three." His wife gives him a funny look and asks, "What'd you say 'one, two, three' for?" And **that** is why you never end a sentence with a preposition!

HOLY MOLY!
(OR, INTERJECTIONS)

An **interjection**—often followed by an exclamation mark—is used to show emotion. It is not grammatically linked to other parts of a sentence.

Bah! Darn! Eek! Good Lord! God bless you! Heavens! Yikes! Hey! Ouch! Oh no! No way! Nonsense! D'oh!

Well, that was easy, wasn't it? We're not even going to bother to say, "Don't overdo exclamation marks!" at this stage, because there'll be plenty of that when we get to punctuation (see page 145).

3
Sentence Structure

Do I Get Time Off for Good Behavior? (or, Sentences)

> "A perfectly healthy sentence, it is true, is extremely rare.
> For the most part we miss the hue and fragrance
> of the thought; as if we could be satisfied
> with the dews of the morning without their colors,
> or the heavens without their azure."
> —Henry David Thoreau

According to the dictionary, a **sentence** is "a sequence of words capable of standing alone to make an assertion, ask a question or give a command." All sentences…

1. Have a subject and a predicate (see page 111)
2. Begin with a capital letter
3. End in a period, a question mark, or an exclamation mark

There are various types of sentences, depending on how complicated they are:

A **simple sentence** consists of a single main clause or statement (we'll come back to what a clause is shortly—see page 125): *I like pink roses,* or *You prefer white roses.*

A **compound sentence** consists of two or more main clauses: *I like pink roses best, but I expect you'll choose white ones.*

Sentence Structure

Complex sentences have main clauses and subordinate clauses:

The roses, when they finally arrived, were yellow.

Really complex sentences (or **compound-complex sentences**, if we're going to be technical) have clauses coming out of their ears and often get a bit carried away with themselves: *The roses, which you say you ordered several days ago, didn't arrive until this morning, and were yellow, not pink or white by the way, so the bride is not happy.*

> 🖐 **Smart Aleck:** The longest sentence in English literature is spoken by Molly Bloom in James Joyce's *Ulysses*. It contains 4,391 words, which makes it far too long to be quoted here.

Fragments

Complete sentences need a subject and a verb. Without these, they are known as **fragments**.

That wretched dress.
Waiting in the mall for her prescription.
Never in agreement about anything.

Fragments need the context of other sentences in order to convey their meaning:

I had an awful time at the party. Sally again. Going on and on about having worn the same dress as that new actress. That wretched dress.

I saw Sally again this morning. Waiting in the mall for her prescription. At least, that's what she was pretending to do. I'm sure she was really watching to see if I bought anything for the weekend.

What Kind of a Sentence Is That?

Many sentences simply make statements. The formal term for this is a declarative sentence. But sentences can also ask questions, give instructions or make exclamations:

A **declarative sentence:** *I saw you copying the files.*
An **interrogative sentence:** *Did you copy the files?*
An **imperative sentence:** *Don't even think of copying the files.*
An **exclamatory sentence:** *I repeat, I did not copy the files!*

Note, by the way, that an imperative sentence doesn't need a subject. In this instance the pronoun *you* is clearly implied.

Imperatives don't have to be bossy, just gently persuasive—which is probably why advertisers love them:

Just do it.
Let your fingers do the walking.
Don't *leave home without it.*

SUBJECT-VERB-OBJECT

Here's a simple sentence: *I wrote a simple sentence.* It is made up of a subject, a verb, and an object. We know about verbs, so we can probably tell that in the above sentence the verb is *wrote*. The rest of the sentence consists of a subject and an object...

Rule 1: The **subject** is the person or thing carrying out the action in a sentence. (In this case *I*. Who wrote the simple sentence? I did.) The **object** is on the receiving end of the action. It is the thing being done to. (In this case, *a simple sentence*. What did I write? A simple sentence.) To determine the subject of a sentence, first find the **verb** and then ask *who?* or *what?* is doing the action. The answer will be the subject.

Sentence Structure

Rule 2: In a straightforward English sentence the subject will come first, the verb second, and the object third. (Grammarians refer to this as SVO.)

Subject	**Verb**	**Object**
Simple Simon	*met*	*a pieman*
Mary	*had*	*a little lamb*
Little Bo Peep	*has lost*	*her sheep*

Another useful piece of terminology here is the **predicate**. This is the verb and the object (or indirect object, or anything else that isn't the subject) considered together. So, in the above examples, *met a pieman, had a little lamb* and *has lost her sheep* are all predicates. So are *sat on a wall, jumped over the moon, sat on a tuffet* and *went up the hill to fetch a pail of water*. Who would have thought that nursery rhymes could prove so useful?

"Proper words in proper places
make the true definition of a style."
—Jonathan Swift, *Letter to a Young Clergyman*

*

"I have the words already. What I am seeking is the
perfect order of words in the sentence.
You can see for yourself how many different ways
they might be arranged."
—James Joyce

Breaking the Subject-Verb-Object (SVO) Rule

The SVO rule can be broken for emphasis or stylistic effect:

> *John I can convince* ...but James would never let me get away with such nonsense.
>
> *Chicken I can live without* ...though I am rather partial to duck.

It's also broken with questions, when the verb commonly precedes the subject: *Who was that lady I saw you with last night?*

Direct and Indirect Objects

So far, so good. In some sentences, however, there is more than one object—a direct one and an indirect one.

Take this sentence: *My boss paid me a bonus.*

If you have been paying attention so far, you know that *my boss* is the subject of the verb *paid*. But now you have to ask:

What did the boss pay?	*He paid a **bonus***	**direct object**
To ***whom*** did he pay it?	*To **me***	**indirect object**

Hang on, you may say, how about *The boss paid me?* Doesn't that make *me* the direct object? Well, no. The test here is to see if you can rework the sentence to put a preposition in front of the object. If you can, it's an indirect object. You could easily rephrase the above example to become *My boss paid a bonus to me.* Clumsy, perhaps, but it makes sense (and it would be absolutely fine if you wanted to say *My boss paid a bonus to everyone in my department*).

Don't trip up on a sentence that begins with *there* and a form of the verb *to be*. *There* is not the subject in this case: *there were lots of people out for a walk today.* To find the correct subject, ask *who?* or *what?* before the verb. *Who was out for a walk today?* Answer: *lots of people.*

The Exception: It Would Be, Wouldn't It?

The exception to the subject-verb-object rule concerns—guess what—the verb *to be*. It doesn't take an object, it takes a **complement**. *To be,* and verbs used in a similar way, such as *to become, to seem, to taste* are called **copulative verbs** (honestly, they are—look it up in the dictionary yourself if you don't believe us)—they express a state rather than performing an action. So in sentences such as:

> *I am a New Yorker*
> *You became an artist*
> *He seems respectable enough*
> *The chocolates tasted of arsenic*

the words after the verb are the complement, and they may be nouns, pronouns, adjectives or adverbs, or phrases serving the same purpose (in the above example, *of arsenic* is an adverbial phrase qualifying the verb *tasted*).

On the Subject of I and the Object of Me (or, Subject and Object)

Unlike Latin, English nouns don't bother much with cases (different endings to show their relationship with other words in the sentence) because we express that sort of thing with prepositions (see page 101) and word order. In Latin a noun would have a different ending depending on whether it was the **subject** or the **object** of the verb, and if you wanted to say *to the noun* or *of the noun*, the endings would be different again. Then you could put the words in pretty much any order you liked and the endings would sort the meaning out for you. But English sentences such as *the dog chased the cat* and *the cat chased the dog* have exactly the same words in them and it is the order that establishes the meaning.

Pronouns don't follow this no-change rule. They do their own thing. Or their own thing is done to them.

Rule: I = subject
           me = object

I is used for the subject of a sentence—the person doing the action.

Me is used for the object of the sentence—the person the verb is acting upon.

> Not *Me telephoned Jim* but *I telephoned Jim*.   Because I performed the action.
>
> Not *Jim rang I back* but *Jim rang me back*.   Because Jim performed the action.

Sentence Structure

Similarly: he/she/it/they = subject
him/her/it/them = object

Not *I adore he*	He is the *object* of my
but *I adore him*.	affection.
Not *Them were responsible*	They *subjected* us to the
but *They were responsible*.	horror.

This rule applies, but may be less obvious, when you have a **compound subject** or a **compound object**—that is, a subject or object that consists of more than one noun or pronoun.

*John and **I** (compound subject) went fishing.*

*He gave the bait to John (or **him**) and **me** (compound object).*

*My husband and **I** (compound subject) are both going to the wedding.*

*The groom has invited my husband (or **him**) and **me** (compound object) to the wedding.*

Hint: If you are unsure whether to use *I* or *me*, or *he* or *him*, in a compound subject or object, take out the other part. If you omit your husband from the last two examples you are left with:

I am going to the wedding (OK, you've had to change the verb from *are* to *am* because there's only one person involved now, but that's not the point here).

The groom has invited me to the wedding.

On the Subject of I and the Object of Me

What's Wrong with Songwriters?

Beach Boys: *"My buddies and me are gettin' real well known…"*

The Beatles: *"Take a good look, you're bound to see that you and me were meant to be for each other…"*

Rule: The rules don't apply to songwriters. But surely they can't get no satisfaction from their writing.

Who Goes There? I or Me?

*It is **I** or It is **me**?*
*It wasn't **I** who said it or It wasn't **me** who said it?*
*It is **I** who am at fault or It is **me** who is at fault?*

"'Somebody's sharp.' 'Who is?' asked the gentleman, laughing. I looked up quickly, being curious to know. 'Only Brooks of Sheffield,' said Mr. Murdstone. I was relieved to find that it was only Brooks of Sheffield; for, at first, I really thought it was I."
—Charles Dickens, *David Copperfield*

Traditionally, *It is I* is correct, because Latin rules state that subject forms are found after the verb *to be*. However, modern thinking is that this sounds rather pretentious and old-fashioned. Most people will not bat an eyelid if you say *It was me*.

Sentence Structure

If that isn't good enough for you, try avoiding the issue by rephrasing:

He can't run as fast as me (or *I*) becomes

*He can't run as fast as I **can**.*

He's earning more than her (or *she*) becomes

*He's earning more than she **is**.*

Or, if you aren't happy with that, just decide which way you are going to go and stick to it. This sentence—heard on a radio news bulletin recently—fails on every count: *It was he who fired the gun and it was him who was killed.*

"Heedless of grammar, they all cried, 'That's him!'"
—Rev. R. H. Barham, *A Lay of Saint Gengulphus*

Between You and I

Here's the **I-me error** creeping in again. Lots of people are anxious about using *me*. But—between you and me—it is wrong to say *between you and I*.

Rule: Always use an object pronoun (*me*) after a preposition (*between*). (See page 101 for a list of prepositions.)

They can't take that away from me…

I've been to paradise but I've never been to me…

It's good night from me, and it's good night from him.

> "Between you and me and the grand piano, I'm afraid my father was rather a bad hat."
> —*The Uninvited* (film), 1944

My Grammar and I (or should that be "me"?)

Few of us will have cause to ask (or answer, or give a darn about) this question in real life. However, this book does ask it, so it seems only courteous to try to answer it:

*This book is **about** (preposition) my grammar and **me** (object pronoun).*

***My grammar** (subject) and **I** (subject pronoun) are not on good terms.*

In a book title, we think it is safe to assume that *Grammar and I* form a compound subject (see page 116).

Remember Your Manners

If you are talking about yourself and another person, it is polite to mention the other person first.

Wishing you both great happiness from me and Gary. ☒
Wishing you both great happiness from Gary and me. ☑

I and my wife would like to thank everyone for coming. ☒
My wife and I would like to thank everyone for coming. ☑

But there's no need to be too humble:

With lots of love from the children, the dog and me...

Nor too full of oneself:

*James and **myself** went fishing.*
*James and **I** went fishing* will do very well.

Sentence Structure

On the Subject of Who and the Object of Whom

> "What is fame? The advantage of being known by
> people of whom you yourself know nothing,
> and for whom you care as little."
> —Lord Byron
>
> *
>
> "As far as I'm concerned,
> *whom* is a word that was invented
> to make everyone sound like a butler."
> —Calvin Trillin

Rule 1:   who = subject
                whom = object

*This is the woman **who** swallowed a fly.*	The woman swallowed the fly. The woman is the subject of the verb.
*This is the woman **whom** the fly choked.*	The fly choked the woman. She is now the object of the verb.

Rule 2: As with other pronouns, the object form is used after a preposition (see page 101):

*The people **to whom** I spoke didn't seem to know anything about it.*

*That boy **above whom** we all towered when we were at school is taller than any of us now.*

*Send not to ask **for whom** the bell tolls.*

DON'T YOU AGREE? (OR, AGREEMENT)

Rule: Parts of a sentence must agree with each other. A singular subject takes a singular verb, while a plural subject takes a plural verb.

*I **was born** in a caravan.*
***She is** only a bird in a gilded cage.*
*What **were we** talking about?*
***They don't** make them like that any more.*

Straightforward enough? Less obvious, perhaps, are:

*He is one of those **men** **who sing** in the shower.*	*Those men*, plural, are the subject of the verb *sing*.
*A **person knows** when **he/she is** being rude.*	Many people nowadays would say, *A person **knows** when they are being rude.* Perhaps better to avoid the issue by saying, *People **know** when **they are** being rude* instead.

And what about:

*My brother **and** his girlfriend (two people) **have** taken the spare room.*

*It sounds as if my brother **or** his girlfriend (one or the other but not both) **has** used all the hot water.*

Rule: Use a plural verb with two or more subjects when they are connected by *and*. Two singular subjects connected by *or* or *nor* take the singular form of the verb.

Sentence Structure

And another rule: *Either* and *neither* are both singular. ***Neither of them has*** *thought about my needing to wash.* ***Either he*** *or* ***she is*** *bathing last tomorrow, if I have any say in the matter.*

Along Came a Distraction

Sometimes an expression may creep between a subject and its verb. Don't let this lead you astray.

The nanny*, along with the cook and the housekeeper,* ***has*** *caught chicken pox from the children.*

Poisoning*, as well as the shock of the bite,* ***was*** *the cause of death.*

My husband*, with our neighbor and his dog,* ***is*** *walking the coastal path.*

We'll have a closer look at those parenthetical commas in the next chapter, but for the moment just note that they are precisely that—a parenthesis or bracket—and everything between them could be lifted out of the sentence without altering the grammatical relationship between the subject and the verb.

> ☞ **See Me after Class:**
> ***Each*** *of the boys* ***were*** *good at grammar.*
> Were he indeed?
> ***Every*** *cat* ***have their*** *own bowl.*
> No: ***every cat*** **has its** *own bowl.*
> Just as ***every cat*** **has** *a tail.*
>
> Useful mnemonic: think of these words as *each one* and *every one*, and you'll remember to use a singular verb and a singular pronoun.

Rule: The following words are singular and require singular verbs:

anybody	*every*	*one*
anyone	*everybody*	*somebody*
each	*everyone*	*someone*

However, *any*, *all*, *most*, and *some* can be either singular or plural. It depends whether they are being applied to countable or non-countable nouns (see page 47).

*All of the petty cash **has** been stolen.*
*All of the suspects **have** gone to the pub together.*
*Some of their discarded kebabs **have** been discovered.*
*Some of the money **has** been found.*
*Most of it **is** still missing.*
*Most of the culprits **are** nursing hangovers.*

Rule: *Many, both, a few,* and *several* are always followed by a plural verb.

I've Got Your Number

Numerical expressions can be rather tricky, but just remember that the expression *the number* is singular, which means it should be followed by a singular verb:

*The number **is** 6.*
*The number in question **is** 666.*
*The number of people unaccounted for **is** 6,000.*
*The number of people who died **was** 60,000.*

Exception: *A number of* is used with plural nouns and takes a plural verb:

*A number of people **were** in shock after the incident.*

Numerical expressions, however, take either the singular or plural

Sentence Structure

form of the verb, according to whether they are being referred to as a single entity or as individuals within a group.

*A million dollars **is** a lot of money.*
*A million homes **are** reported to be without power today.*
***Two** years **is** a long time to wait.*
*The **two** years since I saw you **have** dragged by.*
***Half** the people at the party **have** food poisoning.*
***The remainder** of the guests **are** still enjoying the party.*

And Then There Was None...

You're likely to come across conflicting views on this one. Many people believe that *none* is a contraction of *not one*, and therefore should always take the singular verb. *None* may also mean *not any*, however, in which case it takes a plural verb.

Rule: *None* is singular only when it means *no amount*. If you mean *not one* you could always say *not one*, particularly if you want to add emphasis.

***None** of the wine **was** left in the bottle.*
***None** of the drinks **are** paid for.*
***None** of the food **is** fresh.*
***None** of the people **are** well.*

How Many Objects Exactly?

Another common area of confusion between singular and plural comes in sentences such as:

Many men cheat on their wife/wives?
The boys put their hands on their head/s?

Are we talking about bigamists as well as adulterers here? Or a number of men sharing a single wife? Many-headed boys? Or boys sharing a single head?

[124]

Rule: The two elements should agree. ***Men***, plural, even monogamous ones, *have **wives***, plural. ***Boys***, even non-freaky ones, *have **heads***.

Or you can write the sentences differently and duck the issue:
Many a man cheats on his wife.
Each boy put his hands on his head.

FROM MAJOR TO MINOR (OR, CLAUSES)

A **clause** is a sentencelike construction with a subject and predicate, including a finite verb (see pages 72 and 123 for an explanation of those things). Some clauses, but by no means all, stand alone as sentences. A clause that can stand alone as a sentence is known as the **main clause**; anything else is a **subordinate clause**.

I can't play the piano as well as my sister, even though I practice more than she does.

I can't play the piano as well as my sister is a perfectly good sentence on its own. It has a subject (*I*) and a finite verb (*play*) and makes a complete statement. *Even though I practice more than she does* is not. It has a subject (*I*) and a finite verb (*practice*), but it depends on the first clause (*I can't play the piano as well as my sister*) to become a complete statement.

But it's perfectly possible for a sentence to have two main clauses, in which case they are called **coordinating clauses** and are usually linked by *and, but,* or *or*:

*I'm going to play the piece by Mozart, **and** she will play the piece by Chopin.*

Sentence Structure

*I wanted to play the Chopin, **but** she had first choice.*
*I might play in the concert, **or** I might decide to go to a bar instead.*

In all these examples either of the two clauses can stand alone.

As its name suggests, a **subordinate clause** carries information that is of secondary importance to that contained in the main clause.

A subordinate clause often begins with a subordinate conjunction such as *after, although, as, because, though, if, in order to, rather than, since, so that, unless,* and so on.

*Unfortunately I won't be playing, **because I've broken my finger**.*
*She won the role, **although nobody thought she had a chance**.*

Or it may begin a relative pronoun (*that, which, whichever, who, whoever, whom, whose, whosoever, whomever*), in which case it is called a **relative clause**.

*I used to know the spy **who came in from the cold**.*
*I used to know the spy **whom the Russians codenamed Smirnoff**.*
*I will claim to have known **whichever of the spies you bring into the conversation**.*

Which Is That?

Restrictive clauses (also sometimes called **defining clauses**) define or classify a noun or pronoun in the main clause. **Non-restrictive** or **non-defining clauses** offer further description. A non-restrictive clause is usually preceded by a pause in speech or a comma in writing, whereas a restrictive clause is not. A non-restrictive clause is also usually *followed* by a pause or a comma, if it does not end the sentence.

Rule: Non-restrictive clauses are dispensable. Their role is merely to give additional information.

Sorry, have we lost you? Let's look at some examples. Although the following sentences make grammatical sense without their subordinate clauses, they do not convey much information—the restrictive clause is essential.

*The man **that died on the trip** was once my history teacher.*
*The car **that broke down** is now in the garage.*
*You look like the cat **that got the canary**.*

Take out that clause and you are left with:

The man was once my history teacher.	Which man? Why are you telling me this? Why should I care?
The car is now in the garage.	Again, which car? So what?
You look like the cat.	Duh? I think you'll find I don't have whiskers or a tail.

On the other hand,

*The history teacher, **who had a trusty aim with the eraser**, ensured that we never forgot important dates.*
*The car, **which broke down halfway through France**, had to be towed back to England.*
*My new cat, **which somehow jumped on the counter and ate the hot dogs last night**, came home with someone's trout today.*

Sentence Structure

You don't feel obliged to ask *Which history teacher?*, *Which car?*, *Which cat?* at the end of these sentences. The information given in the subordinate clause is a bonus.

Now consider the difference between these:

The dogs that barked at night did not recognize the thief.	**Restrictive:** Some of the dogs *did* recognize the thief and therefore did not bark.
The dogs, which barked in the nighttime, did not recognize the thief.	**Non-restrictive:** None of the dogs recognized the thief and all of them barked.

Or

I cut down all the trees that were evergreen.	**Restrictive:** Some of them were deciduous and I left them alone.
I cut down all the trees, which were evergreen.	**Non-restrictive:** I've destroyed the entire forest and, by the way, all the trees were evergreen.

In both cases illustrated above, restrictive clauses are introduced by that. Non-restrictive clauses are introduced by the relative pronouns *who, whom, whose,* and *which,* but never by *that.*

It boils down to this: if you can tell what is being discussed without the *which* or *that* clause, use *which*; if you can't, use *that*. Or, as a rule of thumb, if the phrase needs a comma, you probably should use *which*.

> ### Is It Which or That?
> Grammarians are divided over whether *which* or *that* should be used in restrictive clauses. While researching this book, we came across all of the following in apparently respectable sources:
>
> > "Many grammarians insist on a distinction without any historical justification."
> >
> > "*Which* and *that* are equally acceptable in restrictive relative clauses; *that* is perhaps the less formal of the two."
> >
> > "Don't mix *which* clauses with *that* clauses."
>
> It boils down to this: if you can tell what is being discussed without the *which* or *that* clause, use *which*; if you can't, use *that*. Or, as a rule of thumb, if the phrase needs a comma, you probably mean *which*.
>
> A paradoxical mnemonic: use *that* to tell which, and *which* to tell that.

HOW DO YOU PHRASE THAT? (OR, PHRASES)

A **phrase** is a group of words that has either no subject or no predicate, meaning it cannot form a complete sentence on its own. You can have verb phrases (*may sink in gradually*), noun phrases (*grammatical rules*), and adjectival phrases (*even the most complicated*) but until you put them all together (*even the most complicated grammatical rules may sink in gradually*), you don't have a sentence.

Sentence Structure

Actually there are lots of other kinds of phrases, too:

Participial phrases: *Having to get up in the morning is the worst part of my day.*

Infinitive phrases: *My ambition is to retire by the time I am fifty.*

Adverbial phrases: *I work a long way away, so I need to leave home before my wife.*

Prepositional phrases: *I would love to be able to stay in bed.*

But you don't really have to worry about these technical terms—as long as you remember *to set the alarm*.

4
Punctuation

PUNCTUATION: THE VIRTUE OF THE BORED?

Author Evelyn Waugh once said that *punctuality* was the virtue of the bored, but he doesn't seem to have said anything witty about punctuation, so we thought we'd just paraphrase him in the title above.

Punctuation can be defined as "the act, practice, or system of using certain standardized marks and signs in writing and printing," and punctuation marks are symbols that are used in sentences and phrases to make their meaning clearer. Those most commonly used in English are the period (.), comma (,), question mark (?), exclamation point (!), semi-colon (;), colon (:), apostrophe ('), and quotation marks (" ").

Cecil Hartley's poem from *Principles of Punctuation* or *The Art of Pointing* (1818) reveals the old-fashioned way that people were advised on how to interpret punctuation when reading sentences out loud.

> The stops point out, with truth, the time of pause
> A sentence doth require at ev'ry clause.
> At ev'ry comma, stop while *one* you count;
> A semicolon, *two* is the amount;
> A colon doth require the time of *three*;
> The period *four*, as learned men agree.

Punctuation

Though it's not a verse that most grammarians would encourage these days, it does give you an idea of the difference between the most common punctuation marks.

> ☛ **Teacher's Corner:** Punctuation existed in Greek texts from at least the fourth century B.C., although Greek and Latin scribes rarely used more than two marks, the equivalent of the period and the comma.

STOP! (OR, PERIODS)

The **period** is the strongest mark of punctuation. It shows its muscle by telling us we need to make a definite pause at the end of a sentence, giving us time to gather our breath or our thoughts, before moving on to the next sentence. Ignore the pause and sentences run together: meaning becomes confused. Periods are also used in (some) abbreviations (see below). They are not used:

- when we end a sentence with another punctuation mark, a question mark or an exclamation point, for example. *Understand? Of course you do!*
- if a sentence ends with an abbreviation. In this case, the period indicating the abbreviation does the job of two: *I have to go out at 9:00 P.M.*

From the Long to the Short of It

An **abbreviation** (from Latin *brevis*, meaning *short*) is a shortened form of a word or phrase that for whatever reason we do not choose

Stop!

to write out in full. Strictly speaking, an abbreviation is a word or words with the end(s) left off (*Prof., vol., CD, VP*), whereas one where something is left out of the middle (*Mr., Dr.*) is a **contraction**, but most people use *abbreviation* indiscriminately to cover both. If an abbreviation of several words forms something that is pronounced as a word in itself (*UNESCO, radar, scuba, AIDS*), this is an **acronym**.

Unlike British English, American English uses the period after contractions such as *Mr., Mrs.,* and *Dr.* Both, however, still use the period for *No., A.M., and P.M.*

A number of common words such as *cello, flu,* and *phone* are actually abbreviations or clipped forms (of *violoncello, influenza,* and *telephone*) and would once have been written with an apostrophe (or two): *'cello, 'flu', 'phone*. Some people still do this, but most would say it was old-fashioned. Some shortenings have become so accepted that to use the long form of the word would sound pompous:

> *Jane will not be at work today because she thinks she might have* **influenza**.
>
> *Tim works out at the* **gymnasium** *every day and then catches the* **omnibu***s home.*

On the other hand, *stache* instead of *moustache, doc* instead of *doctor,* or *gator* instead of *alligator* may be too casual for formal writing.

> ✋ **Smart Aleck:** How come the word *abbreviation* is so long?

Punctuation

TAKE A DEEP BREATH (OR, COMMAS)

> "For want of merely a comma, it often occurs
> that an axiom appears a paradox."
> —Edgar Allan Poe, *"Marginalia"* (1848)

Historically, the **comma** marks a short pause, a place where you might pause for breath after reading a fragment of text aloud. In grammar, the comma is used to facilitate meaning by separating the different elements of a sentence. Some people are comma-happy; they put commas anywhere and everywhere:

Dear Professor Purvis, [comma, pause for breath]
Please may I have an extra, short, extension on my very late,
and, at this point in time, largely unfinished, English
dissertation?

Other people prefer to leave them out altogether:

Dear Professor Purvis
Please may I have an extra short extension on my very late
and at this point in time largely unfinished English
dissertation?

In the first example, there are so many pauses that it takes forever to get to the point. In the second, with no pauses at all, we risk losing the plot. How should we interpret *an extra short extension?* Is it *an extra, short extension* (that is, a short extension in addition to the longer extension already granted) or *an extra-short extension* (an extremely short one, much shorter than the sort of extension that would usually be requested)? Just a smattering of punctuation would have helped here.

> ### Ha-Ha
> My apologies for using this terribly old joke, but it illustrates the point.
>
> A college professor wrote on his blackboard: *a woman without her man is nothing.* He then asked his students to punctuate the sentence. All of the males in the class wrote: *a woman, without her man, is nothing.* All of the females in the class wrote: *a woman: without her, man is nothing.*

So Where Does a Comma Go?

We spent most of our time sitting on the back porch watching the cows playing Scrabble and reading.

A comma can go in lots of places. Here are seventeen examples:

1. At a place in a sentence where you wish your readers to pause:

    Take a breather, will you?

2. After introductory words or phrases that come before the main clause:

    In the autumn of 1066, the English lost the Battle of Hastings.
    Once upon a time, there lived a boy called Jack.
    Of course, .../However, .../Finally, .../Yes, ...

3. Between separate clauses within a sentence:

   In the beginning, when God created the universe, the earth was formless and desolate.

4. Before direct speech:

   He asked, "Can you tell me why I should pay attention to these rules?"

5. In addresses and place names where one part of the place name gives further information about the other:

   The White House, 1600 Pennsylvania Ave., Washington, D.C.

   The President was assassinated by a gunman in Dallas, Texas (as opposed to any other Dallas).

6. On either side of parenthetical phrases or clauses (those non-restrictive parts that contain extraneous information; see page 139). These are known as paired or parenthetical commas, so there must always be two of them:

   She backed up into the traffic barrier, which she could have sworn was not there an hour before, causing considerable damage to her car.

   One day in the near future, if we can believe what scientists tell us, this planet will run out of oxygen.

7. After items in a list:

   My favorite Victorian novelists are the Brontë sisters, Wilkie Collins, Charles Dickens, and Thomas Hardy.

8. In large numbers. In numbers of more than three digits, use a comma after every third digit (reading

from right to left):

I make that 6,000 people.

20,000 leagues under the sea.

The population of Argentina is 34,663,000.

But note that in scientific texts and particularly in tables of figures the comma is sometimes replaced by a space: *6 000, 20 000, 34 663 000.*

9. Around a non-restrictive clause. Be careful with commas here. They change what you mean to say:

I pulled up all the flowers that looked like weeds.	**Restrictive:** I pulled up only the flowers that looked like weeds.
I pulled up all the flowers, which looked like weeds.	**Non-restrictive:** I heartlessly tore all the flowers out of the ground; they also looked like weeds.

10. Before and after an appositive (that's a word or phrase that defines or modifies a noun or pronoun that comes before it):

I, Jane Jones, declare that I was at home on the evening of September 25.

Chérie Blair, wife of former Prime Minister Tony Blair, was accused of not liking cats.

And again, note the difference between:

My upstairs neighbor Bill plays loud music.	There could also be an upstairs neighbor called Ben, for all we know.
My upstairs neighbor, Bill, plays loud music.	Bill is the only upstairs neighbor.

Punctuation

11. Between a dependent clause and an independent clause, where the dependent clause comes first:

    After lunch, my stomach was upset.

    The comma here is optional, but it does indicate (the possibility of) a pause for breath. However, you wouldn't pause for breath in the sentence *My stomach was upset after lunch,* so no comma is necessary.

12. After consecutive adjectives that are equally important in describing a noun:

    In the dreary light of the morning, the rows of gray, pebble-dashed houses, with their unkempt, litter-strewn gardens, failed to inspire tender thoughts of home.

13. In front of conjunctions such as *like, although, but, or, so, and* and *yet* when they are used to link two independent clauses:

    The show was over, but the crowd refused to leave.
    It's going to be a long night, so let's get those coffees in.

14. In place of a word that has been deliberately omitted:

    The room was cold, the bed hard.

15. Before the word *too* when it means *also*:

    Two pairs of ballet shoes and two tutus, too.

    Parenthetical commas can also add emphasis to the word *too* if it appears in the middle of a sentence:

    He'd never really thought about where to put commas in a sentence, but then, too, he'd never thought much about punctuation at all.

16. To emphasize an adverb:

I wrote it down, quickly, which is why I went to the wrong address.

17. After greetings and before closings in letters:

Dear Sir,

Sincerely,

This used to be a hard-and-fast rule, but it is beginning to fall out of favor. Now the hard-and-fast rule is *be consistent:* if you use a comma after *Dear Sir,* use one after *Sincerely,* too.

> ☛ **See Me after Class:** *I find writing English essays really difficult, I'm sure everyone finds that inspiration does not always come instantly, I think you'll find that is so.*
>
> These could be treated as three distinct sentences, separated by periods; or they could be clauses, separated by semicolons. Or, in informal writing, if you wanted to make them sound a bit breathless, you could use dashes. But, sorry, the commas here are just wrong wrong wrong.

Are you feeling tired? Bored? Confused? Let's move on to something more straightforward.

The Serial Comma

The Oxford, Harvard, or serial comma is placed before the final *and, or,* or *nor* in a list of more than two elements. (The names are derived from the Oxford University Press and Harvard University Press, both advocates of this usage.) In British English, it is mostly used to avoid ambiguity, but it is more often used in American English.

He introduced me to Mr. Brown, his teacher and his friend. (He introduced me to one person, Mr. Brown, who happened to be both his teacher and his friend.)

He introduced me to Mr. Brown, his teacher, and his friend. (He introduced me to two people: his unnamed friend and a teacher, whose name was Mr. Brown. Or indeed, if the speaker is particularly grammatically unaware, to three people: Mr. Brown, plus the teacher of either Mr. Brown or the speaker, plus a friend of the teacher, Mr. Brown or the speaker.)

Serial commas are particularly useful if one of the items in a list already contains the word *and*, or in sentences such as this one, where the items of the list are a complicated collection of phrases or clauses. Dick King-Smith's novel *Poppet* contains this perfect example: "He asked beetles and grubs and worms and caterpillars and little lizards and small frogs, and some replied jokily and some replied angrily and some didn't answer."

WHAT IS THIS, THE SPANISH INQUISITION? (OR, QUESTION MARKS)

> 'To whom, then, must I dedicate my wonderful, surprising and interesting adventures? to whom dare I reveal my private opinion of my nearest relations? the secret thoughts of my dearest friends? my own hopes, fears, reflections and dislikes? Nobody!'
> —Frances Burney

Question: When do you use a **question mark**?
Answer: At the end of a direct question.

Well, we'd probably better go into just a little more detail.

Direct questions are things such as:

Where were you when I needed you?
When did you last see your father?
Who's the best team this year?

Indirect questions are things such as:

I wonder who's kissing her now.
I didn't hear what he said.
I know where you are coming from.

These sentences aren't questions, they are statements: *I wonder, I didn't hear, I know,* so they don't need a question mark.

Rule: A direct question needs a ?; an indirect question does not.

Hint: To spot an indirect question, look out for the words *ask* or *wonder,* often followed by *if.*

A question in the form of a statement, known as an **embedded question**, also doesn't require a question mark: *The question whether children learn enough grammar remains to be answered.*

Hint: Look out for the words *whether* or *if*—they often indicate embedded questions.

But *The question is, "Do today's children learn enough grammar?"* The opening words plus the comma have set the scene for direct speech, and the direct speech takes the form of a direct question. So—yes, you've guessed, go to the head of the class—it needs a question mark.

Note: One *asks* a question.
"How much does it cost?" he said. ☒
"How much?" he asked/inquired/questioned. ☑

Rhetorical questions—questions to which we do not expect an answer—are still questions and deserve to end with a question mark: *How much longer must our people endure this injustice?*

Question upon Question

Sometimes a question will be followed with a series of brief questions. When that happens, especially when the brief questions are more or less follow-up questions to the main one, the little questions can begin with a lower-case letter and end with a question mark. Both of the following are correct:

Who is responsible for this? The boy who cheated? The girl who told? Or the teacher who left the answers on her desk?

Who is responsible for this? the boy? Sarah? or Mrs. Dean, who was out smoking a cigarette in the middle of the exam?

But, as so often when there are alternative ways of doing things, you should decide which style you are going to use and use it consistently.

Rule: Do not put a period after a sentence that ends with a question mark. But when a question ends with an abbreviation, end the abbreviation with a period and then add the question mark. *Do you mean 3:00 P.M. or 3:00 A.M.?*

Are You Questioning My Orders?

When a question is really an instruction, use a period instead of a question mark.

Would you take these books back to the library for me?	A polite request. Is it convenient for you to do this?
Would you take back the books as I asked you to do yesterday.	An order. You'd better or else.

Something to Shout About (or, Exclamation Marks)

"Cut out all these exclamation points.
An exclamation point is like laughing at
your own joke."
—F. Scott Fitzgerald, quoted in *Beloved Infidel* (1958)

The **exclamation point** may be used at the end of a sentence in the place of a period, in order to express strong emotion, such as excitement, delight, fear, anger, or surprise.

> *Hey!*   *Watch out!*
> *Boo!*   *Stop!*
> *Woohoo!*   *Run!*
> *Wow!*   *Fire!*
> *Ouch!*   *Detention! Now!*

They may also be used to catch the reader's attention. Compare:

> *Slow workmen in road.*
> *Slow! Workmen in road.*
> *Elephants please stay in your car.*
> *Elephants! Please stay in your car.*

But beware of overkill. Too many exclamation points make writing overheated. There are no real rules about using them, except *Please restrain yourself.* If you overdo it—

I'd love to! Thank you so much for asking! I'll be there in plenty of time! Oh, I'm so excited!

I'll kill you!!!!!!

Get out!!!!!

It tastes disgusting!!!!!

—you lose the impact that a single, well-placed exclamation point might have. A well-written sentence should be able to pack its own punch. Besides which, exclamation points are visually distracting and can get really annoying!!!!

Rule: An exclamation point ends a sentence in place of a period and should be followed by a capital letter.

> ☛ **See Me after Class:**
> *"You won't give me detention, will you?!"*
> *"What is the meaning of this '?!'"*
>
> (**Answer: An interrobang**. In formal writing, don't use a question mark in combination with other marks.)

Two Dots
(or, Colons)

Rule: A **colon** informs the reader that what follows sums up or explains what has come before.

For example, it may be used to link two main clauses, where the second clause explains the first.

She was delighted to have the offer accepted: It was the third time she had bid on the house.

Or to introduce a list of items (or, indeed, an example):

The cake contained ingredients found lying in the back of the kitchen cupboard: flour, baking soda, dried orange peel, sultanas, raisins, brown sugar, nutmeg, cinnamon, and mixed spices. To this, we just added some milk and an egg from the fridge.

You will need: strong footwear, waterproof clothing, a change of clothes, high-energy snacks, a small first-aid kit, a good map, and a flashlight.

Punctuation

SUPERCOMMA TO THE RESCUE (OR, SEMICOLONS)

"There were pears and apples, clustered high in blooming pyramids; there were bunches of grapes, made, in the shopkeepers' benevolence, to dangle from conspicuous hooks, that people's mouths might water gratis as they passed; there were piles of filberts, mossy and brown, recalling, in their fragrance, ancient walks among the woods, and pleasant shufflings ankle deep through withered leaves; there were Norfolk Biffins, squat and swarthy, setting off the yellow of the oranges and lemons, and, in the great compactness of their juicy persons, urgently entreating and beseeching to be carried home in paper bags and eaten after dinner."
—Charles Dickens, *A Christmas Carol*

Now fighting a losing battle against the less elegant dash (see page 150), the **semicolon** connects two or more independent clauses that don't *quite* justify being sentences in their own right. It often replaces *and* or *but*. It may be helpful to think of it as a "supercomma."

I have tickets for the U.S. Open tomorrow. I bet it rains.	These two short sentences read a bit jerkily.
I have tickets for the U.S. Open tomorrow but I bet it rains.	A little clumsy.
I have tickets for the U.S. Open tomorrow; I bet it rains.	Much better!

Rule 1: You must have a finite clause sentence (see page 125) on both sides of the semicolon.

[148]

Rule 2: Semicolons are followed by a lower-case letter, unless the word in question is a proper noun. A semicolon is also used instead of a comma to break up items in a long and complicated list, particularly when the list has plenty of commas in it already, as in the Dickens quote above.

DASH AWAY ALL
(OR, DASHES)

A **dash** (—) is a horizontal line that may be used alone, or as a pair in place of brackets. It introduces an aside, an interruption, or an additional piece of information, indicates a sudden change of emotion or thought, or shows that words have been omitted at the end of a sentence that has been broken off.

He had said that he would marry her when he got his next promotion—and she, poor girl, believed him.
She—poor girl—believed him.
After hours of careful preparation the experiment actually worked—eureka!
They want that contract—which means they get that contract—by the end of today.
He is an excellent employee, but—

A dash can also indicate that we are carrying on where we left off: *—as I was telling you, I wouldn't be seen dead in a ditch with her.*

Nowadays, dashes are riding roughshod over the poor old semi-colon (*I have tickets for the U.S. Open tomorrow—I bet it rains*), and this is becoming more acceptable, especially in informal writing.

Punctuation

Americans use the longer em-dash (—) and no spaces, while British English usually uses an en-dash (–) with a space on either side of it.

A dash also sometimes takes the place of letters in order to "disguise" curse words (does this really fool anybody?). In this case, the closed-up em-dash, or something longer, is usual on both sides of the Atlantic:

That man who hit me was a real b——d.
Oh, s——.

> ✋ **Smart Aleck:** An en-dash is named for the width of a typesetter's *n* key. The longer em-dash is the width of a typesetter's *m* key.

JOINED-UP WRITING (OR, HYPHENS)

> "A knave, a rascal, an eater of broken meats, a base proud, shallow, beggarly, three-suited, hundred-pound, filthy-worsted-stocking knave; a lily-livered, action-taking, whoreson glass-gazing super serviceable finical rogue, one-trunk-inheriting slave."
> —William Shakespeare, *King Lear*

A **hyphen** looks like a short dash but isn't used in the same way. Its function is to join two or more words to show that they belong to each other, and also to separate syllables when necessary—for example, when a word is split in half at the end of a line of type. Hyphens are rather going out of fashion these days, particularly in American English, but they are often useful (and sometimes essential) in clarifying meaning, as the examples below illustrate.

Hang glider pilots in training today.
He wore a new dress shirt and jacket to the dinner.
Fox hunting supporters.
It was a long overdue visit.
They were speaking a nonnative language.
Thirteen year-old boys take placement exams here tomorrow.
She went through it with a fine tooth-comb.

In the above examples, common sense tells us where a hyphen would have been useful. (*Fine-toothed comb*, please!)

Some hyphen rules:

- Be careful with compound adjectives. Hyphenating these incorrectly, or not hyphenating them at all, can cause confusion because we don't know which words go together: *Thirteen-year-old* boys take placement exams; *thirteen year-old boys* would be far too young, and are an unlucky number anyway.

- A hyphen is unnecessary if other punctuation makes the meaning clear without it:

    The old English teacher droned on and on.
    The Old English teacher droned on and on.

    The fact that the word old is capitalized in the second sentence makes all the difference: in the first sentence we know that the teacher is old; in the second, it is the English that is old.

Punctuation

The usefulness of the hyphen in forming compounds that serve as adjectives before nouns is demonstrated in the entries ill- ajd well-.

Example: *She wore a well-tailored suit.*

But the hyphen is omitted when the words follow the noun they modify: The suit was well tailored.

"QUOTATION MARKS"

"'You are old, Father William,' the young man said,
'And your hair has become very white;
And yet you incessantly stand on your head—
Do you think, at your age, it is right?'"
—Lewis Carroll, *You Are Old, Father William*

Rule: In direct speech (when we write the actual words that are spoken) we need quotation marks. These may be single or double. Both are correct, in some instances although if you quote within speech, use single within double: *"I find the government's 'nanny state' attitude really irritating,"* he said.

Another rule: Punctuation goes inside the closing quotation mark:

"Punctuation goes inside the closing quotation mark," I said.
"Where did you say the punctuation should go?" he asked for the umpteenth time.
"Inside the inverted comma!" I snapped.

If the spoken words end the sentence, there is no need for extra punctuation:

He asked, "Is this the end?"
They replied, "This is the end."
She screamed, "Help!"

Note that in such a sentence as *"Can anybody hear me?" she yelled.* there is no capital letter after the question mark, because it is all the same sentence despite all that punctuation.

Something to Report?

Rule: Do not use quotation marks for **indirect** (or **reported**) **speech**.

They say that you can't have too much of a good thing.
He asked me how to use a comma.

What's All the Fuss?
(or, Apostrophes)

The **apostrophe** (') is probably the most misunderstood piece of punctuation we have. At its simplest, it is used to show possession (*his master's voice*) or omission (*you wouldn't dare*). But, of course, it isn't as simple as that.

Thoughts on *Ain't*
"A*in't* ain't a word, so you ain't going to
find it in no dictionary."

✱

"Ignorant people think it is the noise which fighting cats
make that is so aggravating, but it ain't so; it is
the sickening grammar that they use."
—Mark Twain

Punctuation

Leave It Out, Will You?

Rule: When you omit a letter or letters in a word, you should replace it/them with an apostrophe.

If you choose to write *can't* instead of *cannot*, *we've been here before* rather than *we have been...*, *'or 80s* instead of *1980s,,* you need to replace the missing letters with an apostrophe. Note that the apostrophe in *'80s* tells us that something is missing from the *front* of the word, but it is still an apostrophe. Do not reverse the apostrophe and write '80s. And if you write *rock 'n' roll rather* than *rock and roll*, you need apostrophes before and after the *n*.

> ➤ **Teacher's Corner:** The ancient Greeks invented the rhetorical device *apostrephein* (meaning "to turn away"). This had nothing to do with grammar. It described the moment when a speaker turned away from the audience to address a usually absent person or a thing personified—" O Liberty, what things are done in thy name!" This is still known as *apostrophe* today. However, over time, the word's meaning has widened to include "something missing," such as letters and sounds.

Common contractions requiring an apostrophe include:

aren't	*hadn't*	*they're*
can't	*hasn't*	*they've*
couldn't	*isn't*	*weren't*
didn't	*it's**	*won't*
don't	*shouldn't*	*wouldn't*

Such contractions aren't normally used in formal writing, unless someone's speaking, but in a friendly book such as this one they're OK. But remember—the apostrophe is replacing a missing letter, so please put it in the right place.

> "There ain't nothing more to write about, and I am rotten glad of it, because if I'd a' knowed what a trouble it was to make a book I wouldn't a' tackled it, and I ain't agoing to no more."
> —Mark Twain, *The Adventures of Huckleberry Finn*

What's Not in a Name? (or, Possessive Apostrophes)

At one time in the history of the English language, a common way of indicating that something belonged to someone was to add the suffix *-es*.

---

*But only when it's short for *it is*. See page 67.

Punctuation

Singular	Possessive singular
mann	*mannes*
James	*Jameses*

At some point, however, people omitted to pronounce and write the *es*. So instead of an *e* we gained an apostrophe.

The man's hand.
James's book.

This use of apostrophes to indicate possession caught on. In fact, people started adding them to any old word, whether they carried the suffix *-es* or not.

Rule: The apostrophe is placed at the end of a noun to indicate that something belongs to someone or something. It replaces the word *of* in a sentence. If the noun is singular, add *'s*. If the noun is plural, just add the apostrophe.

The boss's chair is for the boss only.	The chair **of the boss**
The animals' feed is insufficient to last the winter.	The feed **of the animals**

Another rule: In the singular the apostrophe is always on the left of its *s*; in the plural it is usually on the right.

The school's rules (one school)
The schools' rules (two or more schools)
The princess's slippers (one princess)
The princesses' slippers (more than one princess)

What the Heck Do I Do with That Apostrophe?

There are—of course—**exceptions** to the apostrophe rules. These are they:

1. When the plural doesn't end in *s*, add an apostrophe followed by an *s*:

   *The **children's** party*
   *The **mice's** lack of eyesight*

2. Names ending in an *s* should be followed by *'s* if singular and *-es'* if plural:

   ***Charles's** last name was Dickens.*
   *Charles **Dickens's** novels are well loved.*
   *The **Joneses'** standards weren't worth keeping up with.*

   Our old friend euphony (see page 94) also crops up here: the moment the word becomes a mouthful, you stop adding an *s*. So:

   *St. **Agnes's** Church*
   ***Jesus's** sandals*
   but ***Barabbas'** criminal record*

3. If the last syllable is pronounced *-iz* or *-eeze*, stick to *s'*, don't add the extra *s*—***Sophocles'** plays*—although, with longer words, it's often easier to paraphrase:

   The inventions of Archimedes rather than *Archimedes'* (or *Archimedes's*) inventions.
   The odyssey of Odysseus rather than *Odysseus'* (or *Odysseus's*) odyssey.

   It also sounds better—and makes you less likely to spit at the person you are speaking to.

4. Then there are organizations that have simply decided that they are above having to employ correct grammar:

   Diners Club International and Walgreens, for instance.

There appears to be no logic to this, but presumably an organization has the right to choose how to spell its own name. That said, ten out of ten for *Macy's*, *McDonald's*, and *Bloomingdales*.

But Who Really Care's?

The problem is that, in the course of the last few decades, lots of people have become confused about this and—rather than, as they fear, looking ignorant by leaving the apostrophes out—they have started putting apostrophes in places they shouldn't. This is often called the **greengrocer's apostrophe**.

APPLE'S HERE! FREE BANANA'S! FAIR DEAL'S! NO DOG'S!

Free Margarita's before 7:00 P.M.

But free Margarita's what? You could write *Free Margarita's lover before 7:00 P.M.*, if you wanted him to get out of the office in time to go to the movies. However, assuming that Margarita is an alcoholic drink, there is no need for a possessive apostrophe in either of these examples.

Similarly *VPs, GIs, and the 1970s* don't need apostrophes, unless they are followed by a possessive or attribute. *An* (individual) *VP's expenses*, (all) *GIs' uniform requirements. A 1970s' trend* would belong to the whole decade; *1970's music* is specifically music from the year 1970.

Conclusion: Using an apostrophe in a plural that is not a possessive form is to be frowned on. No if's, and's, or but's.

To avoid confusion, it is permissible—but not necessarily necessary—to include an apostrophe in:

do's and don'ts
the three R's
There are two s's in that word
dotting one's i's
Minding your p's and q's

But in all of these cases, it is a matter of personal taste, and the apostrophe is included only for ease of reading.

The Typo Hunt

Jeff Deck of Somerville, Massachusetts, and his friend Benjamin Herson of Virginia Beach, Virginia, decided they had seen one too many signs with misspelled words.

Armed with chalk and adhesive letters, the duo, who called themselves the Typo Eradication Advancement League, set out in 2008 on a nationwide search to stamp out grammatical errors. After correcting a misplaced comma and apostrophe on a sign in Grand Canyon National Park, they were arrested and charged with conspiracy to vandalize a historic marker. They were ordered to pay restitution and were banned for one year from national parks.

Punctuation

Yours, Mine, and Ours

Rule: The personal pronouns *yours, theirs, its, his, hers* and *ours* never need an apostrophe.

*The **boys'** burgers, but the burgers are **theirs**.*
*The **girl's** cakes but the cakes are **hers**.*

The only possessive personal pronoun that needs an apostrophe is *one's*. However, be careful when using it. *One's well* could mean either *one is well* or *the well that one owns*—though with a bit of luck, the context will help you work out which!

> ✋ **Smart Aleck:** We also use an apostrophe in possessive indefinite pronouns: *Is that someone's idea of a joke? That's anyone's guess.*

What Happens When Two People Own Something?

Rule: An apostrophe is placed after the second name when the possession belongs to two people who are mentioned in the same sentence: *Jane and Peter's dog*, not *Jane's and Peter's dog*.

That one is easy because you only have to add *'s*. If, however, you—yes, you—co-owned Jane's dog, you would have to say *Jane's and my dog*, because you can't say *Jane and my's* nor, God forbid, *Jane and I's*.

> ✋ **Smart Aleck:** Achilles heel is the Achilles heel here. Neither Achilles heel nor Achilles tendon has an apostrophe.

And Finally...

Useful mnemonics for remembering the difference between a plural form and a singular form in need of a possessive apostrophe.

Rose's are red
Violet's are blue
Which color underwear
Belongs to these two?

Got that? Oh good. Because we're exhausted.

5
Odds and Ends (or, Elements of Style)

BEING A BIT FANCY

There's more to grammar than knowing the difference between a dangling conjunction, a subordinate object, and a non-restrictive apostrophe. So this chapter rounds up a few other points that sometimes cause bafflement.

A BIG NO-NO (OR, DOUBLE NEGATIVES)

> "...nor your name is not Master Cesario;
> nor this is not my nose neither."
> —Shakespeare, *Twelfth Night*

Double negatives may not have mattered to Shakespeare, but they do matter in standard modern English.

Rule: Two negatives equal a positive and therefore negate each other. If you want to be negative, use only one.

Sometimes a double negative is obvious—

*I did**n't** do **nothing** right*

*I did**n't** **never** do well in that*

– while others are more elusive:

*His essay **scarcely** needs **no** correction*

*There is**n't** **nowhere** I'd rather be than here with you.*

They are all equally wrong.

Odds and Ends (or, Elements of Style)

> ☞ **See Me after Class:** *I ain't never heard of no one by no name like that.*
>
> On the other hand, when Al Jolson said, "Wait a minute, you ain't heard nothin' yet." in *The Jazz Singer* in 1927, he made movie history.

Yes-Yes to No-Nos

Double negatives are permissible—indeed, useful—when they convey cunning nuances of meaning:

*It was a **not unusual** reaction for someone who has been given bad news.*	Sounds more sympathetic than *It was a usual reaction.*
*I **wouldn't** say I **don't** like your new house.*	I am too polite to admit that I hate it.

And they are allowed for emphasis when they belong to different phrases or clauses:

*I will **not** give up, **not** now, **not** ever.*

*You **don't** ask for much, **no** more than the rest of them, anyhow.*

Positive or Negative?

Interpretation of a **deliberate double negative** may depend on context and intonation.

A Big No-No

*She's **not un**attractive.*	This may mean that she is not ugly, but neither is she beautiful—she's not **un**attractive. On the other hand, we may be leaping to the lady's defense—she's **not** unattractive!
*Your visits are **not in**frequent.*	You could visit more often—or you visit regularly enough.
I can't not come if you're singing.	I don't want to come but I'm obliged to if you are singing—or I wouldn't miss your singing for the world.
*That's **not bad**.*	That's good—or it could be better.

Sometimes double negatives contradict themselves to make positive statements:

I'm not not doing my job!	I *am* doing my job!
There isn't a day when I don't think about him.	I think about him every day.
*He **cannot** just do **nothing**.*	He doesn't understand the concept of idleness.

Odds and Ends (or, Elements of Style)

> **Ha-Ha**
>
> A linguistics professor was lecturing to his class.
>
> "In English," he said, "a double negative forms a positive. In some languages, such as Russian, a double negative is still a negative. However, there is no language wherein a double positive can form a negative."
>
> "Yeah, right," said a voice in the back of the room.

PLEONASM, PROLIXITY, AND TAUTOLOGY (OR, WORDINESS)

Wordiness—also known as long-windedness, pleonasm, prolixity, redundancy, verboseness, verbosity, windiness, wordage, verbiage, garrulousness, redundancy, tautology, or logorrhoea—is to be avoided at all costs.

> "Vigorous writing is concise. A sentence should contain no unnecessary words, a paragraph no unnecessary sentences, for the same reason that a drawing should have no unnecessary lines and a machine no unnecessary parts. This requires not that the writer make all his sentences short, or that he avoid all detail and treat his subjects only in outline, but that every word tell."
> —William Strunk Jr., *The Elements of Style*

Imagine what Mr. Strunk would have had to say about either of these examples:

As the firemen climbed up the steps of the ladder to reach the people trapped in the building that was on fire (people with no escape!), the piercing sound of a shrill cry could be audibly heard from up high on the rooftop. Above the loud roar of the burning flames, we heard a woman screaming out at the top of her voice to the rescuing fireman. We sighed a sigh of relief when they finally reached her and she was brought down.

This quarter, we are presently focusing with determination on an all-new, innovative integrated methodology and framework for rapid expansion of customer-oriented external programs designed and developed to bring the company's consumer-first paradigm shift into the marketplace as quickly as possible.

Rule: Be clear; be concise; be simple.

Odds and Ends (or, Elements of Style)

Some Thoughts on Pomposity

"We must have a better word than 'prefabricated.' Why not 'ready-made?'"
—Winston Churchill

✳

"His speeches left the impression of an army of pompous phrases moving over the landscape in search of an idea."
—U.S. politician William McAdoo about President Warren Harding

✳

"Speak properly, and in as few words as you can, but always plainly; for the end of speech is not ostentation, but to be understood."
—William Penn

✳

"Clutter is the disease of American writing. We are a society strangling in unnecessary words, circular constructions, pompous frills, and meaningless jargon."
—William Zinsser

A Waste of Space

Try not to punctuate your speech (and certainly don't litter your writing) with **verbal apologies** such as *and that sort of thing, as it were, do you know what I mean?, to all intents and purposes, needless to say*. Nine times out of ten, they will add nothing. Mark Twain had it right when he said, "Substitute 'damn' every time you're inclined to write 'very'; your editor will delete it and the writing will be just as it should be." The same applies to these empty phrases.

Many of us also diminish powerful words by using them in a trivial way. What we mean is, don't use *awfully*, *fearfully*, *terribly*, or *horribly* when you mean *very*. In formal writing, keep these words for when they are needed: *He was horribly scarred by the accident.*

Er, Um, Room for Improvement

Recent research concludes that English speakers use a meaningless word about every nine seconds and that 10 percent of English speech consists of **filler words**. And, um, you know, if you don't mind our saying so, it's sort of boring to listen to.

Rule: If it is possible to cut out a word, do so.

It's Déjà-Vu All Over Again...

Tautological phrases or synonyms (words that mean the same) simply repeat a meaning with different words. Making free with these weakens your writing and suggests that you don't know what the words mean. Our pet peeves are *safe haven* (what other kind of haven is there?) and *PIN number* (what do people think the *N* stands for?) but we seem to be fighting a losing battle on these two. However, there are lots of other nonsenses against which we can still fight:

absolute certainty	*factual information*	*honest truth*
accidental mistake	*fall down*	*new innovation*
added bonus	*fictional story*	*stupid idiot*
awful tragedy	*final conclusion*	*sum total*
climb up	*free gift*	*terrible disaster*
close scrutiny	*grab hold*	*true fact*
complete opposite	*end result*	*unconfirmed rumor*
8:00 P.M. in the evening	*HIV virus*	*variety of different*

Odds and Ends (or, Elements of Style)

> ✋ **Smart Aleck:** How come *needless to say* is always followed by something being said?

Note: One particularly common misuse is of the word *unique*. *Unique*, from the Latin for *one*, means "being the only one of a kind; without parallel." So it is (just about) possible for something to be *almost unique* (that is, there might be two of them, whatever they are) but not for it to be *quite unique* or *very unique*.

"It was a sudden and unexpected surprise."
—BBC correspondent

✱

"Every Superbowl is totally unique—and
this one is just the same."
—Young football athlete

Let Me Repeat Myself
Not all **repetition** is bad. The repetition of key words, phrases and sentence patterns is obviously important in poetry.

> It was many and many a year ago,
> In a kingdom by the sea,
> That a maiden there lived whom you may know
> By the name of ANNABEL LEE;
> And this maiden she lived with no other thought
> Than to love and be loved by me.
> I was a child and she was a child,
> In this kingdom by the sea;

> But we loved with a love that was more than love—
> I and my Annabel Lee;
> With a love that the winged seraphs of heaven
> Coveted her and me.
> —Edgar Allan Poe, *Annabel Lee*

And it can be effective in prose too:

> "She turned towards me immediately. The easy elegance of every movement of her limbs and body as soon as she began to advance from the far end of the room, set me in a flutter of expectation to see her face clearly. She left the window—and I said to myself, *The lady is dark.* She moved forward a few steps—and I said to myself, *The lady is young.* She approached nearer—and I said to myself (with a sense of surprise which words fail me to express), *The lady is ugly!*"
> —Wilkie Collins, *The Woman in White*

Of course, as with all good things in life, this can be taken to extremes:

> *If one doctor doctors another doctor does the doctor who doctors the doctor doctor the doctor the way the doctor he is doctoring doctors? Or does the doctor doctor the way the doctor who doctors doctors?*

Odds and Ends (or, Elements of Style)

Say That Again

A word that has two meanings that are the opposite of each other is called an **antagonym** or **contranym**.

*That horse will **bolt** unless you **bolt** the stable door.*

*The soldier was **bound** for home, when they caught him and **bound** him.*

*Having **clipped** off his baby hair, she **clipped** the pieces in his baby book.*

*We escaped from the mudflats as **fast** as we could, before we were stuck **fast**.*

These examples are all grammatically correct, every word is used accurately, but they still manage to sound silly. It's best to avoid them.

> 👋 **Smart Aleck:** What's another word for *thesaurus*?

Choose Your Words Carefully

As we said earlier, English is full of easily confused, similar-sounding words, with plenty of opportunity for deliberate puns and inadvertent verbal gaffes.

Visiting relatives can be boring.	Are they visiting you or are you visiting them?
I had been driving for forty years when I fell asleep at the wheel and had an accident.	No wonder, I expect you were rather tired.
Q: *What gear were you in at the moment of the impact?*	A: Gucci sweats and Reeboks.

Pleonasm, Prolixity, and Tautology

Yogi Berra was a master of this form of miscommunication—"He hits from both sides of the plate. He's amphibious."—but while not many of us would aspire to his heights, he is an object lesson in what can happen if you don't watch what you say. On the other hand, you can have a lot of fun with words if you don't mind what you say. See what we mean?

Enjoy These Other Reader's Digest Best-Sellers

Featuring all the memory-jogging tips you'll ever need to know, this fun little book will help you recall hundreds of important facts using simple, easy-to-remember mnemonics from your school days.

$14.95 hardcover
ISBN 978-0-7621-0917-8

Make learning fun again with these light-hearted pages that are packed with important theories, phrases, and those long-forgotten "rules" you once learned in school.

$14.95 hardcover
ISBN 978-0-7621-0993-1

This laugh-out-loud collection of heartwarming jokes, quips, and truisms about the joys of aging will keep you entertained for hours.

$14.95 hardcover
ISBN 978-1-60652-025-8

Reader's Digest books can be purchased through retail and online bookstores. In the United States books are distributed by Penguin Group (USA), Inc. For more information or to order books, call 1-800-788-6262.